S0-EAU-316

EXECUTIVE'S YELLOW PAGES

SETH GODIN, EDITOR

Houghton Mifflin Company
Boston   New York   1995

No part of this work may be reproduced or transmitted in any form or by any means, electronic or mechanical, including photocopying and recording, or by any information storage or retrieval system without the prior written permission of Houghton Mifflin Company unless such copying is expressly permitted by federal copyright law.

Copyright © by Seth Godin Productions, Inc.

All rights reserved

For information about permission to reproduce selections from this book, write to permissions, Houghton Mifflin Company, 215 Park Avenue South, New York, New York 10003.

For information about this and other Houghton Mifflin trade and reference books and multimedia products, visit The Bookstore at Houghton Mifflin on the World Wide Web at http://www.hmco.com/trade/.

ISBN: 0-395-74282-X

Printed in the United States of America

BIN 10 9 8 7 6 5 4 3 2 1

Editorial and Production Staff

EDITOR IN CHIEF: Seth Godin

SENIOR EDITOR: Amy N. Winger

HOUGHTON MIFFLIN: Steven M. Lewers

PRODUCTION EDITOR: Julie Maner

BOOK DESIGN: Julie Maner, Seth Godin

EDITORIAL ASSISTANCE: Karen Watts, Carol Markowitz, Lisa DiMona, Anne Shepherd

COPY EDITING: Jolanta Benal

RESEARCH ASSISTANCE: Louise Anderson, Mark Underwager, Becky McPeters, Vic Lapuszynski, Lauren Fox, Nikki Coddington

PROOFREADING: Cynthia Liu, Nicole Goldstein, David Bloom, David Levine

Acknowledgments

We could not have put this book together without the help of people who contributed their knowledge and insight. Thanks to the following for their time and cooperation:

INDIVIDUALS: Phyllis McKenzie, Capitol Speakers Bureau; Joanne Paulino, the Information Broker's Directory; Larry Rotundi, Associate Publisher, Gift & Decorative Accessories; Jennifer Miller, VP of Marketing, and Stephanie Lifland, Membership Coordinator, ICIA; Alfred Lagasse, International Taxicab Association; Jennifer Zane, Equipment Leasing Association; Bruce Steinberg, National Association of Temporary Services; Cheryl Johnson, Jones Printing Service; Walter Bacak, American Translators Association; John Rhamstine, Norfolk Scope; Ken Njenga, Oxbridge Communications; Jack O'Dwyer; Jill Denman, YPPA; Harvey Wynn, YPPA; Susan Gary, Hampton Roads Admirals.

ORGANIZATIONS: Securities Industry Association; *Worth* Magazine

Contents

OFFICE MANAGEMENT

ORGANIZATIONS

TRAVEL/TRANSPORTATION

How to Use the Executive's Yellow Pages

The *Executive's Yellow Pages* contains more than 9,000 telephone numbers essential to any executive or administrative assistant. This directory covers many topics not found in the regular yellow pages.

We've focused on fifty large American metropolitan areas, taking care to include those most frequently visited by business travelers. Some categories are a compilation of national industry leaders. Others, where appropriate, are arranged by city.

Several listings include additional information for contacting associations, or for ordering annual directories, magazines, and CD-ROMs. We recommend these resources to you.

The book is arranged by ten logical subject headings ranging from "Business Services" to "Travel/Transportation." Related topics are alphabetically arranged within each subject heading. Use the running heads at the top of each page to guide you. An index is also included at the back of the book to access topics alphabetically.

The telephone numbers in this edition were collected from a variety of sources. They are accurate to the best of our ability. If you find a number that's incorrect, please notify us at EYP@yoyo.com or send mail to Box 321, Dobbs Ferry, New York 10522.

Should you have suggestions for other useful listings, please drop us a line. If we include your suggestion, we'll send you a free copy of the next edition.

This book is available for bulk sales to organizations. If your customers find it as useful as you do, they'll use it constantly. For details, contact Maire Gorman at Houghton Mifflin Special Sales, 222 Berkeley Street, Boston, Massachusetts 02116.

Accounting Firms

Altschuler, Melvoin & Glasser, Chicago, IL .....(312) 207-2800
American Express Tax & Business Services,
    Minneapolis, MN..(612) 635-1900
Amper Politziner & Mattia, Edison, NJ ....(908) 287-1000
Anchin, Block & Anchin, NY ....(212) 840-3456
Aronson Fetridge Weigle & Stern,
    Rockville, MD...(301) 231-6200
Arthur Andersen & Co., New York, NY..........(212) 708-4000
Baird Kurtz & Dobson, Springfield, MO ....(417) 831-7283
BDO Seidman, New York, NY..........................(212) 885-8000
Berry, Dunn, McNeil & Parker, Portland, ME ..(207) 797-5877
Blackman Kallick Bartlestein, Chicago, IL........(312) 207-1040
Blue, Indianapolis, IN ....(317) 633-4705
Blum Shapiro, West Hartford, CT.....................(203) 561-4000
Brady Martz & Assocs., Grand Forks, ND.........(701) 775-4685
Buchbinder Tunick, New York, NY ....(212) 695-5003
C. W. Amos, Baltimore, MD..............................(410) 727-5341
Campos & Stratis, Teaneck, NJ ....(201) 692-0300
Charles Bailly, Fargo, ND..................................(701) 239-8500
Checkers Simon & Rosner, Chicago, IL............(312) 346-7499
Cherry Bekaert & Holland, Richmond, VA.......(804) 673-4224
Clark, Schaefer, Hackett, Middletown, OH ......(513) 424-5000
Clifton Gunderson, Peoria, IL...........................(309) 671-4500
Cohen, Cleveland, OH ....(216) 579-1040
Comprehensive Business Services,
    Carlsbad, CA ....(619) 431-2150
Coopers & Lybrand, New York, NY..................(212) 536-2000
Crowe, Chizek, South Bend, IN ....(219) 232-3992
David Berdon, New York, NY...........................(212) 832-0400
Deloitte & Touche, Wilton, CT ....(203) 761-3000
Dixon Odom, High Point, NC ....(910) 889-5156
Doeren Mayhew, Troy, MI................................(313) 244-3000
Edward Isaacs, New York, NY ....(212) 297-4800
Eide Helmeke, Fargo, ND ....(701) 237-3343
Elliott Davis, Greenville, SC ....(803) 242-3370
Ernst & Young, New York, NY ....(212) 773-3000
Follmer, Rudzewicz, Southfield, MI ....(810) 355-1040
Friedman, Eisenstein, Raemer & Schwartz,
    Chicago, IL ....(312) 644-6000
General Business Service & E. K. Williams & Co.,
    Waco, TX..(817) 756-6181
Geo. S. Olive, Indianapolis, IN ....(317) 383-4000
Goldstein Golub Kessler & Co.,
    New York, NY...(212) 869-1818
Goodman, Norfolk, VA......................................(804) 624-5100
Grant Thornton, Chicago, IL ....(312) 856-0200
H & R Block Tax Services,
    Kansas City, MO...(816) 753-6900
Habib, Arogeti & Wynne, Atlanta, GA ....(404) 892-9651
Hausser & Taylor, Cleveland, OH ....(216) 523-1900
Hemming Morse, San Mateo, CA ....(415) 574-1900
Hill Barth & King, Youngstown, OH ....(216) 758-8613
Hood & Strong, San Francisco, CA ....(415) 781-0793
J. H. Cohn, Roseland, NJ...................................(201) 228-3500
Jackson Hewitt, Virginia Beach, VA ....(804) 431-0326
Joseph Decosimo, Chattanooga, TN..................(615) 756-7100
Kafoury, Armstrong, Reno, NV ....(702) 689-9100
Katz, Sapper & Miller, Indianapolis, IN ....(317) 580-2000
Kaufman Rossin, Miami, FL...............................(305) 858-5600

Keller Bruner, Frederick, MD..............................(301) 663-8918
Kemper CPA Group, Robinson, IL....................(618) 546-1502
Kennedy & Coe, Salina, KS..............................(913) 825-1561
Kenneth Leventhal, Los Angeles, CA...............(310) 277-0880
Kerber Eck & Braeckel, Springfield, IL ....(217) 789-0960
Konigsberg, Wolf, New York, NY ....(212) 685-7215
KPMG Peat Marwick, New York, NY ....(212) 909-5000
Larson, Allen, Weishair, Minneapolis, MN.......(612) 376-4500
LeMaster & Daniels, Spokane, WA...................(509) 928-1714
Lopez, Edwards, Frank, Valley Stream, NY.......(516) 872-3400
Lurie Besikof Lapidus, Minneapolis, MN ....(612) 377-4404
M. R. Weiser, New York, NY ....(212) 641-6700
Mahoney Cohen, New York, NY ....(212) 490-8000
Margolin Winer Evans, Garden City, NY..........(516) 747-2000
Mauldin & Jenkins, Albany, GA ....(912) 883-3343
Mayer Hoffman McCann, Kansas City, MO .....(816) 968-1000
McGladrey & Pullen, Davenport, IA ....(319) 326-5111
Meaden & Moore, Cleveland, OH ....(216) 241-3272
Mitchell, Titus, New York, NY ....(212) 709-4500
Morrison, Brown, Argiz, Miami, FL..................(305) 667-3500
Mortenson & Associates, Cranford, NJ.............(908) 272-7000
Moss Adams, Seattle, WA..................................(206) 223-1820
Padgett Business Services, Athens, GA.............(706) 548-6843
Parente, Randolph, Orlando, Carey & Assocs.,
   Wilkes-Barre, PA ....(717) 820-0100
Philip Rootberg, Chicago, IL ....(312) 930-9600
Plante & Moran, Southfield, MI.......................(810) 352-2500
Price Waterhouse, New York, NY.....................(212) 596-7000
Rachlin Cohen & Holtz, Coral Gables, FL ....(305) 667-0412
Rehmann Robson, Saginaw, MI........................(517) 799-9580
Reznick Fedder & Silverman, Bethesda, MD....(301) 652-9100
Richard A. Eisner, New York, NY ....(212) 355-1700
Rothstein Kass, Roseland, NJ............................(201) 994-6666
Rubin, Brown, Gornstein, St. Louis, MO..........(314) 727-8150
S. R. Snodgrass, Wexford, PA ....(412) 934-0344
Schenck & Associates, Appleton, WI...............(414) 731-8111
Schumaker, Romenesko & Associates,
   Appleton, WI..(414) 733-7385
Suby, von Haden & Associates, Madison, WI ..(608) 831-8181
Thomas Havey, Chicago, IL..............................(312) 368-0500
Tobias, Fleishman, Shapiro, Cambridge, MA....(617) 547-5900
Triple Check, Burbank, CA ....(818) 840-9077
Urbach, Kahn & Werlin, Albany, NY...............(518) 449-3166
Virchow Krause, Madison, WI ....(608) 249-6622
Walpert, Smullian & Blumenthal,
   Baltimore, MD..(410) 296-4600
Windes & McClaughry, Long Beach, CA ....(310) 435-1191
Wipfli Ullrich Bertelson, Wausau, WI..............(715) 845-3111
Wolpoff, Baltimore, MD....................................(410) 837-3770
Yergen & Meyer, Portland, OR........................(503) 295-1288
Zelenkofske, Axelrod, Jenkintown, PA ....(215) 572-7410

Advertising Agencies

Ackerman McQueen, Oklahoma City, OK.......(918) 250-9511
Adler Boschetto Peebles & Partners,
   New York, NY..(212) 684-5220
Ally & Gargano, New York, NY.......................(212) 688-5300
Anderson & Lembke, New York, NY ....(212) 886-2100
Angotti, Thomas, Hedge, New York, NY..........(212) 420-0030

Arnold Fortuna Lawner & Cabot,
  Boston, MA ....(617) 737-6400
Arvett, Free & Ginsberg, New York, NY ....(212) 832-3800
Barkley & Evergreen, Shawnee Mission, KS.....(913) 432-2600
Bates USA, New York, NY ....(212) 297-7000
Bayer Bess Vanderwarker, Chicago, IL...............(312) 861-3800
BBDO, New York, NY......................................(212) 459-5000
Bernstein-Rein, Kansas City, MO.....................(816) 756-0640
Bozell, New York, NY......................................(212) 727-5000
Campbell, Mithun, Esty, Minneapolis, MN ......(612) 347-1000
Carmichael Lynch, Minneapolis, MN ....(612) 334-6000
Chiat/Day, Venice, CA ....(310) 314-5000
Cliff Freeman & Partners, New York, NY ....(212) 463-3200
Cramer-Krasselt, Milwaukee, WI.....................(414) 227-3500
D'Arcy Masius Benton & Bowles,
  New York, NY..(212) 468-3622
Dahlin Smith White, Salt Lake City, UT ....(801) 364-0919
Dailey & Assocs., Los Angeles, CA...................(213) 386-7823
Davis, Ball & Colombatto, Los Angeles, CA....(213) 688-7000
DDB Needham, New York, NY ....(212) 415-2000
Earle Palmer Brown, Bethesda, MD...................(301) 986-0510
Eire Partners, Chicago, IL................................(312) 335-4330
Eisaman, Johns & Laws, Los Angeles, CA ....(213) 932-1234
Evans Group, Salt Lake City, UT ....(801) 364-7000
Fahlgren Martin, Parkersburg, WV...................(304) 424-3591
Fallon McElligott, Minneapolis, MN................(612) 332-2445
Fogarty Klein & Partners, Houston, TX............(713) 862-5100
Foote, Cone & Belding, Chicago, IL...........(312) 751-7000
Gianettino & Meredith, Short Hills, NJ ....(201) 376-2100
Gillespie, Princeton, NJ ....(609) 799-6000
Goldberg Moser O'Neill, San Francisco, CA ....(415) 677-1800
Goodby, Berlin, Silverstein,
  San Francisco, CA..(415) 392-0669
Gray Kirk/VanSant, Baltimore, MD ....(410) 539-5400
Grey, New York, NY...(212) 546-2000
GSD&M, Austin, TX..(512) 327-8810
Hal Riney & Partners, San Francisco, CA ....(415) 981-0950
Hameroff/Milenthal/Spence, Columbus, OH....(614) 221-7667
Hill, Holliday, Connors, Cosmopulos,
  Boston, MA ....(617) 437-1600
Houston Effler Herstek & Favat, Boston, MA ..(617) 267-5050
Ingalls, Quinn & Johnson, Boston, MA............(617) 954-1000
Italia/Gal, Los Angeles, CA..............................(213) 937-4400
J. Walter Thompson, New York, NY ....(212) 210-7000
Jack Levy Assocs., Chicago, IL ....(312) 337-7800
Jordan, McGrath, Case & Taylor,
  New York, NY..(212) 326-9100
Ketchum, Pittsburgh, PA..................................(412) 456-3500
Kirshenbaum & Bond, New York, NY...............(212) 633-0080
Kresser Stein Robaire, Los Angeles, CA ....(310) 315-3000
LCF&L, New York, NY.....................................(212) 213-4646
Leo Burnett, Chicago, IL..................................(312) 220-5959
Lintas USA, New York, NY ....(212) 605-8000
Lois/USA, New York, NY ....(212) 373-4700
Lord, Dentsu & Partners, New York, NY ....(212) 408-2100
Lowe & Partners/SMS, New York, NY...............(212) 708-8800
Margeotes Fertitta Donaher & Weiss,
  New York, NY..(212) 979-6600
The Martin Agency, Richmond, VA ....(804) 254-3400
Martin/Williams, Minneapolis, MN ....(612) 340-0800
McCann-Erickson, New York, NY.....................(212) 697-6000

McKinney & Silver, Raleigh, NC......................(919) 828-0691
Meldrum & Fewsmith, Cleveland, OH.............(216) 241-2141
Merkley Newman Harty, New York, NY...........(212) 366-3500
Mezzina Brown, New York, NY........................(212) 251-7700
Mullen, Wenham, MA.......................................(508) 468-1155
N. W. Ayer & Partners, New York, NY.............(212) 474-5000
Ogilvy, Adams & Rinehart, New York, NY......(212) 880-5200
Partners & Shevack, New York, NY..................(212) 596-0200
Publicis/Bloom, New York, NY........................(212) 370-1313
The Richards Group, Dallas, TX......................(214) 891-5700
Richardson, Myers & Donofrio,
    Baltimore, MD...(410) 576-9000
Robinson, Yesawich & Pepperdine,
    Orlando, FL...(407) 875-1111
Ross Roy Communications,
    Bloomfield Hills, MI..................................(313) 433-6000
Rotando Partners, Stamford, CT......................(203) 358-2100
Rubin Postaer & Associates,
    Santa Monica, CA......................................(310) 394-4000
Rumrill-Hoyt, Rochester, NY...........................(716) 272-6100
Saatchi & Saatchi Direct, New York, NY..........(212) 463-3600
Seiniger Advertising, Los Angeles, CA.............(310) 777-6800
Sosa, Bromley, Aguilar, Noble & Associates,
    San Antonio, TX...(210) 227-2013
Tatham EURO RSCG, Chicago, IL..................(312) 337-4400
TBWA, New York, NY......................................(212) 725-1150
Team One, El Segundo, CA..............................(313) 615-2000
Trahan, Burden & Charles, Baltimore, MD......(410) 347-7500
Tucker Wayne/Luckie & Co., Atlanta, GA......(404) 347-8700
Uniworld, New York, NY..................................(212) 219-1600
Valentine-Radford, Kansas City, MO...............(816) 842-5021
W. B. Doner & Co., Southfield, MI..................(810) 354-9700
Waring & LaRosa, New York, NY....................(212) 755-0700
Warwick Baker & Fiore, New York, NY...........(212) 941-4200
The Weightman Group, Philadelphia, PA.........(215) 561-6100
Wells Rich Greene/BDDP, New York, NY........(212) 303-5000
WestGroup, Tampa, FL....................................(813) 224-9378
Wieden & Kennedy, Portland, OR...................(503) 228-4381
Wyse Advertising, Cleveland, OH...................(216) 696-2427
Yaffe & Co., Southfield, MI.............................(313) 262-1700
Young & Rubicam, New York, NY...................(212) 210-3000

Advertising Specialty Companies

Accessory Advertising.......................................(512) 335-3935
AccuCraft Pocket Scales..................................(501) 326-4700
Action Print Wear..(800) 880-5307
The Adcap Apron & Bag Line.........................(800) 868-7111
Aero Rubber..(800) 662-1009
AGC..(800) 989-1876
All Shore Trading...(800) 959-0548
Allstar Plastic Industries..................................(800) 337-0524
Amenities Unlimited..(800) 739-9058
American Design Group...................................(800) 541-1888
Anthony & Co..(800) 548-3450
Apsco Enterprises..(800) 789-2342
Arlington Crystal...(800) 848-4224
B.C.D.K..(800) 760-3052
B-D Printing..(800) 518-2515
Brueckman Specialties.....................................(313) 272-4710
Bulova...(800) 423-3553

BuzTronics...(800) 878-3413
C.R. Mfg. ....(800) 328-3984
C. W. Marsh...(616) 722-3781
Case Products Div. Casecraft ....(800) 795-1337
Commercial Sewing ....(800) 905-5509
Competitive Edge ....(800) 458-3343
Concept Promotions...................................(800) 327-6098
The Crazy Hatter..(516) 475-0023
Creative Classics.......................................(812) 537-2275
Crest Products...(800) 343-0711
Cromex America ....(800) 876-5705
Designed Printed Products ....(708) 697-3882
Dolsey Ltd..(800) 969-7473
Dri Mark U.S.A...(800) 645-9118
E.W. Hannas ....(800) 864-2750
Fitness Industries ....(800) 791-0131
Flexmag Industries ....(800) 543-4426
Gemini Technologies ....(800) 788-3891
Graphex ....(800) 524-9525
Graphically Speaking ....(517) 269-9200
Graphic Imprints ....(800) 806-6758
Guild Paper & Plastic Products ....(800) 266-8934
Head West ....(800) 826-0759
Hologram World..(800) 806-6015
Image Time ....(800) 938-0171
Imperial Promotions ....(312) 481-1616
Inflatable Image ....(800) 783-5441
J K Enterprises ....(800) 248-3441
JRM Industries..(201) 779-9340
K-Products ....(800) 959-0422
LBU..(800) 969-2468
M&B Headwear..(804) 648-1603
MagneCorp..(612) 546-8244
Magnetic Productions.................................(800) 806-6046
Maryland China ....(800) 638-3880
Medallic Art ....(800) 843-9854
Merrick Industries......................................(800) 426-5454
Mespo Umbrellas ....(800) 991-1427
Mitchellace..(800) 848-8696
Montco Graphics ....(610) 825-2525
Morgan/Artcraft Screenprint ....(800) 786-0687
New Image ....(800) 836-0523
Nite Lite Balloons ....(800) 423-4800
PAGEfinder ....(617) 239-9899
Polyman Plastics ....(800) 563-0814
Pop Tops Sportswear..................................(800) 647-8677
Precision Incentives ....(800) 509-0544
Prime Manufacturing Technologies ....(800) 818-4922
Print Plus ....(800) 977-0695
Progressive Promotions...............................(201) 945-0500
RBG Cannons ....(203) 245-1216
RBI Industries ....(800) 942-8463
Rhode Island Textile ....(800) 556-6488
Right Choice Advertisement ....(800) 535-8256
Sakar International.....................................(800) 949-1089
Screened Images ....(800) 959-0062
SGI...(800) 667-7418
The Sherwood Group ....(800) 939-2450
Shirtz Unlimited...(800) 728-4291
Showcase Specialties ....(800) 739-9102
Shumsky Enterprises...................................(800) 326-2203

Solar World	(719) 635-5125
Southington Tool & Manufacturing	(203) 276-0021
Specialized Promotions	(800) 739-9154
Spectratek	(310) 473-4966
Stanton Manufacturing	(314) 365-2441
Tweel Home Furnishings	(800) 273-6308
U.S. Box	(800) 221-0999
Unitron	(516) 589-6666
West Hawk Industries	(800) 678-1286
Yale Sportswear	(800) 503-3879
Zuse	(203) 458-3295

Information Brokers

ANCHORAGE, AK
InformAlaska .... (907) 563-4375

ATLANTA, GA
Integrated Research & Information Services .... (404) 321-9459
Library Specialists .... (404) 523-0628

BALTIMORE, MD
Carr Research Group .... (410) 719-8630
The Information Consultancy .... (410) 532-7275

BOSTON, MA
Rumrill Information Service .... (617) 787-6905

BUFFALO, NY
Information Plus .... (716) 852-2220

CHARLOTTE, NC
Information/Access Online .... (704) 364-7987

CHICAGO, IL
CombsMoorhead Associates .... (312) 944-4020
Information Age Resources .... (312) 334-8083
The Litdis Group .... (312) 918-3218
Newsclip .... (312) 751-7300

CINCINNATI, OH
Information Advantage .... (513) 723-1400

CLEVELAND, OH
Information Specialists .... (216) 321-7500
ZETA Intelligence .... (216) 579-0327

COLUMBUS, OH
Frautschi Information Services .... (614) 457-5445
Infinity Information Network .... (614) 329-3832

DALLAS, TX
F1 Services .... (214) 528-9895

DENVER, CO
Access/Information .... (303) 778-7691
Knowledge Brokers .... (303) 777-8653

FORT WORTH, TX
D. Hanson, Consulting .... (817) 738-0646

GRAND RAPIDS, MI
Beaumont Information Services .... (616) 942-0013

Honolulu, HI
Honolulu Information Service ....(808) 732-8778

Houston, TX
Burwell Enterprises ....(713) 537-9051
InfoResearch Services...(713) 463-3863
Williams Information Services...........................(713) 667-2868

Indianapolis, IN
HARRIS Marketing ....(317) 251-9729

Kansas City, MO
Information Retrieval...(816) 444-4253

Las Vegas, NV
Immedia Results Information
  Consulting Services ....(702) 645-0619
IQ: InfoQuick ....(702) 895-1570

Los Angeles, CA
Cal Info...(213) 957-5035
Law Offices of B. Mark Nordman ....(310) 202-9192

Miami, FL
BioInformation Resources ....(305) 854-0070
HNz Marketsearch & Information.....................(305) 381-9999

Milwaukee, WI
Information Express..(414) 272-5250
The LITDIS Group. ....(414) 271-0909
Worldlink..(414) 225-0700

Minneapolis, MN
Ann Potter & Associates ....(612) 338-5750
Nancy Jackson Gronbeck, Information Broker .(612) 332-1866

New York, NY
Alternative Research.. (212) 683-3478
Diamant Business Information (DBI) ....(212) 678-8907
Docutronics Information Services......................(212) 730-7140
Gretes Research Services.....................................(212) 535-7472
Harold L. Hubbard, Consultant ....(212) 861-2464
Joat Information ....(212) 370-9589
Knowledge = Power..(212) 251-0470
MBRS Information Services ....(212) 799-7533
The Merlo Company ....(516) 653-8911
Welker Research & Translation.........................(212) 787-3556

North Miami Beach, FL
Computer Assisted Research On Line...............(305) 944-2111

Oakland, CA
Information Finders...(510) 654-7730
Isis Information Services ....(510) 268-8675
Krauss Research ....(510) 482-8760
PFC Information Services ....(510) 653-0666
RISA SACKS Information Services...................(510) 530-6154
The Rugge Group ....(510) 530-3635

Philadelphia, PA
Ayers Information Network ....(215) 842-9450
Cooper Hydock Rugge...(215) 823-5490
DIALOG's DIALSEARCH................................(800) 634-2564

The Marketing Audit ....(215) 545-6620

PHOENIX, AZ
NDR..(800) 829-5578

PITTSBURGH, PA
Suzanne Paul Information Services...................(412) 683-1719

PORTLAND, OR
InfoQuest! Information Services........................(503) 228-4023

RALEIGH, NC
The New Synergy Partnership ....(919) 839-8811
PiSYS IQ Information Quest ....(919) 829-8918

ST. LOUIS, MO
LCM Research...(314) 352-1700
M. V. Gaffey...(314) 726-9013
Patent Information Services..............................(314) 434-6812

SALT LAKE CITY, UT
Information Ink ....(801) 273-0997

SAN ANTONIO, TX
Information Research Center............................(210) 829-0001

SAN DIEGO, CA
Deward Houck, Attorney at Law ....(619) 544-1492

SAN FRANCISCO, CA
Access Information Services ....(415) 564-9096
UMI Information Store......................................(415) 433-5500

SEATTLE, WA
DataQuad Information Services........................(206) 363-8662
Golden Information Group ....(206) 547-5662
Skillful Scholar..(206) 325-3625

WASHINGTON, DC
Alex Kramer Private
    Research and Investigations ....(202) 234-5410
Bates Information Services................................(202) 332-2360
Docutronics Information Services.....................(202) 347-5600

Source: a selection of the thousands of firms named in the Information
Broker's Directory. *This annual directory is available in book form and
on disk from Burwell Enterprises. To order, contact Burwell Enterprises,
3742 F.M. 1960 West, Suite 214, Houston, TX 77068; phone
(713) 537-9051, fax (713) 537-8332.*

Insurance Companies

Aetna Life & Casualty ....(203) 273-0123
Allstate Life ....(708) 402-5000
American Express Financial Advisers................(612) 671-3131
Cigna..(203) 726-6000
The Equitable Company ....(212) 554-1234
Jackson National Life ....(517) 394-3400
John Hancock Mutual Life.................................(617) 572-6000
Lincoln National Life Insurance Company ....(219) 455-2000
Massachusetts Mutual Life
    Insurance Company.......................................(413) 788-8411
Metropolitan Life Insurance..............................(212) 578-2211
Mutual Life Insurance of New York ....(212) 708-2000

Nationwide Insurance Enterprise ....(614) 249-7111
The New England ....(617) 578-2000
New York Life Insurance ....(212) 576-7000
Northwestern Mutual Life ....(414) 271-1444
Pacific Mutual ....(714) 640-3011
Principal Financial Group ....(515) 247-5111
The Prudential Insurance
   Company of America ....(201) 802-6000
State Farm Automobile Mutual Insurances ....(309) 766-2311
Teachers Insurance & Annuity ....(212) 490-9000
Travelers Insurance Companies ....(203) 277-0111
Variable Annuity Life Insurance Company ....(713) 526-5251

Market Research Firms

Abt Associates ....(617) 492-7100
The Arbitron ....(212) 887-1300
Audits & Surveys ....(212) 627-9700
The BASES Group ....(606) 655-6000
Burke Marketing Research ....(513) 241-5663
D&B Marketing Information Services ....(203) 834-4200
Elrick & Lavidge ....(404) 938-3233
Information Resources ....(312) 726-1221
Intersearch ....(215) 442-9000
J. D. Power & Associates ....(818) 889-6330
The M/A/R/C Group ....(214) 506-3400
Marco International ....(301) 572-0200
Maritz Marketing Research ....(314) 827-1610
Market Facts ....(708) 590-7000
Millward Brown ....(708) 505-0066
The National Research Group ....(213) 549-5000
NFO Research ....(203) 629-8888
The NPD Group ....(516) 625-0700
Opinion Research ....(908) 281-5100
Roper Starch Worldwide ....(914) 698-0800
Walker Group ....(317) 843-8843
Walsh America/PMSI ....(602) 381-9500
Westat ....(301) 251-1500

Paging Companies

International Communications Link ....(800) 448-3004
Metrocall ....(800) 800-2337
Mobilecomm Nationwide Messaging ....(800) 305-1616
MobileMedia ....(800) 437-2337
Moore Paging ....(800) 638-2893
Pagenet of New Jersey ....(800) 365-2337
US Paging ....(800) 473-0846
VCP ....(800) 442-7001

Polling Companies

ALABAMA

Southern Opinion Research, Tuscaloosa ....(205) 349-3916

ALASKA

Alaska Analysts/Dittman Research Corporation
   of Alaska, Anchorage ....(907) 243-3345

ARIZONA

The Insight Group Incorporated, Phoenix ....(602) 340-1610
O'Neil Associates, Tempe ....(602) 967-4441

CALIFORNIA

Asian Marketing Communication
    Research, Belmont..(415) 595-5028
Charlton Research, San Francisco....................(415) 981-2343
Commsciences, Los Angeles ....(213) 937-7607
Computer-Assisted Survey Methods
    Program, Berkeley...(510) 642-1104
Fairbank, Maslin, Maullin Assoc.,
    Santa Monica..(310) 828-1183
Field Research Corporation, San Francisco.......(415) 392-5763
Gene Bregman & Assocs., San Francisco..........(415) 957-9700
Hispanic & Asian Marketing Communication
    Research, Belmont..(415) 595-5028
Institute for Social Science Research,
    Los Angeles...(310) 825-0712
Interviewing Service of America, Van Nuys .....(818) 989-1044
J. D. Franz Research, Sacramento ....(916) 488-1550
Juárez and Assocs., Los Angeles.......................(310) 478-0826
Market Development, San Diego......................(619) 232-5628
PRIMER, Carmel...(408) 626-4309
Rand Survey Research Group, Santa Monica ...(310) 393-0411
SRI International, Menlo Park ....(415) 859-4164
Survey Methods Group, San Francisco.............(415) 495-6692
Survey Operations Center, San Diego ....(619) 553-7602
Survey Research Center, Berkeley .. ..(510) 642-6578

COLORADO

Ciruli Assocs., Denver.......................................(303) 595-0748
Rocky Mountain Research Group,
    Colorado Springs ....(719) 634-6824
Talmey-Drake Research & Strategy, Boulder ....(303) 443-5300

CONNECTICUT

Goldstein/Krall Marketing Resources,
    Stamford...(203) 359-2820
The Roper Center for Public Opinion
    Research, Storrs ....(203) 486-4440
Survey Sampling, Fairfield ....(203) 255-4200
Yankelovich Partners, Westport........................(203) 227-2700

DISTRICT OF COLUMBIA

Belden & Russonello ....(202) 789-2400
Center for Communication Dynamics...............(202) 842-1010
Hamilton & Staff ....(202) 686-5900
Market Facts ....(202) 429-6990
Mathew Greenwald and Assocs. ....(202) 686-0300
National Research ....(202) 686-9350
Price Waterhouse/Survey Research Center ....(202) 828-9061

FLORIDA

Oppenheim Research, Tallahassee ....(904) 386-9100
Survey Research Laboratory, Tallahassee...........(904) 644-5270

GEORGIA

Ayres & Assocs., Roswell ....(404) 594-7898
E & P Research, Atlanta....................................(404) 391-0224
The Marketing Workshop, Norcross..................(404) 449-6767
SDR, Atlanta...(404) 451-5100

ILLINOIS

A. C. Nielsen Company, Northbrook................(708) 498-6300
American Medical Association, Chicago ....(312) 464-5135

Creative & Response Research Services,
    Chicago ....(312) 828-9200
The Gary Siegel Organization, Chicago.............(312) 539-2922
L. C. Williams & Assocs., Chicago ....(800) 837-7123
National Opinion Research Center, Chicago ...(312) 753-7500
Northern Illinois University Public
    Opinion Laboratory, De Kalb ....(815) 753-0555
Northwestern University Survey Laboratory,
    Evanston ....(708) 491-8759
Organizational Studies
    International, Chicago ....(312) 977-9040
Richard Day Research, Evanston ....(708) 328-2329
Sawtooth Software, Evanston ....(708) 866-0870
Survey Research Laboratory, Chicago...............(312) 996-5300

INDIANA

Center for Survey Research, Bloomington ....(812) 855-2573

IOWA

Central Surveys, Shenandoah............................(712) 246-1630
Social Science Institute, Iowa City....................(319) 335-2367
Starr Litigation Services, West Des Moines ......(515) 224-1616

KANSAS

Central Research Corporation, Topeka ....(913) 233-8948

MAINE

Market Decisions, South Portland ....(207) 799-2226
Survey Research Center, Portland ....(207) 780-4430

MARYLAND

The Arbitron Company, Laurel ....(301) 497-4835
Aspen Systems Corporation, Silver Spring ....(301) 585-8181
Coda, Silver Spring ....(301) 588-0177
Herschel Shosteck Assocs., Silver Spring..........(301) 589-2259
Hollander, Cohen & McBride, Baltimore ....(410) 337-2121
Interviewing Service of America,
    East Grasonville...(410) 827-4855
The Mayatech Corporation, Silver Spring........(301) 587-1600
R/S/M, Lanham ....(301) 306-0844
Schaefer Center Survey Research Assocs.,
    Baltimore...(410) 837-6188
Survey Research Assocs., Baltimore ....(410) 377-5660
Survey Research Center, College Park ....(301) 314-7831
Westat, Rockville ....(301) 251-1500

MASSACHUSETTS

ABT Assocs., Cambridge ....(617) 492-7100
Cambridge Reports/Research International,
    Cambridge...(617) 661-0110
Center for Survey Research, Boston ....(617) 287-7200
Chadwick Martin Bailey, Boston ....(617) 350-8922
Kochevar Research Assocs., Cambridge ....(617) 868-0024
Opinion Dynamics, Cambridge.........................(617) 492-1400

MICHIGAN

Center for Urban Studies, Detroit ....(313) 577-8353
Datastat, Ann Arbor ....(313) 994-0540
Information Transfer Systems, Ann Arbor ....(313) 994-0003
Project for Urban and Regional Affairs, Flint ...(810) 762-3383
Survey Design & Analysis, Ann Arbor ....(313) 663-0424
Survey Research Center, Ann Arbor.................(313) 763-5039

MINNESOTA

Minnesota Center for Survey Research,
Minneapolis ....(612) 627-4282
Mori Research, Minneapolis ....(612) 835-3050
Research Solutions, Minneapolis ....(612) 825-8887

MISSOURI

Marketeam/Doane Marketing Research,
St. Louis ....(314) 878-7707

NEVADA

Center for Survey Research, Las Vegas..............(702) 895-3322

NEW HAMPSHIRE

Dudley Research, Exeter....................................(603) 778-1583
The Survey Center, Durham ....(603) 862-2186

NEW JERSEY

Datan, Princeton ....(609) 921-6098
The Eagleton Poll, New Brunswick ....(908) 828-2210
The Gallup Organization, Princeton ....(609) 924-9600
Hypotenuse, Verona ....(201) 857-8500
Jennifer Macleod Assocs., Princeton
Junction...(609) 799-0378
John G. Stryker, Kendall Park...........................(908) 297-7251
Mathematica Policy Research, Princeton..........(609) 799-3535
Mathtech, Princeton ....(609) 520-3860
Princeton Survey Research Assocs.,
Princeton..(609) 924-9204
Research 100, Princeton....................................(609) 924-6100
Research Strategies Corporation, Princeton......(609) 683-1119
Response Analysis Corporation, Princeton ....(609) 921-3333
Schrader Research & Rating Service,
Cranbury ....(609) 395-1200
Statistical Research, Westfield ....(908) 654-4000
Total Research Corporation, Princeton ....(609) 520-9100

NEW YORK

A. Foster Higgins & Co., New York ....(212) 574-9082
AHF Marketing Research, New York ....(212) 941-5555
Audits & Surveys, New York ....(212) 627-9700
Blum & Weprin Assocs., New York...................(212) 929-6510
Chelsea Research Group, New York ....(212) 362-0360
David & Assocs., New York ....(212) 393-9100
EDK Assocs., New York ....(212) 582-4504
Eric Marder Assocs., New York ....(212) 986-2130
Fact Finders, Albany..(518) 439-7400
Goldhaber Research Assocs., Amherst ....(716) 689-3311
Gordon S. Black Corporation, Rochester..........(716) 272-8400
Intermarket Research, New York ....(212) 929-2901
Jeanne Anderson Research, New York ....(212) 243-4252
Louis Harris & Assocs., New York ....(212) 698-9600
Keleman Assocs., New York...............................(212) 666-1822
The Ketchum Public Relations Research &
Measurement Department, New York............(212) 536-8765
KRC Research & Consulting, New York...........(212) 484-7250
Madden Public Opinion Research, New York...(201) 659-3644
Marketing Answers Consultants, Ardsley ....(914) 693-7737
Mitofsky International, New York ....(212) 582-5675
Monroe Mendelsohn Research, New York ....(212) 677-8100
Opatow Assocs., New York ....(212) 421-4837

Renaissance Research & Consulting,
   New York ....(212) 319-1833
Roper Starch Worldwide, New York..................(212) 599-0700
Ruth Diamond Market Research Services,
   Buffalo..(716) 836-1110
Schulman, Ronca & Bucuvalas, New York ....(212) 779-7700
Voter News Service, New York ....(212) 947-7280

NORTH CAROLINA

Institute for Research in Social Science,
   Chapel Hill..(919) 962-0781
Marketwise, Charlotte...(704) 332-8433
Research Triangle Institute,
   Research Triangle Park ....(919) 541-6220

OHIO

The Craig Group, Columbus...............................(614) 241-2222
Institute for Policy Research, Cincinnati ....(513) 556-5028
NFO Research, Toledo ....(419) 661-8209
Polimetrics Laboratory for Political and
   Social Research, Columbus ....(614) 292-1061
Senecio Software, Bowling Green ....(419) 352-4371
The Social Dynamics Group, Cleveland ....(216) 351-2972
Survey Research Center, Akron..........................(216) 972-5111

PENNSYLVANIA

Chilton Research Services, Radnor ....(215) 964-4632
Genesys Sampling Systems, Philadelphia ....(215) 521-6747
ICR Survey Research Group, Media...................(215) 565-9280
Institute for Survey Research, Philadelphia.......(215) 204-8319
National Analysts, Philadelphia ....(215) 496-6800
Survey America, Morrisville ....(215) 736-1600

TEXAS

Shell Oil Company, Houston..............................(713) 241-6161

UTAH

Survey Research Center, Salt Lake City.............(801) 581-6491

VIRGINIA

Isis, Fairfax ....(703) 425-6319
Q S & A Research and Strategy, Fairfax ....(703) 273-7007
Survey Research Laboratory, Richmond.............(804) 367-8813
Virginia Tech Center for Survey Research,
   Blacksburg...(703) 231-3676
The Wirthlin Group, McLean ....(703) 556-0001

WASHINGTON

Elway Research, Seattle.......................................(206) 728-1620
Social & Economic Sciences Research Center,
   Pullman...(509) 335-1511

WISCONSIN

Computer Assisted Survey Systems, Madison ...(608) 231-1217
HBRS, Madison...(608) 232-2800
Letters and Science Survey Center, Madison....(608) 262-1688
Wisconsin Survey Research Laboratory,
   Madison...(608) 262-3122
Zigman Joseph Stephenson, Milwaukee ....(414) 273-4680

Source: Taken from The Blue Book of the American Association
for Public Opinion Research/World Association for Public Opinion
Research.

Business Services (Public Relations)

Public Relations Firms, National

Anthony M. Franco	(313) 567-2300
Bader Rutter & Assocs.	(414) 784-7200
Burson-Marsteller	(212) 614-4000
Cohn & Wolfe	(404) 688-5900
Cone Comms.	(617) 227-2111
Copithorne & Bellows	(415) 284-5200
Cunningham Comms.	(408) 982-0400
Dennis Davidson Assocs.	(213) 954-5858
Dewe Rogerson	(212) 688-6840
Dix & Eaton	(216) 241-0405
Dye, Van Mol & Lawrence	(615) 244-1818
Earle Palmer Brown	(301) 657-6000
Edelman PR Worldwide	(312) 240-3000
Edward Howard & Co.	(216) 781-2400
EvansGroup PR Division	(801) 364-7000
Financial Relations Board	(312) 266-7800
Fleishman-Hillard	(314) 982-1700
GCI Group	(212) 546-2200
Gibbs & Soell	(212) 697-2600
Gross Townsend Frank Hoffman	(212) 886-3111
E. Bruce Harrison	(202) 638-1200
Edward Howard & Co.	(216) 781-2400
Hill and Knowlton	(212) 885-0300
Jasculca/Terman & Assocs.	(312) 337-7400
The Jefferson Group	(202) 626-8500
KCSA PR	(212) 682-6300
The Kamber Group	(202) 223-8700
Ketchum PR	(212) 878-4600
Lobsenz-Stevens	(212) 684-6300
Makovsky & Co.	(212) 532-6300
Manning, Selvage & Lee	(212) 213-0909
Morgan & Myers	(414) 674-4026
Morgen-Walke Assocs.	(212) 850-5600
MWW/Strategic Comms.	(201) 507-9500
Nelson Comms. Group & Nelson, Robb, Duval & DeMenna	(714) 957-1010
Ogilvy Adams & Rinehart	(212) 880-5200
Omnicom PR Network	(206) 442-9900
Pacific/West Comms. Group	(206) 442-9900
Padilla Speer Beardsley	(612) 871-8877
Powell Tate	(202) 347-6633
Public Comms.	(312) 558-1770
Robinson Lake/Sawyer Miller/Bozell	(212) 484-7700
The Rockey Co.	(206) 728-1100
The Rowland Co.	(212) 527-8800
Ruder Finn	(212) 593-6400
S&S Public Relations	(708) 291-1616
Shandwick	(212) 972-8080
Stoorza, Ziegaus & Metzger	(619) 236-1332
Taylor-Rafferty Assocs.	(212) 889-4350
Watt, Roop & Co.	(216) 566-7019
The Weber Group	(617) 661-7900

Source: O'Dwyers 1995 Directory of Public Relations Firms, *published by the Jack O'Dwyer Co., 271 Madison Ave., New York, NY 10016.*

Public Relations Firms, Local

ANCHORAGE, AK
Bradley Reid Comms. ....(907) 274-9563
Bruce Pozzi Public Relations ....(907) 272-8880
Corporate Comms. Strategies..............................(907) 345-4406

ATLANTA, GA
A. Brown-Olmstead Assocs................................(404) 659-0919
Cohn & Wolfe...(404) 688-5900
Pringle Dixon Pringle ....(404) 688-6720

BALTIMORE, MD
Adams Sandler ....(410) 558-2100
Image Dynamics ....(410) 539-7730
Trahan, Burden & Charles...................................(410) 347-7500

BOSTON, MA
Agnew, Carter, McCarthy ....(617) 437-7722
Bridgeman Comms. ....(617) 742-7270
Miller Comms...(617) 536-0470

BUFFALO, NY
Collins & Co. ....(716) 884-4520
Singer PR & Promotions......................................(716) 884-8885
Weekes Writes ....(716) 832-5894

CHARLOTTE, NC
Epley Assocs ....(704) 522-1220
Luquire George Andrews.....................................(704) 366-0999
Selz, Seabolt & Assocs. ....(704) 541-0429

CHICAGO, IL
FSC Group...(312) 943-8116
Media Strategy...(312) 944-7398
Minkus & Dunne Comms. ....(312) 541-8787

CINCINNATI, OH
Dan Pinger PR ....(513) 751-6161
Martiny PR ....(513) 489-4600
Northlich, Stolley, Lawarre ....(513) 421-8840

CLEVELAND, OH
Edward Howard & Co.,...(216) 781-2400
McKinney/PR...(216) 621-5133

COLUMBUS, OH
Cochran Public Relations ....(614) 224-0600
Lord Sullivan & Yoder PR ....(614) 846-7777
Werth, Paul Assocs...(614) 224-8114

DALLAS, TX
Bustin & Co. ....(214) 720-3700
Laurey Peat & Assocs...(214) 871-8787
Meltzer & Martin PR ....(214) 953-0808

DENVER, CO
Darcy Comms. ....(303) 480-0123
Kostka, William, and Assocs...............................(303) 623-8421

DETROIT, MI
Anthony M. Franco...(313) 567-2300
Bassett & Bassett ....(313) 567-4150

Lovio-George ....(313) 832-2210

GRAND RAPIDS, MI

Sefton Assocs. ....(616) 957-0600
Seyferth & Assocs. ....(616) 776-3511

HARRISBURG, PA

Andrews, Sacunas & Saline ....(717) 233-8853

HARTFORD, CT

O'Neal & Prelle ....(203) 527-3233
Salius Comms. ....(203) 231-7770

HONOLULU, HI

Hill & Knowlton ....(808) 521-5391
Professional Comms. ....(808) 528-3159
Stryker Weiner Assocs. ....(808) 523-8802

HOUSTON, TX

Booker Hancock & Assocs. ....(713) 439-7581
Darcy Communications ....(713) 942-0002
Rives Carlberg ....(713) 965-0764

INDIANAPOLIS, IN

Borshoff Johnson & Co. ....(317) 923-2300
Caldwell Vanriper ....(317) 632-6501

KANSAS CITY, MO

Everett, Klamp, Bernauer & Assocs. ....(816) 421-0000
Icon Marketing Comms. ....(816) 561-8120
Spectrum Comms. ....(816) 891-7644

LAS VEGAS, NV

Carrara Group ....(702) 362-7700

LOS ANGELES, CA

Bohle ....(310) 785-0515
Cerrell Assocs. ....(213) 466-3445
Dennis Davidson Assocs. ....(213) 954-5858

MEMPHIS, TN

Archer & Malmo ....(901) 523-2000
Walker & Assocs. ....(901) 522-1100

MIAMI, FL

Beare, Nikki & Assocs. ....(904) 539-9955
Meyer, Hank, Assocs. ....(305) 576-5700
Rubin Barney & Birger ....(305) 448-7450

MILWAUKEE, WI

Peter Acly Comms. ....(414) 347-7866
Meyer & Wallis ....(414) 224-0212
Ron Sonntag PR ....(414) 354-0200

MINNEAPOLIS, MN

Carmichael Lynch Spong ....(612) 334-6000
Padilla, Speer, Beardsley ....(612) 871-8877
Swenson/Falker Assocs. ....(612) 371-0000

NASHVILLE, TN

Buntin PR ....(615) 256-8844
Ericson PR ....(615) 242-1050
McNeely, Pigott & Fox ....(615) 259-4000

New Orleans, LA

Bauerlein ....(504) 522-5461

New York, NY

Anreder & Co. ....(212) 421-4020
Cairns & Assocs. ....(212) 421-9770
Kennedy, Daniel Comms. Services ....(212) 580-3454
Sims & Assocs. ....(212) 725-3838

Norfolk, VA

Brickell & Assocs. ....(804) 491-1985

Orlando, FL

Cramer-Krassell ....(407) 236-8300
Greenstone Roberts PR...(407) 422-0014
Robinson, Yesawich & Pepperdine ....(407) 875-1111

Philadelphia, PA

Harris Baio & McCullough ....(215) 440-9800
Tierney Group...(215) 732-4100

Phoenix, AZ

Kur Carr Group ....(602) 253-5838
Mullen PR..(602) 222-4343
Phillips & Partners ....(602) 381-6644

Pittsburgh, PA

Blattner/Brunner...(412) 263-2979
Skutski & Assocs. ....(412) 281-5656
Walshak Comms. ....(412) 835-7770

Portland, OR

Hastings, Humble, Giardini ....(503) 221-1063
Karakas VanSickle Ouellette.................................(503) 221-1551
Waggener Edstrom..(503) 245-0905

Providence, RI

Duffy & Shanley...(401) 274-0001
Martin Thomas PR ....(401) 331-8850
Rivers Doyle & Walsh...(401) 521-2700

Raleigh, NC

Brewer PR ....(919) 833-9353
Rockett, Burkhead, Lewis & Winslow...............(919) 848-2600

Sacramento, CA

Cooper Comms. ....(818) 348-8030
Latimer Burch PR ....(916) 448-2021
Revell Communications ....(916) 443-3816

St. Louis, MO

Farrell Group ....(314) 991-3555
Hughes Advertising..(314) 721-3400
The Vandiver Group ....(314) 394-4129

Salt Lake City, UT

EvansGroup PR ....(801) 364-7000
The Orton Group ....(801) 596-2100
Zabriskie & Assocs. ....(801) 484-7272

San Antonio, TX

Dublin-McCarter & Assocs....................................(210) 227-0221
S&C Advertising & PR ....(210) 342-7000

Business Services (Public Relations–Translators)

SAN DIEGO, CA

Gable Group ....(619) 234-1300
MacCracken & McGaugh............................(619) 696-8282
Palmer, Sharrit & Co. ....(619) 675-3300

SAN FRANCISCO, CA

Barnes Clarke ....(415) 788-1000
Fineman Assocs PR ....(415) 777-6933
Hi-Tech PR...(415) 904-7000

SEATTLE, WA

Ager & Assocs. PR ....(206) 343-5400
McKnight & Co. ....(206) 464-0884
The Rockey Company............................(206) 728-1100

TAMPA, FL

Fahlgren Benito ....(813) 222-1400
Roberts & Cline ....(813) 281-0088
Tucker/Hall...(813) 228-0652

VIRGINIA BEACH, VA

Barker Campbell & Farley.....................(804) 497-4811
Brickell & Assocs. ....(804) 491-1985

WASHINGTON, DC

Devillier Comms....................................(202) 833-8121
E. Bruce Harrison Co. ....(202) 638-1200
John Adams Assocs..............................(202) 737-8400

WEST PALM BEACH, FL

Kathy Kazen & Co. ....(407) 659-5660

Source: O'Dwyers 1995 Directory of Public Relations Firms *published by the Jack O'Dwyer Co., 271 Madison Ave., New York, NY 10016.*

Speakers Bureaus

Barnes Dyer Marketing.........................(714) 768-2943
Capital Speakers ....(202) 393-0772
Contemporary Comms ....(604) 224-2384
Harry Walker Agency............................(212) 563-0700
Lanktree Sports Celebrity Network ....(312) 266-9558
National Speakers Bureau ....(708) 295-1122
Royce Carlton..(212) 355-7700
Speakers Guild......................................(508) 888-6702
Standing Ovations.................................(619) 455-1850
Washington Speakers Bureau................(703) 684-0555

Translators/Interpreters

American Linguists, New York, NY...................(212) 213-8888
Arabic Business Center (Arabic)......................(817) 469-1612
Asian Translation & Typesetting,
   Alexandria, VA (Japanese, Korean) ....(703) 823-9773
C&E Translation & Desk Top Publishing,
   Vancouver, B.C. (Chinese) ....(800) 663-1884
Century, San Jose, CA ....(408) 249-0452
ComNet International,
   Westlake Village, CA (Arabic)......................(818) 991-1277
Copper Translation Service, Schenectady, NY..(518) 372-8940
The Corporate Word, Pittsburgh, PA ....(412) 391-0378
Diversified Language Institute, Torrance, CA...(310) 373-8433
Dynamic Language Center, Seattle, WA...........(206) 244-6709

East-West Concepts, Plainsboro, NJ ....(609) 275-7211

Eunkyung Na Korean Consulting,
Miami, FL (Korean)......................................(305) 220-6552

Foreign Language Services,
Charlottesville, VA...(804) 974-9090

Foreign Language Services, Huntsville, AL.......(205) 881-1120

Global Solutions, Wellesley Hills, MA..............(617) 431-2610

IME Corporation, Hoffman Estates, IL
(Russian, Ukrainian) ....(708) 310-3355

Inter-Contact, Miami, FL
(Spain, Latin America) ....(5114) 46 25 21

InterNation Communication, New York, NY ...(212) 274-8200

International Language Services,
Minneapolis, MN...(612) 934-5678

Japanese Technical Translations Orientation,
Marlborough, MA (Japanese) ....(508) 481-7220

Language Bridge Translations,
Columbus, OH (Russian, Ukrainian) ....(614) 548-4385

The Language Service, Poughkeepsie, NY ....(914) 473-4303

Mellon Bank Foreign Language Services,
Pittsburgh, PA..(412) 234-5751

MUS, St. Petersburg, FL (Spanish/English) ......(813) 895-2589

OMNI Interpreting and Translating Network...(800) 543-4244

OmniLingua, Cedar Rapids, IA ....(319) 365-8565

Philippine Languages Translators and
Interpreters, Benicia, CA ....(707) 745-1324

Premier Translation Services,
North Brunswick, NJ ....(908) 940-0470

Professional Thai Translations,
Lakeside, MT (Thai) ....(406) 844-2623

ProTrans, Providence, RI..................................(401) 274-1776

SH3, Kansas City, MO ....(816) 767-1117

Speak Easy Languages, Plymouth, MI...............(313) 459-5556

Spiridonov & Assocs., Berkeley, CA ....(510) 549-3516

Stevens Language Center, Long Island, NY
(Dutch, French, German) ....(516) 261-0216

Sykes Enterprises, Boulder, CO........................(303) 440-0909

Terra Pacific, Seattle, WA.................................(206) 343-7102

Translation Aces, New York, NY ....(212) 269-4660

Translingua, Columbia, MD.............................(410) 730-9700

Universal Translation Agency,
Sherman Oaks, CA ....(213) 626-0011

Verbatim, Pittsburgh, PA
(Spanish, French, Portuguese) ....(412) 621-0635

Vision Graphics International,
New York, NY (Korean)................................(212) 268-9733

Whitman Language Services,
Palo Alto, CA...(415) 325-4192

The Wordmill, Healdsburg, CA........................(707) 431-7414

Wordnet Incorporated, Acton, MA..................(508) 264-0600

Source: American Translators Association, 1800 Diagonal Rd., Suite 220, Alexandria, VA 22314, (703) 683-6100.

Computer Supply Mail Order Companies

ACS	(800) 774-7014
APC	(800) 800-4272
APS Technologies	(800) 235-9125
Club Mac	(800) 258-2622
CompUSA Direct	(800) 266-7872
Computer Discount Warehouse	(800) 279-4239
Data Comm Warehouse	(800) 328-2261
Egghead	(800) 344-4323
First Source International	(800) 439-9866
Insight Direct	(800) 998-8025
Macintosh Accessory Center	(800) 931-9711
MacMall	(800) 222-2808
Mac's Place	(800) 367-4222
Mac Zone	(800) 248-2088
Megahaus Hard Drives	(800) 473-0972
Micro Systems Warehouse	(800) 660-3222
Micro Warehouse	(800) 367-7080
Midwest Micro	(800) 682-7248
NECX Direct	(800) 961-9208
Nevada Computer	(800) 982-2946
PC and Mac Connection	(800) 800-1111
PCs Compleat	(800) 598-4727
Sunshine Computers	(800) 854-7754
Tiger Direct	(800) 666-2562
US Computer Supply	(800) 987-7877
USA Flex	(800) 766-1940
Worldwide Technologies	(800) 636-6792

Computer Hardware/Software Companies

The following is a list of computer hardware and software companies throughout the country. The first telephone number listed is a sales number. The second is a technical support number. If no second number is listed, the first number may be used for technical support.

Abacus Accounting Systems	(403) 488-8100
Abacus Software	(800) 451-4319
technical support	(616) 698-0330
ABL Electronics	(800) 726-0610
ABS-American Business Systems	(800) 356-4034
Acculogic	(800) 234-7811
technical support	(714) 454-2441
AceCad	(800) 676-4223
Acer America	(800) 733-2237
Acme Electric	(800) 325-5848
Action Plus Software	(800) 766-7229
technical support	(801) 255-0600
Acucobol	(800) 262-6585
technical support	(800) 399-7220
Adaptec	(408) 945-8600
technical support	(408) 934-7240
Addtron Technology	(800) 998-4638
technical support	(800) 998-4646
ADI Systems	(800) 228-0530
Adobe Systems	(800) 833-6687
Advanced Gravis Computer Technology	(800) 663-8558
technical support	(604) 431-5020
Advanced Logic Research	(800) 444-4257

Advanced Matrix Technology............................(800) 992-2264
Advanced Media ....(714) 965-7122
Advantage Memory ....(800) 245-5299
Affinity ....(800) 367-6771
   technical support ....(303) 442-4840
Agfa..(800) 424-8973
AimTech ....(800) 289-2884
Alacrity Systems ....(800) 252-2748
   technical support ....(908) 813-2501
Aladdin Systems ....(408) 761-6200
Aldus..(800) 333-2538
Altec Lansing Multimedia...............................(800) 648-6663
Altima Systems ....(800) 356-9990
Altsys ....(214) 680-2060
   technical support ....(415) 252-9080
American Power Conversion ....(800) 800-4272
AMP ....(800) 522-6752
Amrel Technology...(800) 882-6735
Analog & Digital Peripherals...........................(513) 339-2241
Analog Devices...(800) 262-5643
Analog Technology ....(818) 357-0098
Andromeda Systems ....(818) 709-7600
Antec ....(510) 770-1200
Antex Electronics ....(800) 338-4231
Apple Computer..(800) 538-9696
   technical support ....(800) 767-2775
Applied Micro Circuits ....(619) 450-9333
Appoint...(800) 448-1184
Apricorn ....(800) 458-5448
Archive Software...(800) 821-8782
Areal Technology ....(408) 436-6800
   technical support ....(843) 436-6843
Arnet..(800) 366-8844
Artek Computer Systems ....(510) 490-8402
Artisoft..(800) 846-9726
   technical support ....(602) 670-7000
Asanté Technologies ....(800) 662-9686
askSam Systems ....(800) 800-1997
   technical support ....(904) 584-6590
ASP Computer Products ....(800) 952-6277
Aspen Imaging International ....(800) 955-5555
AST Research..(800) 876-4278
Asymetrix ....(800) 448-6543
   technical support ....(206) 637-1600
ATI Technologies ....(905) 882-2600
Attachmate...(800) 426-6283
   technical support ....(800) 688-3270
Austin Computer Systems...............................(800) 752-1577
Autodesk...(800) 228-3601
Avance Logic ....(510) 226-9555
Award Software ....(415) 968-4433
Axelen (USA)..(206) 643-2781
Axis Comms. ....(617) 938-1188
Baler Software...(800) 327-6108
   technical support ....(708) 506-1770
Beame & Whiteside Software ....(800) 463-6637
Beaver Computer..(800) 827-4222
   technical support ....(800) 827-4888
Behavior Tech Computer (USA) ....(510) 657-3956
Belkin Components..(800) 223-5546
Bell & Howell..(800) 247-3724

Berkeley Speech Technologies	(510) 841-5083
Berkeley Systems	(510) 540-5535
Best Data Products	(800) 632-2378
technical support	(818) 772-9600
Best Power Technology	(800) 356-5794
Bit 3 Computer	(612) 881-6955
Bits Technical	(713) 735-9900
Blue Sky Software	(800) 677-4946
Boca Research	(407) 997-6227
technical support	(407) 241-8088
Bold Data Technology	(510) 490-8296
Borland International	(800) 331-0877
BOS National	(214) 956-7722
Brier Technology	(404) 564-5699
Brøderbund Software	(415) 382-4400
technical support	(415) 382-4700
Brooks Power Systems	(800) 523-1551
Brother International	(908) 356-8880
technical support	(901) 373-6256
Brysis Data	(818) 810-0355
Bureau of Electronic Publishing	(800) 828-4766
technical support	(201) 808-2780
BusLogic	(408) 492-9090
technical support	(408) 654-0760
Byte Brothers	(206) 271-9567
C-Power Products	(800) 800-2797
CA Retail Solutions	(800) 668-3767
technical support	(905) 793-9302
Cache Computers	(510) 226-9922
Caere	(800) 535-7226
technical support	(800) 462-2373
Calculus	(305) 481-2334
Camintonn/Z-Ram	(714) 454-1500
Campbell Services	(800) 345-6747
Canon USA	(800) 848-4123
technical support	(800) 423-2366
Cardiff Software	(800) 659-8755
technical support	(619) 931-4565
CarNel Enterprises	(800) 962-1450
Carroll Touch	(512) 244-3500
Casio	(800) 962-2746
CBIS	(404) 446-1332
CD Technology	(408) 752-8500
Central Point Software	(800) 445-4208
technical support	(800) 491-2764
Centrepoint	(613) 235-7054
Certified Management Software	(801) 534-1231
CH Products	(800) 624-5804
technical support	(619) 598-2518
Champion Business Systems	(800) 243-2626
Chaplet Systems U.S.A.	(408) 732-7950
technical support	(408) 732-6159
Cherry Electrical Products	(708) 662-9200
Chicony America	(714) 380-0928
Chinon America	(800) 441-0222
Chipsoft	(602) 295-3110
Chronocom	(418) 449-4378
Chuck Atkinson Programs	(800) 826-5009
technical support	(800) 829-4005
Cimmetry Systems	(800) 361-1904
Cipher Data Products	(800) 424-7437

Cirrus Logic	(510) 623-8300
Citizen America	(800) 477-4683
technical support	(310) 453-0614
Citrix Systems	(800) 437-7503
Clarion Software	(800) 354-5444
technical support	(305) 785-4556
Claris	(800) 325-2747
technical support	(408) 727-9054
Clark Development	(800) 356-1686
technical support	(801) 261-1686
Clary	(800) 442-5279
CMG Technology	(800) 426-3832
Codenoll Technology	(914) 965-6300
Colorado Memory Systems	(303) 635-1500
Command Comms	(800) 288-3491
technical support	(800) 288-6794
Commax Technologies	(800) 526-6629
technical support	(408) 435-8272
Commercial & Industrial Design	(714) 556-0888
Compaq Computer	(800) 345-1518
technical support	(800) 652-6672
CompSee	(800) 628-3888
CompuAdd	(800) 999-9901
CompuLan Technology	(800) 486-8810
CompuRegister	(314) 365-2050
Computer Aided Technology	(214) 350-0888
Computer Assocs. International	(800) 225-5224
Computer Friends	(800) 547-3303
technical support	(503) 626-2291
Computer Law Systems	(800) 328-1913
Computer Modules	(408) 496-1881
Computer Peripherals	(800) 854-7600
technical support	(714) 454-2441
Computone	(800) 241-3946
CompuTrend Systems	(818) 333-5121
technical support	(800) 568-6388
Comy Technology	(408) 437-1555
technical support	(800) 505-4295
Concurrent Controls	(800) 487-2243
Connect Tech	(519) 836-1291
Connect-Air International	(800) 247-1978
Conner Peripherals	(408) 456-3167
Consumer Technology NW	(800) 356-3983
Contact Software International	(800) 365-0606
Core International	(407) 997-6044
technical support	(407) 997-6033
Corel Software	(800) 772-6735
Corel Systems	(800) 836-7274
technical support	(800) 818-1848
Corollary	(800) 338-4020
Cougar Mountain Software	(800) 388-3038
technical support	(800) 727-0656
CPU Products	(800) 882-1842
Creative Labs	(800) 998-5227
technical support	(405) 742-6622
Crystal Semiconductor	(512) 445-7222
technical support	(512) 445-3554
CrystalGraphics	(408) 496-6175
CTX International	(800) 289-2189
technical support	(800) 888-2012
Cybex	(205) 430-4000

CyCare Software Publishing	(800) 545-2488
technical support	(800) 548-2660
CYMA Systems	(800) 292-2962
DacEasy	(800) 222-8778
Dallas Semiconductor	(214) 450-8170
technical support	(214) 450-3850
Danpex	(408) 437-7557
Dassault Electronic	(212) 909-0550
Data Access	(800) 451-3539
technical support	(305) 232-3142
Data Entry Systems	(205) 430-3023
technical support	(205) 837-8715
Data General	(800) 328-2436
technical support	(800) 344-3577
Data I/O	(800) 247-5700
Data Race	(800) 749-7223
technical support	(800) 940-7223
Data Technology	(408) 942-4000
technical support	(408) 262-7700
Databook	(716) 292-5720
technical support	(716) 292-5725
Datacap	(914) 332-7515
Datacap Systems	(215) 699-7051
Datalux	(800) 328-2589
Datasouth Computer	(800) 476-2120
DataSym	(519) 758-5800
Dataware	(800) 426-4844
Daystar	(800) 962-2077
technical support	(404) 967-2077
DD & TT Enterprise USA	(213) 780-0099
Dell Computer	(800) 289-3355
technical support	(800) 624-9896
DeLorme Mapping	(207) 865-4171
Delrina Technology	(800) 268-6082
technical support	(416) 443-4390
DeltaPoint	(800) 367-4334
technical support	(408) 375-4700
Deltec Electronics	(800) 854-2658
Deneba Software	(800) 622-6827
Denistron	(310) 530-3530
DesignCAD	(918) 825-4844
Deskstation Technology	(913) 599-1900
technical support	(913) 599-0911
DFM Systems	(800) 223-4791
Diamond Computer Systems	(408) 325-7000
technical support	(408) 325-7100
DigiBoard	(800) 344-4273
Digicom Systems	(800) 833-8900
technical support	(408) 934-1601
Digital Communications Assocs.	(800) 348-3221
technical support	(404) 740-0300
Digital Equipment	(800) 332-4636
technical support	(800) 354-9000
Digital Products	(800) 243-2333
Digital Vision	(800) 346-0090
technical support	(617) 329-5400
Digitalk	(800) 922-8255
Digitan Systems	(408) 954-8270
Discoversoft	(510) 769-2902
Disctec	(407) 671-5500
Distributed Processing Technology	(407) 830-5522

Dolch Computer Systems......................................(800) 538-7506
Dover Electronics Manufacturing ....(800) 848-1198
Dragon Systems ....(800) 825-5897
   technical support ....(617) 965-7670
Dycam..(818) 998-8008
   technical support ....(818) 407-3970
Dynamic Software ....(800) 627-1218
Dynapro ....(800) 667-0374
DynaTek Automation Systems.............................(416) 636-3000
   technical support ....(800) 267-6007
Eastman Kodak ....(800) 242-2424
Edimax Computer...(408) 496-1105
   technical support ....(408) 988-6092
EFA of America..(408) 987-5400
EFI Electronics ....(800) 877-1174
Electro Products..(800) 423-0646
Electrohome Limited ....(800) 265-2171
   technical support ....(716) 874-3630
Electronic Arts ....(800) 245-4525
Electronic Frontier Foundation.........................(202) 347-5400
Electronic Imagery ....(800) 645-9657
Elographics..(615) 482-4100
Emigre ....(916) 451-4344
Empress Software ....(301) 220-1919
Emulex ....(800) 854-7112
Enable Software ....(800) 888-0684
   technical support ....(518) 877-8236
Epson America ....(800) 922-8911
Ergotron ....(800) 888-8458
ETC Computer ....(510) 226-6250
ETEQ Microsystems ....(408) 432-8147
Everex Systems ....(800) 821-0806
   technical support ....(510) 498-4410
Exabyte ....(303) 442-4333
   technical support ....(800) 445-7736
Exide Electronics ....(800) 554-3448
ExperVision..(800) 732-3897
   technical support ....(408) 428-9234
Facit ....(800) 879-3224
Farallon Computing ....(510) 814-5000
FileNet ....(714) 966-3400
   technical support ....(714) 966-9990
Folex Film Systems ....(800) 631-1150
Folio ....(800) 543-6546
FontBank ....(708) 328-7370
   technical support ....(305) 445-6304
Fora ....(800) 367-3672
Foresight Resources ....(800) 231-8574
   technical support ....(816) 891-8418
Franklin Quest Technologies...............................(800) 877-1814
Free Computer Technology ....(408) 945-1118
Fuji Photo Film...(914) 789-8100
Fujitsu America ....(800) 626-4686
   technical support ....(408) 894-3950
Funk Software...(800) 828-4146
   technical support ....(617) 497-6339
Future Domain ....(800) 879-7599
   technical support ....(714) 253-0440
FutureSoft Engineering..(713) 496-9400
Futurus ....(800) 327-8296
   technical support ....(404) 825-0379

Gazelle Systems	(800) 786-3278
technical support	(801) 377-1288
GEC Plessey Semiconductors	(408) 438-2900
General Parametrics	(800) 223-0999
technical support	(510) 524-1060
General Ribbon	(800) 423-5400
Genesis Integrated Systems	(800) 325-6582
technical support	(612) 557-9226
Genoa Systems	(800) 934-3662
technical support	(408) 432-8324
Genovation	(714) 833-3355
Glenco Engineering	(800) 562-2543
GMC Technology	(909) 468-5686
Golden Power Systems	(805) 582-4400
Goldstar Technology	(800) 777-1192
Graphic Enterprises of Ohio	(800) 321-9874
Great Plains Software	(800) 456-0025
Group 1 Software	(800) 368-5806
GVC Technologies	(800) 289-4821
Hayes Microcomputer Products	(800) 426-7704
Health Software	(216) 759-2103
Hercules Computer Technology	(800) 532-0600
technical support	(510) 623-6050
Hewlett-Packard	(800) 752-0900
Hitachi America	(800) 369-0422
technical support	(800) 241-6558
Hooleon	(800) 937-1337
Horizons Technology	(619) 292-8320
HyperData	(909) 468-2955
Hyundai Electronics America	(408) 473-9200
technical support	(800) 289-4986
IBC/Integrated Business Computers	(800) 468-5847
IBM	(800) 426-3333
In Focus Systems	(800) 327-7231
Indiana Cash Drawer	(317) 398-6643
Infomatic Power Systems	(310) 948-2217
Intel	(800) 538-3373
technical support	(503) 264-7000
Intellicom	(800) 992-2882
International Keytech	(909) 598-6219
International Power Machines	(800) 527-1208
Interphase	(214) 919-9000
Intuit	(800) 624-8742
Iomega	(800) 456-5522
IPC America	(512) 339-3500
technical support	(800) 752-4171
Iterated Systems	(800) 437-2285
J-Mark Computer	(818) 814-9472
JetFax	(800) 753-8329
JMR Electronics	(818) 993-4801
Joindata Systems	(818) 330-6553
Jovian Logic	(510) 651-4823
JVC Co. of America	(201) 808-2100
Kalok	(408) 747-1315
KAO Infosystems	(800) 274-5520
KentMarsh	(800) 325-3587
technical support	(713) 522-8906
Key Power	(310) 699-2438
KeyTronic	(800) 262-6006
KFC USA	(800) 253-2872

Kingston Technology	(800) 845-2545
technical support	(800) 435-0640
Knowledge Adventure	(800) 542-4240
KnowledgePoint	(800) 727-1133
Kofax Image Products	(714) 727-1733
Koutech Systems	(310) 699-5340
Microspeed	(510) 490-1403
KYE International	(800) 456-7593
technical support	(909) 923-2417
Kyocera Electronics	(800) 323-0470
L.A. Computer	(310) 533-7177
Labtec Enterprises	(206) 896-2000
LaserTools	(510) 420-8777
Leading Edge Products	(800) 874-3340
Legacy Storage Systems	(800) 966-6442
Linco Computer	(714) 990-2288
Link Technologies	(800) 448-5465
Logical Operations	(800) 456-4677
Logitech	(800) 231-7717
technical support	(570) 795-8100
Longshine Electronics	(310) 903-0899
Lotus Development	(800) 343-5414
Lucas Deeco	(510) 471-4700
M. Bryce & Assocs.	(813) 786-4567
MA Laboratories	(408) 954-8188
Mag InnoVision	(800) 827-3998
Magic Solutions	(201) 587-1515
technical support	(201) 587-1517
Mannesmann Tally	(800) 843-1347
Manzanita Software Systems	(800) 447-5700
MapInfo	(800) 327-8627
technical support	(800) 552-2511
Mass Memory Systems	(407) 629-1081
Mass Optical Storage Technologies	(714) 898-9400
Matrix Digital Products	(800) 227-5723
Matrox Electronic Systems	(800) 361-1408
technical support	(514) 685-0270
Maxell of America	(800) 533-2836
Maxoptix	(800) 848-3092
Maxpeed	(415) 345-5447
Maynard Electronics	(800) 821-8782
Media Vision	(800) 845-5870
technical support	(800) 638-2807
Megahertz	(800) 527-8677
technical support	(801) 320-7777
Megatel Computer	(416) 245-2953
Meridian Data	(800) 767-2537
technical support	(800) 755-8324
Mextel	(800) 888-4146
Micro Design International	(800) 228-0891
Micro Direct International	(714) 251-1818
Micro Palm Computers	(800) 832-0512
Micro Solutions Computer Products	(815) 756-3411
Micro Star Software	(800) 444-1343
technical support	(619) 931-4949
Micro-Integration Bluelynx	(800) 642-5888
Micrografx	(800) 733-3729
technical support	(214) 234-2694
MicroMat Computer Systems	(800) 829-6227
MicroNet Computer Systems	(714) 453-6100
technical support	(714) 453-6060

Microprose	(410) 771-0440
technical support	(410) 771-1151
Microrim	(800) 628-6990
technical support	(206) 649-9551
MicroSlate	(514) 444-3680
Microsoft	(800) 426-9400
Microspeed	(800) 232-7888
MicroStep	(818) 964-5048
Microtest	(800) 526-9675
MicroTouch Systems	(800) 866-6873
Minuteman UPS	(800) 238-7272
Mitsubishi Electronics America	(800) 843-2515
technical support	(800) 344-6352
Monterey Electronics	(408) 437-5496
Moses Computers	(408) 358-1550
Mountain Network Solutions	(800) 458-0300
Multi-Industry Technology	(800) 366-6481
Multi-Tech Systems	(800) 328-9717
technical support	(800) 972-2439
Mustang Software	(800) 999-9619
technical support	(805) 873-2550
Mylex	(800) 776-9539
Myriad	(510) 659-8782
Nanao USA	(800) 800-5202
National Instruments	(800) 433-3488
National Semiconductor	(800) 272-9959
NCL America	(408) 737-2496
NCR	(800) 531-2222
NEC Technologies	(800) 632-4636
technical support	(800) 388-8888
Network Security Systems	(800) 755-7078
New Media Graphics	(800) 288-2207
Newer Technology	(800) 678-3726
NewGen Systems	(800) 756-0556
technical support	(714) 436-5150
Nikon	(800) 645-6687
NMB Technologies	(800) 662-8321
technical support	(818) 341-3355
Northgate Computer Systems	(800) 548-1993
Novell	(800) 638-9273
Now Software	(503) 274-2800
technical support	(503) 274-2815
Ntergaid	(203) 380-1280
technical support	(203) 882-0838
Numonics	(800) 247-4517
nView	(800) 736-8439
technical support	(800) 775-7575
Ocron	(800) 933-1399
technical support	(510) 252-0200
Odyssey Development	(800) 992-4797
Omnicomp Graphics	(713) 464-2990
OnTrack Computer Systems	(800) 872-2599
OPTi	(408) 980-8178
Optibase	(800) 451-5101
Optical Devices	(310) 320-9768
Optima Technology	(714) 476-0515
Orchid Technology	(800) 767-2443
technical support	(510) 683-0323
Orientec of America	(818) 442-1818
Output Technology	(509) 536-0468
Overland Data	(800) 729-8725

Pacific Data Products ....(619) 552-0880
Pacific Magnetics...(619) 474-8216
Pacific Rim Systems..(800) 722-7461
Packard Bell..(800) 733-4411
Panamax ....(800) 472-5555
   technical support ....(415) 499-3900
Panasonic Comms. & Systems...........................(800) 742-8086
Panduit ....(800) 777-3300
Parity Systems..(800) 514-4080
Passport Designs ....(415) 726-0280
   technical support ....(415) 726-3826
Passport Software..(800) 969-7900
Peachtree Software..(800) 554-8900
   technical support ....(404) 923-4318
Pelikan ....(615) 794-9000
Perceptive Solutions..(800) 486-3278
Percon...(800) 873-7266
Peripheral Land ....(800) 288-8754
Phoenix Technologies ....(800) 677-7300
Physician Micro Systems ....(206) 441-8490
Pinnacle Micro ....(800) 553-7070
Pioneer Comms. of America ....(800) 527-3766
Pivar Computing Services ....(800) 266-8378
PKware...(414) 354-8699
Plasmaco ....(914) 883-6800
PowerCom America ....(800) 288-9807
Practical Peripherals ....(404) 840-9966
Prima Storage Solutions ....(408) 727-2600
Primavera Systems...(800) 423-0245
   technical support ....(610) 668-3030
Prime Portable Manufacturer ....(800) 966-7237
   technical support ....(818) 444-7606
Procom Technology ....(800) 800-8600
Procomp USA ....(216) 234-6387
Progen Technology ....(714) 549-5818
Progress Software ....(800) 327-8445
Prolink Computer..(213) 780-7978
Prometheus Products ....(800) 477-3473
   technical support ....(503) 692-9601
Proxim...(800) 229-1630
Proxima...(800) 447-7694
PS Solutions ....(214) 980-2632
QMS ....(800) 523-2696
Qualitas...(800) 733-1377
   technical support ....(301) 907-7400
Quantum..(800) 624-5545
   technical support ....(800) 826-8022
Quantum Designs Computer.................................(310) 908-1029
Quark ....(800) 788-7835
   technical support ....(303) 894-8822
QuaTech ....(800) 553-1170
Radiometrics Midwest ....(708) 932-7262
Radius ....(800) 227-2795
   technical support ....(408) 541-5700
Rainbow Technologies ....(800) 852-8569
Rancho Technology..(909) 987-3966
RCI ....(908) 874-4072
RealWorld..(800) 678-6336
Recognita of America..(800) 255-4627
Red Wing Business Systems ....(800) 732-9464
Relialogic ....(510) 770-3990

Relisys	(408) 945-9000
Reply	(800) 955-5295
Rexon/Tecmar	(800) 422-2587
Ricoh	(800) 955-3453
Riso	(508) 777-7377
technical support	(508) 750-8497
Rockwell International	(800) 436-9988
technical support	(800) 854-8099
Roland Digital Group	(213) 685-5141
S-MOS Systems	(408) 954-0120
Sampo of America	(404) 449-6220
Sampson MIDI Source	(800) 726-6434
Samsung Electronics America	(800) 624-8999
technical support	(310) 453-0614
Samtron	(800) 726-8766
Santa Cruz Operation (SCO)	(800) 726-8649
SBT	(800) 944-1000
technical support	(415) 444-9700
SCI Systems	(205) 882-4800
Scitor	(415) 570-7700
Seagate Technology	(800) 468-3472
technical support	(408) 438-8222
Security Microsystems	(800) 345-7390
technical support	(718) 667-4720
Shape Electronics	(800) 367-5811
Sharp Electronics	(800) 237-4277
Shiva	(617) 252-6300
technical support	(617) 270-8400
Shuttle Computer International	(408) 945-1480
Silicon Graphics	(800) 800-7441
Silicon Star International	(510) 623-0500
Silicon Systems	(800) 624-8999
Smart Technologies	(403) 245-0333
Softkey/Spinnaker	(800) 227-5609
technical support	(404) 428-0008
SoftSolutions Technology	(801) 226-6000
technical support	(800) 861-2140
Software Directions	(800) 346-7638
technical support	(201) 584-3882
Software Products International	(800) 937-4774
Software Publishing	(800) 282-6003
The Software Toolworks	(800) 234-3088
technical support	(415) 883-5157
Sola Electric	(800) 879-7652
Soletek Computer Supply	(800) 437-1518
Sonera Technologies	(800) 932-6323
technical support	(908) 747-6886
Sony of America	(800) 582-7669
SourceMate Information Systems	(800) 877-8896
technical support	(415) 381-1793
Sprite	(408) 773-8888
SRW Computer Components	(800) 547-7766
Stac Electronics	(800) 522-7822
technical support	(619) 929-3900
Star Gate Technologies	(800) 782-7428
Star Micronics	(800) 227-8274
Statpower Technologies	(604) 420-1585
STB Systems	(800) 234-4334
Storage Technology	(800) 733-7381
Summit Micro Design	(408) 739-6348
Sun Microsystems	(800) 872-4786

Suncom Technologies	(708) 647-4040
SuperMac	(800) 541-7680
SuperTime	(905) 764-3530
Supra	(800) 727-8772
Symantec	(800) 441-7234
Symphony Laboratories	(408) 986-1701
Synchronics	(800) 852-5852
technical support	(800) 852-8755
Synergystex International	(216) 225-3112
Syntel Comms.	(908) 651-0415
SyQuest Technology	(800) 245-2278
Sysgration USA	(415) 306-7860
Syspro Impact Software	(800) 369-8649
Systems Plus	(800) 222-7701
technical support	(415) 969-7066
Systems Strategies	(212) 279-8400
Tandy	(817) 390-3011
technical support	(800) 843-7422
Tatung Co. of America	(800) 827-2850
TDK Electronics	(516) 625-0100
Teac America	(213) 726-0303
technical support	(213) 727-7674
Telemagic	(800) 835-6244
Telex Comms.	(612) 887-5531
technical support	(800) 331-2623
Texas Instruments	(800) 527-3500
Texas Microsystems	(800) 627-8700
TextWare	(801) 645-9600
THEOS Software	(510) 935-1118
Thomas-Conrad	(800) 332-8683
technical support	(800) 334-4112
TimeKeeping Systems	(216) 361-9995
T/Maker	(415) 962-0195
TMC Research	(408) 262-0888
Toshiba America	(800) 334-3445
technical support	(800) 999-4273
TOSOH USA	(800) 238-6764
TouchStone Software	(800) 531-0450
Trace Mountain	(408) 441-8040
technical support	(800) 468-7223
Transition Engineering	(800) 325-2725
Transitional Technology	(800) 437-4884
Traveling Software	(800) 662-2652
technical support	(206) 483-8088
Trident Microsystems	(415) 691-9211
Tripp Lite Manufacturing	(312) 329-1777
Triton Technologies	(800) 322-9440
Truevision	(800) 344-8783
Tseng Labs	(215) 968-0502
Twelve Tone Systems	(800) 234-1171
technical support	(617) 924-6275
Twinhead	(800) 545-8946
U.S. Robotics	(800) 342-5877
technical support	(800) 550-7800
UDP Fonts	(800) 888-4413
UDS Motorola	(800) 631-4869
technical support	(800) 221-4380
Ultima Electronics	(510) 659-1580
UltraStor	(714) 581-4100
technical support	(714) 581-4016
Unlimited Systems	(619) 622-1400

Upsonic	(800) 877-6642
US Logic/HM System	(800) 777-4875
technical support	(619) 467-1100
Varta Batteries	(914) 592-2500
Verbatim	(704) 547-6500
Videomedia	(408) 227-9977
Videx	(503) 758-0521
ViewSonic	(800) 888-8583
Visionetics International	(310) 316-7940
VLSI Technology	(602) 752-8574
technical support	(602) 752-6367
Voyetra Technologies	(800) 233-9377
technical support	(914) 966-0600
Wallaby Software	(201) 490-3100
technical support	(800) 638-4726
WangDat	(216) 349-0600
Wangtek	(800) 992-9916
Western Telematic	(800) 854-7226
Westrex	(617) 254-1200
Wolfram Research	(800) 441-6284
technical support	(217) 398-6500
WordPerfect	(800) 451-5151
WordStar	(800) 227-5609
technical support	(404) 428-0008
XDB Systems	(800) 488-4948
technical support	(410) 312-9400
Xing Technology	(805) 473-0145
Xircom	(800) 775-0400
technical support	(805) 376-9200
XyQuest	(410) 576-2040
Y-E Data America	(708) 291-2340
technical support	(708) 855-0890
Yamaha of America	(800) 543-7457
Young Micro Systems	(310) 802-8899
Z-Ram	(800) 368-4726
Zedcor	(602) 881-8101
Zenith Data Systems	(800) 582-0524
Zoom Telephonics	(800) 631-3116
technical support	(617) 423-1076
ZSoft	(404) 428-0008
Zyxel Communications	(800) 255-4101
technical support	(714) 693-0808

Internet Service Providers

Alternet	(800) 488-6384
America Online	(800) 827-6364
ANS	(800) 456-8267
Class	(800) 488-4559
CompuServe	(800) 848-8990
Delphi	(212) 556-8100
EWorld	(408) 996-1010
Infolan	(310) 335-2600
Institute for Global Communications	(415) 442-0220
JVNCNET	(800) 358-4437
MCI Mail	(800) 444-6245
Midnet	(402) 472-5032
MSEN	(313) 998-4562
Netcom	(800) 501-8649
Performance Systems International	(800) 827-7482
Prodigy	(800) 776-3449

Radiomail..(800) 597-6245
Schwartz Communications...................................(617) 431-0770
Sprintlink...(703) 904-2167
Westnet..(303) 491-7260

Commerce Department Desk Officers

Afghanistan	(202) 482-2954
Albania	(202) 482-2645
Algeria	(202) 482-1860
Angola	(202) 482-4228
Anguilla	(202) 482-2527
Antigua/Barbuda	(202) 482-2527
Argentina	(202) 482-1548
Armenia	(202) 482-4655
Aruba	(202) 482-2527
ASEAN	(202) 482-3877
Australia	(202) 482-4958
Austria	(202) 482-2920
Azerbaijan	(202) 482-4655
Bahamas	(202) 482-5680
Bahrain	(202) 482-1860
Balkan States (former Yugoslav republics)	(202) 482-2645
Bangladesh	(202) 482-2954
Barbados	(202) 482-2527
Belarus	(202) 482-4655
Belgium	(202) 482-5401
Belize	(202) 482-2527
Benin	(202) 482-5149
Bhutan	(202) 482-2954
Bolivia	(202) 482-2521
Botswana	(202) 482-4228
Brazil	(202) 482-3871
Brunei	(202) 482-4958
Bulgaria	(202) 482-2645
Burkina Faso	(202) 482-4388
Burma (Myanmar)	(202) 482-4958
Burundi	(202) 482-4388
Cambodia	(202) 482-4958
Cameroon	(202) 482-5149
Canada	(202) 482-3103
Cape Verde	(202) 482-4388
Cayman Islands	(202) 482-5680
Central African Republic	(202) 482-4388
Chad	(202) 482-4388
Chile	(202) 482-1495
China	(202) 482-3932
Colombia	(202) 482-1659
Comoros	(202) 482-4564
Congo	(202) 482-5149
Costa Rica	(202) 482-5680
Cote d'Ivoire	(202) 482-4388
Cuba	(202) 482-5680
Cyprus	(202) 482-3945
Czech Republic	(202) 482-2645
Denmark	(202) 482-3254
Djibouti	(202) 482-4564
Dominica	(202) 482-2527
Dominican Republic	(202) 482-5680
Ecuador	(202) 482-1659
Egypt	(202) 482-5506
El Salvador	(202) 482-2528
Equatorial Guinea	(202) 482-4388
Eritrea	(202) 482-4564
Estonia	(202) 482-2645
Ethiopia	(202) 482-4564

European Community	(202) 482-5276
Finland	(202) 482-3254
France	(202) 482-6008
Gabon	(202) 482-5149
Gambia	(202) 482-4388
Georgia	(202) 482-4655
Germany	(202) 482-2435
Ghana	(202) 482-5149
Greece	(202) 482-3945
Grenada	(202) 482-2527
Guatemala	(202) 482-2528
Guinea	(202) 482-4388
Guinea-Bissau	(202) 482-4388
Guyana	(202) 482-2527
Haiti	(202) 482-5680
Honduras	(202) 482-2528
Hong Kong	(202) 482-3932
Hungary	(202) 482-2645
Iceland	(202) 482-3254
India	(202) 482-2954
Indonesia	(202) 482-3877
Iran	(202) 482-1860
Iraq	(202) 482-1860
Ireland	(202) 482-2177
Israel	(202) 482-1860
Italy	(202) 482-2177
Jamaica	(202) 482-5680
Japan	(202) 482-2425
Jordan	(202) 482-1860
Kazakhstan	(202) 482-4655
Kenya	(202) 482-4564
Korea	(202) 482-4390
Kuwait	(202) 482-5506
Kyrgyz Republic	(202) 482-4655
Laos	(202) 482-4958
Latvia	(202) 482-2645
Lebanon	(202) 482-5506
Lesotho	(202) 482-4228
Liberia	(202) 482-4388
Libya	(202) 482-5545
Lithuania	(202) 482-2645
Luxembourg	(202) 482-5401
Macao	(202) 482-3932
Madagascar	(202) 482-4564
Malawi	(202) 482-4228
Malaysia	(202) 482-4958
Maldives	(202) 482-2954
Mali	(202) 482-4388
Malta	(202) 482-3748
Mauritania	(202) 482-4388
Mauritius	(202) 482-4564
Mexico	(202) 482-0300
Moldova	(202) 482-4655
Mongolia	(202) 482-3932
Montserrat	(202) 482-2527
Morocco	(202) 482-5545
Mozambique	(202) 482-4228
Namibia	(202) 482-4228
Nepal	(202) 482-2954
Netherlands	(202) 482-5401
Netherlands Antilles	(202) 482-2527

New Zealand	(202) 482-4958
Nicaragua	(202) 482-5680
Niger	(202) 482-4388
Nigeria	(202) 482-5149
Norway	(202) 482-4414
Oman	(202) 482-1860
Pacific Islands	(202) 482-4958
Pakistan	(202) 482-2954
Panama	(202) 482-2528
Paraguay	(202) 482-1548
Peru	(202) 482-2521
Philippines	(202) 482-4958
Poland	(202) 482-2645
Portugal	(202) 482-4508
Qatar	(202) 482-1860
Romania	(202) 482-2645
Russia	(202) 482-4655
Rwanda	(202) 482-4388
St. Kitts–Nevis	(202) 482-2527
St. Lucia	(202) 482-2527
St. Martin	(202) 482-2527
St. Vincent–Grenadines	(202) 482-2527
Sao Tome & Principe	(202) 482-4388
Saudi Arabia	(202) 482-1860
Senegal	(202) 482-4388
Seychelles	(202) 482-4564
Sierra Leone	(202) 482-4388
Singapore	(202) 482-4958
Slovak Republic	(202) 482-2645
Somalia	(202) 482-4564
South Africa	(202) 482-5148
Spain	(202) 482-4508
Sri Lanka	(202) 482-2954
Sudan	(202) 482-4564
Suriname	(202) 482-2527
Swaziland	(202) 482-4228
Switzerland	(202) 482-2920
Syria	(202) 482-5506
Taiwan	(202) 482-4390
Tajikistan	(202) 482-4655
Tanzania	(202) 482-4228
Thailand	(202) 482-4958
Togo	(202) 482-5149
Trinidad & Tobago	(202) 482-2527
Tunisia	(202) 482-5506
Turkey	(202) 482-3945
Turkmenistan	(202) 482-4655
Turks/Caicos Islands	(202) 482-5680
Uganda	(202) 482-4564
Ukraine	(202) 482-4655
United Arab Emirates	(202) 482-5545
United Kingdom	(202) 482-3748
Uruguay	(202) 482-1495
Uzbekistan	(202) 482-4655
Venezuela	(202) 482-4303
Vietnam	(202) 482-4958
Virgin Islands (UK)	(202) 482-2527
Yemen	(202) 482-1860
Zaire	(202) 482-4388
Zambia	(202) 482-4228
Zimbabwe	(202) 482-4228

Convention and Visitors Bureaus

Anchorage, AK	(907) 276-4118
Atlanta, GA	(404) 222-6688
Atlantic City, NJ	(609) 348-7130
Baltimore, MD	(410) 659-7300
Boston, MA	(617) 536-4100
Buffalo, NY	(716) 852-0511
Charlotte, NC	(704) 331-2700
Chicago, IL	(312) 567-8500
Cincinnati, OH	(513) 621-6994
Cleveland, OH	(800) 321-1004
Columbus, OH	(614) 221-6623
Dallas, TX	(214) 746-6677
Denver, CO	(303) 892-1505
Detroit, MI	(313) 567-1170
Grand Rapids, MI	(616) 459-8287
Greenville, SC	(803) 233-0461
Harrisburg, PA	(717) 232-4121
Hartford, CT	(203) 728-6789
Honolulu, HI	(808) 923-1811
Houston, TX	(713) 227-3100
Indianapolis, IN	(317) 639-4282
Kansas City, MO	(816) 221-5242
Las Vegas, NV	(702) 892-0711
Los Angeles, CA	(213) 624-7300
Memphis, TN	(901) 543-5300
Miami, FL	(305) 539-3063
Milwaukee, WI	(414) 273-3950
Minneapolis, MN	(612) 661-4700
Nashville, TN	(615) 259-4730
New Orleans, LA	(504) 566-5011
New York, NY	(212) 397-8222
Norfolk, VA	(804) 441-5266
Oklahoma City, OK	(405) 297-8910
Orlando, FL	(407) 363-5800
Philadelphia, PA	(215) 636-3300
Phoenix, AZ	(602) 254-6500
Pittsburgh, PA	(412) 281-7711
Portland, OR	(800) 962-3700
Providence, RI	(401) 274-1636
Raleigh, NC	(919) 834-5900
Sacramento, CA	(916) 264-7777
St. Louis, MO	(314) 421-1023
Salt Lake City, UT	(800) 541-4955
San Antonio, TX	(800) 447-3372
San Diego, CA	(619) 232-3101
San Francisco, CA	(415) 974-6900
Seattle, WA	(206) 461-5840
Tampa, FL	(813) 223-2752
Washington, DC	(202) 789-7000
West Palm Beach, FL	(407) 471-3995

Federal Government Agencies

DEPARTMENT OF AGRICULTURE....................(202) 720-2791

Agricultural Marketing Service	(202) 720-8999
Rural Economic & Community Development	(202) 720-4323
Rural Utilities Service	(202) 720-1255

DEPARTMENT OF COMMERCE ....(202) 482-2000

Bureau of the Census...(301) 457-4608
Bureau of Economic Analysis.............................(202) 606-9900
Bureau of Export Administration.......................(202) 482-2721
Economics and Statistics Administration..........(202) 482-1986
International Trade Administration ....(202) 482-3809
Minority Business Development Agency...........(202) 482-1936
Patent and Trademark Office ....(703) 305-8341
United States Travel and Tourism
    Administration ....(202) 482-3811

DEPARTMENT OF ENERGY...........................(202) 586-5000

DEPARTMENT OF HEALTH AND HUMAN
SERVICES ....(202) 619-0257

Centers for Disease Control and Prevention.....(404) 639-3311
Food and Drug Administration ....(301) 443-1544
Healthcare Financing Administration...............(410) 966-3000
Social Security Administration..........................(410) 965-1234

DEPARTMENT OF HOUSING AND
URBAN DEVELOPMENT ....(202) 708-1422

DEPARTMENT OF THE INTERIOR ....(202) 208-3171

National Biological Survey ....(202) 482-3048
Office of Surface Mining Reclamation
    and Enforcement..(202) 208-2719
United States Bureau of Mines ....(202) 501-9649
United States Geological Survey ....(703) 648-4460

DEPARTMENT OF JUSTICE ....(202) 514-2000

Drug Enforcement Administration ....(202) 307-1000
Federal Bureau of Investigation.........................(202) 324-3000
Immigration and Naturalization Service...........(202) 514-4316

DEPARTMENT OF LABOR.............................(202) 219-5000

Bureau of Labor Statistics..................................(202) 606-5900
Employment Standards Administration ....(202) 219-6191
Mine Safety and Health Administration...........(703) 235-1452
Occupational Safety and
    Health Administration...................................(202) 219-8151
Office of the American Workplace....................(202) 219-6098
Pension and Welfare Benefits Administration ..(202) 219-8921

DEPARTMENT OF STATE ....(202) 647-4000

Economic and Business Affairs ....(202) 647-2720

DEPARTMENT OF TRANSPORTATION ....(202) 366-4000

Federal Aviation Administration.......................(202) 366-4000
Federal Highway Administration.......................(202) 366-0660
Federal Railroad Administration........................(202) 366-4000
Federal Transit Administration ....(202) 366-4043
Maritime Administration ....(202) 366-5807

DEPARTMENT OF THE TREASURY ....(202) 622-2000

Internal Revenue Service....................................(202) 622-5000

INDEPENDENT AGENCIES

Administrative Conference of the
    United States ....(202) 254-7020
African Development Foundation ....(202) 673-3916
Central Intelligence Agency ....(703) 482-1100
Commission on Civil Rights..............................(202) 376-8177

Commodity Futures Trading Commission ....(202) 254-6387
Consumer Product Safety Commision ....(301) 504-0580
Defense Nuclear Facilities Safety Board ....(202) 208-6400
Environmental Protection Agency ....(202) 260-2090
Equal Employment Opportunity
   Commission ....(202) 663-4900
Export-Import Bank of the United States ....(202) 565-3946
Farm Credit Administration ....(703) 883-4000
Federal Communications Commission ....(202) 418-0200
Federal Deposit Insurance Corporation ....(202) 393-8400
Federal Election Commission ....(202) 219-3440
Federal Emergency Management Agency ....(202) 646-4600
Federal Housing Financing Board ....(202) 408-2500
Federal Labor Relations Authority ....(202) 482-6540
Federal Maritime Commission ....(202) 523-5707
Federal Mediation and Conciliation Service .....(202) 606-8080
Federal Mine Safety and Health
   Review Commission ....(202) 653-5625
Federal Reserve System ....(202) 452-3000
Federal Retirement Thrift Investment Board ....(202) 942-1600
Federal Trade Commission ....(202) 326-2222
General Services Administration ....(202) 708-5082
Inter-American Foundation ....(703) 841-3800
Interstate Commerce Commission ....(202) 927-7119
Institute of Museum Services ....(202) 606-8539
Merit Systems Protection Board ....(202) 653-7124
National Aeronautics and
   Space Administration ....(202) 358-1000
National Archives and Records
   Administration ....(202) 501-5400
National Capital Planning Commission ....(202) 724-0174
National Credit Union Administration ....(703) 518-6300
National Endowment for the Arts ....(202) 682-5400
National Endowment for the Humanities ....(202) 606-8438
National Labor Relations Board ....(202) 273-1000
National Mediation Board ....(202) 523-5920
National Railroad Passenger
   Corporation (Amtrak) ....(202) 906-3000
National Transportation Safety Board ....(202) 382-6600
Nuclear Regulatory Commission ....(301) 415-7000
Occupational Safety and Health
   Review Commission ....(202) 606-5100
Office of Government Ethics ....(202) 523-5757
Office of Personnel Management ....(202) 606-1800
Office of Special Counsel ....(202) 653-7188
Panama Canal Commission ....(202) 634-6441
Peace Corps ....(202) 606-3886
Pennsylvania Avenue
   Development Corporation ....(202) 724-9091
Pension Benefit Guaranty Corporation ....(202) 326-4000
Postal Rate Commission ....(202) 789-6800
Railroad Retirement Board ....(202) 272-7742
Resolution Trust Corporation ....(202) 416-6900
Securities and Exchange Commission ....(202) 942-8088
Selective Service System ....(703) 235-2555
Small Business Administration ....(800) 827-5722
Tennessee Valley Authority ....(202) 898-2999
Thrift Depositor Protection Oversight Board ....(202) 416-2650
Trade and Development Agency ....(703) 875-4357
United States Arms Control and
   Disarmament Agency ....(202) 647-8677

United States Information Agency....................(202) 619-4700
United States International Development
   Cooperation Agency..(202) 647-1850
United States International
   Trade Commission ....(202) 205-2000
United States Postal Service ....(202) 268-2000

Governors

Alabama, Fab James ....(344) 242-7100
Alaska, Tony Knowles..(907) 465-3500
Arizona, Fife Symington......................................(602) 542-4331
Arkansas, Jim Guy Tucker...................................(501) 682-2345
California, Pete Wilson ....(916) 445-2841
Colorado, Roy R. Romer ....(303) 866-2471
Connecticut, John Rowland ....(203) 566-4840
Delaware, Thomas Carper...................................(302) 577-3210
Florida, Lawton Chiles ....(904) 488-4441
Georgia, Zell Miller ....(404) 656-1776
Hawaii, Ben Cayetano..(808) 586-0034
Idaho, Phil Batt ....(208) 334-2100
Illinois, Jim Edgar ....(217) 782-6830
Indiana, Evan Bayh ....(317) 232-4567
Iowa, Terry E. Branstad ....(515) 281-5211
Kansas, Bill Graves...(913) 296-3232
Kentucky, Brereton Jones...................................(502) 564-2611
Louisiana, Edwin W. Edwards ....(504) 342-7015
Maine, Angus King ....(207) 287-3531
Maryland, Parris Glendening ....(410) 974-3901
Massachusetts, William F. Weld ....(617) 727-3600
Michigan, John Engler ....(517) 373-3400
Minnesota, Arne Carlson....................................(612) 296-3391
Mississippi, Kirk Fordice.....................................(601) 359-3100
Missouri, Mel Carnahan.....................................(314) 751-3222
Montana, Marc Racicot ....(406) 444-3111
Nebraska, E. Benjamin Nelson ....(402) 471-2244
Nevada, Bob Miller ....(702) 687-5670
New Hampshire, Stephen Merrill ....(603) 271-2121
New Jersey, Christine Todd Whitman ....(609) 292-6000
New Mexico, Gary Johnson ....(505) 827-3000
New York, George Pataki ....(518) 474-8390
North Carolina, James B. Hunt, Jr.....................(919) 733-4240
North Dakota, Edward T. Schafer......................(701) 328-2200
Ohio, George V. Voinovich.................................(614) 644-0813
Oklahoma, Frank Keating ....(405) 521-2342
Oregon, John Kitzhaber......................................(503) 378-3111
Pennsylvania, Tom Ridge ....(717) 787-2500
Rhode Island, Lincoln Almond ....(401) 277-2080
South Carolina, David Beasley ....(803) 734-9818
South Dakota, Bill Janklow.................................(605) 773-3212
Tennessee, Don Sundquist ....(615) 741-2001
Texas, George W. Bush.......................................(512) 463-1762
Utah, Mike Leavitt..(801) 538-1000
Vermont, Howard Dean ....(802) 828-3333
Virginia, George Allen..(804) 786-2211
Washington, Mike Lowry....................................(206) 753-6780
West Virginia, Gaston Caperton........................(304) 558-2000
Wisconsin, Tommy G. Thompson ....(608) 266-1212
Wyoming, Jim Geringer ....(307) 777-7434

Mayors

Anchorage, AK, Rick Mystrom ....(907) 343-4431
Atlanta, GA, Bill Campbell..............................(404) 330-6100
Atlantic City, NJ, James Whelan.......................(609) 347-5400
Baltimore, MD, Kurt Schmoke ....(410) 396-3100
Boston, MA, Thomas M. Menino ....(617) 635-4500
Buffalo, NY, Anthony Masiello.......................(716) 851-4841
Charlotte, NC, Richard Vinroot.......................(704) 336-2241
Chicago, IL, Richard M. Daley ....(312) 744-3300
Cincinnati, OH, Roxanne Qualls.....................(513) 352-3637
Cleveland, OH, Michael R. White.....................(216) 664-3990
Columbus, OH, Greg Lashutka.........................(614) 645-7671
Dallas, TX, Steve Bartlett ....(214) 670-0773
Denver, CO, Wellington E. Webb ....(303) 640-2721
Detroit, MI, Dennis Archer ....(313) 224-3400
Grand Rapids, MI, John H. Logie ....(616) 456-3168
Greenville, NC, Nancy Jenkins ....(919) 830-4422
Harrisburg, PA, Stephen Reed ....(717) 255-3040
Hartford, CT, Mike Peters...............................(203) 543-8500
Honolulu, HI, Jeremy Harris ....(808) 523-4141
Houston, TX, Bob Lanier................................(713) 247-2200
Indianapolis, IN, Stephen Goldsmith...............(317) 327-3601
Kansas City, KS, Carol Marinovich ....(913) 573-5010
Kansas City, MO, Emanuel Cleaver II..............(816) 274-2595
Las Vegas, NV, Jan Laverty Jones.....................(702) 229-6241
Los Angeles, CA, Richard Riordan ....(213) 847-2489
Memphis, TN, Willie W. Herenton..................(901) 576-6000
Miami, FL, Steve Clark ....(305) 250-5300
Milwaukee, WI, John O. Norquist.....................(414) 286-2200
Minneapolis, MN, Sharon Sayles Belton ....(612) 673-2100
Nashville, TN, Philip N. Bredesen ....(615) 862-6000
New Orleans, LA, Mark Morial.......................(504) 565-6400
New York, NY, Rudolph Giuliani ....(212) 788-3000
Norfolk, VA, Paul D. Fraim ....(804) 441-5126
Oklahoma City, OK, Ronald Norick ....(405) 297-2424
Orlando, FL, Glenda Hood ....(407) 246-2221
Philadelphia, PA, Edward Rendell....................(215) 686-2181
Phoenix, AZ, Skip Rimsza...............................(602) 262-7111
Pittsburgh, PA, Tom Murphy ....(412) 255-2626
Portland, OR, Vera Katz..................................(503) 823-4120
Providence, RI, Vincent A. Cianci, Jr. ....(401) 421-7740
Raleigh, NC, Tom Fetzer.................................(919) 890-3050
Sacramento, CA, Joseph Serna, Jr.. ....(916) 264-5300
St. Louis, MO, Freeman R. Bosley, Jr................(314) 622-3201
Salt Lake City, UT, Deedee Corradini...............(801) 535-7704
San Antonio, TX, Nelson W. Wolff ....(210) 299-7060
San Diego, CA, Susan Golding ....(619) 236-6330
San Francisco, CA, Frank Jordan ....(415) 554-6141
Seattle, WA, Norman Rice ....(206) 684-4000
Tampa, FL, Sandra W. Freedman ....(813) 223-8251
Washington, DC, Marion S. Barry....................(202) 727-2980
West Palm Beach, FL, Nancy Graham ....(407) 659-8025

U.S. Representatives

ALABAMA

Spencer Bachus (R)..(202) 225-4921
Thomas Bevill (D) ....(202) 225-4876
Glen Browder (D) ....(202) 225-3261

Government

Robert E. Cramer, Jr. (D) ....(202) 225-4801
    budmail@hr.house.gov
Sonny Callahan (R) ....(202) 225-4931
Terry Everett (R) ....(202) 225-2901
    everett@hr.house.gov
Earl F. Hilliard (D) ....(202) 225-2665

ALASKA

Don Young (R) ....(202) 225-5765

ARIZONA

John Hayworth (R) ....(202) 225-2190
James T. Kolbe (R) ....(202) 225-2542
    jimkolbe@hr.house.gov
Ed Pastor (D)..(202) 225-4065
    edpastor@hr.house.gov
Matthew Salmon (R) ....(202) 225-4065
John Shadegg (R) ....(202) 225-3361
Robert Stump (R)..(202) 225-4576

ARKANSAS

Jay Dickey (R) ....(202) 225-3772
    jdickey@hr.house.gov
Tim Hutchinson (R)...(202) 225-4301
Blanche Lambert-Lincoln (D) ....(202) 225-4076
Raymond Thornton (D)......................................(202) 225-2506

CALIFORNIA

Bill Baker (R) ....(202) 225-1880
Xavier Becerra (D) ....(202) 225-6235
Anthony C. Beilenson (D) ....(202) 225-5911
Howard L. Berman (D) ....(202) 225-4695
Brian P. Bilbray (R) ....(202) 225-2040
Sonny Bono (R) ....(202) 225-5330
George E. Brown, Jr. (D)....................................(202) 225-6161
Ken Calvert (R) ....(202) 225-1986
Gary A. Condit (D) ....(202) 225-6131
Christopher Cox (R) ....(202) 225-5611
Randy Cunningham (R) ....(202) 225-5452
Ronald V. Dellums (D).......................................(202) 225-2661
Julian C. Dixon (D) ....(202) 225-7084
Calvin M. Dooley (D)...(202) 225-3341
John T. Doolittle (R)...(202) 225-2511
Robert K. Dornan (R) ....(202) 225-2965
David Dreier (R) ....(202) 225-2305
Anna G. Eshoo (D)...(202) 225-8104
    annagram@hr.house.gov
Sam Farr (D)..(202) 225-2861
    samfarr@hr.house.gov
Vic Fazio (D) ....(202) 225-5716
Bob Filner (D) ....(202) 225-8045
Elton Gallegly (R) ....(202) 225-5811
Jane Harman (D)..(202) 225-8220
    jharman@hr.house.gov
Walter W. Herger (R)...(202) 225-3076
Stephen Horn (R) ....(202) 225-6676
Duncan L. Hunter (R) ....(202) 225-5672
Jay C. Kim (R)...(202) 225-3201
Thomas Lantos (D) ....(202) 225-3531
    talk2tom@hr.house.gov
Jerry Lewis (R)...(202) 225-5861

Zoe Lofgren (D)......................................(202) 225-3071
zoegram@hr.house.gov
Matthew G. Martinez (D)........................(202) 225-5464
Robert T. Matsui (D).............................(202) 225-7163
Howard P. McKeon (R)..........................(202) 225-1956
tellbuck@hr.house.gov
George Miller (D) ....(202) 225-2095
gmiller@hr.house.gov
Norman Y. Mineta (D)...........................(202) 225-2631
tellnorm@hr.house.gov
Carlos J. Moorhead (R)..........................(202) 225-4176
Ronald Packard (R)................................(202) 225-3906
rpackard@hr.house.gov
Nancy Pelosi (D)...................................(202) 225-4965
sfnancy@hr.house.gov
Richard Pombo (R) ....(202) 225-1947
George P. Radanovich (R) ....(202) 225-4540
george@hr.house.gov
Frank Riggs (R) ....(202) 225-3311
Dana Rohrabacher (R)...........................(202) 225-2415
Lucille Roybal-Allard (D).......................(202) 225-1766
Ed R. Royce (R) ....(202) 225-4111
Andrea H. Seastrand (R) ....(202) 225-3601
andrea22@hr.house.gov
Pete Stark (D) ....(202) 225-5065
petemail@hr.house.gov
Bill Thomas (R) ....(202) 225-2915
Esteban E. Torres (D) ....(202) 225-5256
Walter R. Tucker III (D) ....(202) 225-7924
tucker96@hr.house.gov
Maxine Waters (D) ....(202) 225-2201
Henry A. Waxman (D) ....(202) 225-3976
Lynn C. Woolsey (D) ....(202) 225-5161
woolsey@hr.house.gov

COLORADO

Wayne Allard (R)...................................(202) 225-4676
Joel Hefley (R).......................................(202) 225-4422
Scott McInnis (R) ....(202) 225-4761
Daniel Schaefer (R)...............................(202) 225-7882
schaefer@hr.house.gov
Patricia Schroeder (D) ....(202) 225-4431
David E. Skaggs (D) ....(202) 225-2161
skaggs@hr.house.gov

CONNECTICUT

Rosa DeLauro (D) ....(202) 225-3661
Gary A. Franks (R).................................(202) 225-3822
Samuel Gejdenson (D)...........................(202) 225-2076
bozrah@hr.house.gov
Nancy L. Johnson (R) ....(202) 225-4476
Barbara B. Kennelly (D).........................(202) 225-2265
Christopher Shays (R)............................(202) 225-5541
cshays@hr.house.gov

DELAWARE

Michael N. Castle (R).............................(202) 225-4165

FLORIDA

Michael Bilirakis (R).............................(202) 225-5755
Corrine Brown (D)................................(202) 225-0123
Charles T. Canady (R) ....(202) 225-1252

Peter Deutsch (D) ....(202) 225-7931
                    pdeutsch@hr.house.gov
Lincoln Diaz-Balart (R)..........................(202) 225-4211
Mark Adam Foley (R)..............................(202) 225-5792
Tillie Fowler (R)....................................(202) 225-2501
Samuel M. Gibbons (D)............................(202) 225-3376
Porter J. Goss (R) ....(202) 225-2536
Alcee L. Hastings (D) ....(202) 225-1313
                    hastings@hr.house.gov
Harry Johnston (D) ....(202) 225-3001
William McCollum (R)..............................(202) 225-2176
Carrie Meek (D) ....(202) 225-4506
John L. Mica (R) ....(202) 225-4035
Dan Miller (R) ....(202) 225-5015
Douglas Peterson (D) ....(202) 225-5235
Ileana Ros-Lehtinen (R) ....(202) 225-3931
Joe Scarborough (R)................................(202) 225-4136
E. C. Shaw, Jr. (R) ....(202) 225-3026
Clifford B. Stearns (R) ....(202) 225-5744
                    cstearns@hr.house.gov
Karen Thurman (D) ....(202) 225-1002
                    kthurman@hr.house.gov
Dave Weldon (R)....................................(202) 225-3671
                    fla15@hr.house.gov
C. W. Young (R)....................................(202) 225-5961

GEORGIA

Bob Barr (R) ....(202) 225-2931
Sanford Bishop, Jr. (D)...........................(202) 225-3631
Saxby Chambliss (R)................................(202) 225-6531
                    saxby@hr.house.gov
Mac Collins (R) ....(202) 225-5901
Nathan Deal (R) ....(202) 225-5211
Newt Gingrich (R)..................................(202) 225-4501
                    georgia6@hr.house.gov
Jack Kingston (R)..................................(202) 225-5831
John Lewis (D) ....(202) 225-3801
John Linder (R) ....(202) 225-4272
                    jlinder@hr.house.gov
Cynthia A. McKinney (D)...........................(202) 225-1605
Charles Norwood, Jr. (R) ....(202) 225-4101
                    ga10@hr.house.gov

GUAM

Robert A. Underwood (D)...........................(202) 225-1188

HAWAII

Neil Abercrombie (D)...............................(202) 225-2726
Patsy T. Mink (D)..................................(202) 225-4906

IDAHO

Helen Chenoweth (R) ....(202) 225-6611
Michael D. Crapo (R) ....(202) 225-5531

ILLINOIS

Cardiss Collins (D)................................(202) 225-5006
Jerry F. Costello (D) ....(202) 225-5661
                    jfcil12@hr.house.gov
Philip M. Crane (R)................................(202) 225-3711
Richard J. Durbin (D) ....(202) 225-5271
                    durbin@hr.house.gov
Lane Evans (D)......................................(202) 225-5905

Thomas Ewing (R) ....(202) 225-2371
Harris W. Fawell (R) ....(202) 225-3515
        hfawell@hr.house.gov
Michael Flanagan (R) ....(202) 225-4061
Luis V. Gutierrez (D)..(202) 225-8203
        luisg@hr.house.gov
J. Dennis Hastert (R) ....(202) 225-2976
        dhastert@hr.house.gov
Henry J. Hyde (R) ....(202) 225-4561
Ray LaHood (R) ....(202) 225-6201
William O. Lipinski (D)..(202) 225-5701
Donald A. Manzullo (R) ....(202) 225-5676
John E. Porter (R) ....(202) 225-4835
Glenn Poshard (D)...(202) 225-5201
Bobby L. Rush (D) ....(202) 225-4372
        brush@hr.house.gov
Gerald Weller (R) ....(202) 225-3635
Sidney R. Yates (D) ....(202) 225-2111

INDIANA

Daniel Burton (R) ....(202) 225-2276
Steve Buyer (D)..(202) 225-5037
Lee H. Hamilton (D) ....(202) 225-5315
        hamilton@hr.house.gov
John Hostettler (R) ....(202) 225-4636
        johnhost@hr.house.gov
Andrew Jacobs, Jr. (D) ....(202) 225-4011
David McIntosh (R)..(202) 225-3021
John T. Myers (R)..(202) 225-5805
Timothy Roemer (D)..(202) 225-3915
Mark E. Souder (R) ....(202) 225-4436
Peter J. Visclosky (D) ....(202) 225-2461

IOWA

Greg Ganske (R) ....(202) 225-4426
Tom Latham (R)..(202) 225-5476
James Leach (R) ....(202) 225-6576
James R. Lightfoot (R) ....(202) 225-3806
James Allen Nussle (R) ....(202) 225-2911

KANSAS

Sam Brownback (R)...(202) 225-6601
        brownbak@hr.house.gov
Jan Meyers (R)...(202) 225-2865
Pat Roberts (R)...(202) 225-2715
        emailpat@hr.house.gov
Todd Tiahrt (R) ....(202) 225-6216

KENTUCKY

Scotty Baesler (D) ....(202) 225-4706
James Bunning (R) ....(202) 225-3465
        bunning4@hr.house.gov
Ron Lewis (R) ....(202) 225-3501
Harold Rogers (R) ....(202) 225-4601
Michael Ward (D) ....(202) 225-5401
        mward2@hr.house.gov
Edward Whitfield (R)...(202) 225-3115
        edky01@hr.house.gov

LOUISIANA

Richard H. Baker (R) ....(202) 225-3901
Cleo Fields (D) ....(202) 225-8490

Government

James A. Hayes (D)...(202) 225-2031
William Jefferson (D)..(202) 225-6636
Robert Livingston (R)..(202) 225-3015
James McCrery (R)..(202) 225-2777
W. J. Tauzin (D)..(202) 225-4031

MAINE

John Baldacci (D)..(202) 225-6306
James Longley, Jr. (R)..(202) 225-6116

MARYLAND

Roscoe G. Bartlett (R) ....(202) 225-2721
Benjamin L. Cardin (D)..(202) 225-4016
                                  cardin@hr.house.gov
Robert Ehrlich, Jr. (R)..(202) 225-3061
Wayne T. Gilchrest (R)...(202) 225-5311
Steny H. Hoyer (D)..(202) 225-4131
Kweisi Mfume (D)..(202) 225-4741
Constance Morella (R) ....(202) 225-5341
Albert R. Wynn (D)..(202) 225-8699

MASSACHUSETTS

Peter I. Blute (R)..(202) 225-6101
Barney Frank (D)..(202) 225-5931
Joseph P. Kennedy II (D) ....(202) 225-5111
Edward J. Markey (D)..(202) 225-2836
Martin T. Meehan (D) ....(202) 225-3411
John Joseph Moakley (D).......................................(202) 225-8273
                              jmoakley@hr.house.gov
Richard E. Neal (D)..(202) 225-5601
John W. Olver (D) ....(202) 225-5335
Gerry E. Studds (D)..(202) 225-3111
Peter G. Torkildsen (R)...(202) 225-8020
                              torkma06@hr.house.gov

MICHIGAN

James A. Barcia (D) ....(202) 225-8171
David E. Bonior (D) ....(202) 225-2106
David Camp (R)...(202) 225-3561
                              davecamp@hr.house.gov
Dick Chrysler (R)..(202) 225-4872
                              chrysler@hr.house.gov
Barbara-Rose Collins (D)......................................(202) 225-2261
John Conyers, Jr. (D)..(202) 225-5126
                              jconyers@hr.house.gov
John D. Dingell (D) ....(202) 225-4071
Vern Ehlers (R) ....(202) 225-3831
                              congehlr@hr.house.gov
Peter Hoekstra (R) ....(202) 225-4401
                              tellhoek@hr.house.gov
                              usavoice@hr.house.gov
Dale E. Kildee (D)..(202) 225-3611
Joe Knollenberg (R) ....(202) 225-5802
Sander M. Levin (D) ....(202) 225-4961
Lynn Rivers (D)..(202) 225-6261
Nick Smith (R) ....(202) 225-6276
                              repsmith@hr.house.gov
Bart Stupak (D)..(202) 225-4735
Frederick S. Upton (R) ....(202) 225-3761

MINNESOTA

Gilbert Gutknecht (R)...(202) 225-2472
gil@hr.house.gov
William Luther (D) ....(202) 225-2271
tellbill@hr.house.gov
David Minge (D)..(202) 225-2331
dminge@hr.house.gov
James L. Oberstar (D)..(202) 225-6211
oberstar@hr.house.gov
Collin C. Peterson (D)..(202) 225-2165
to collin@hr.house.gov
James M. Ramstad (D) ....(202) 225-2871
mn03@hr.house.gov
Martin O. Sabo (D)..(202) 225-4755
Bruce F. Vento (D) ....(202) 225-6631
vento@hr.house.gov

MISSISSIPPI

G. V. Montgomery (D)..(202) 225-5031
Mike Parker (D) ....(202) 225-5865
Gene Taylor (D) ....(202) 225-5772
Bennie G. Thompson (D).....................................(202) 225-5876
ms2nd@hr.house.gov
Roger F. Wicker (R) ....(202) 225-4306

MISSOURI

William L. Clay (D) ....(202) 225-2406
Pat Danner (D)..(202) 225-7041
Bill Emerson (R)..(202) 225-4404
bemerson@hr.house.gov
Richard A. Gephardt (D)......................................(202) 225-2671
Melton D. Hancock (R)..(202) 225-6536
Karen McCarthy (D)...(202) 225-4535
Ike Skelton (D) ....(202) 225-2876
James M. Talent (R) ....(202) 225-2561
talentmo@hr.house.gov
Harold L. Volkmer (D)...(202) 225-2956

MONTANA

Pat Williams (D) ....(202) 225-3211

NEBRASKA

William E. Barrett (R)..(202) 225-6435
Douglas Bereuter (R)...(202) 225-4806
Jon Christensen (R) ....(202) 225-4155

NEVADA

John Ensign (R)..(202) 225-5965
Barbara Vucanovich (R) ....(202) 225-6155

NEW HAMPSHIRE

Charles Bass (R) ....(202) 225-5206
William Zeliff, Jr. (R) ....(202) 225-5456
zeliff@hr.house.gov

NEW JERSEY

Robert E. Andrews (D) ....(202) 225-6501
randrews@hr.house.gov
Bob Franks (R) ....(202) 225-5361
franksnj@hr.house.gov
Rodney Frelinghuysen (R) ....(202) 225-5034
Frank LoBiondo (R)..(202) 225-6572

Government (Representatives)

Bill Martini (R) ....(202) 225-5751
Robert Menendez (D) ....(202) 225-7919
Frank Pallone, Jr. (D) ....(202) 225-4671
Donald M. Payne (D)............................(202) 225-3436
Marge Roukema (R)..............................(202) 225-4465
H. James Saxton (R) ....(202) 225-4765
Christopher Smith (R) ....(202) 225-3765
Robert Torricelli (D) ....(202) 225-5061
Richard A. Zimmer (R)..........................(202) 225-5801
zimmer@hr.house.gov

New Mexico

William Richardson (D)..........................(202) 225-6190
Steven H. Schiff (R) ....(202) 225-6316
Joseph Skeen (R)...................................(202) 225-2365

New York

Gary L. Ackerman (D)............................(202) 225-2601
Sherwood Boehlert (R) ....(202) 225-3665
oehlert@hr.house.gov
Eliot L. Engel (D) ....(202) 225-2464
engeline@hr.house.gov
Floyd H. Flake (D) ....(202) 225-3461
Michael Forbes (R)................................(202) 225-3826
mpforbes@hr.house.gov
Daniel Frisa (R) ....(202) 225-5516
Benjamin A. Gilman (R)........................(202) 225-3776
Maurice D. Hinchey (D).........................(202) 225-6335
Amory Houghton (R) ....(202) 225-3161
Sue Kelly (R) ....(202) 225-5441
Peter T. King (R) ....(202) 225-7896
John J. LaFalce (D)................................(202) 225-3231
Rick A. Lazio (R) ....(202) 225-3335
lazio@hr.house.gov
Nita M. Lowey (D)................................(202) 225-6506
Carolyn B. Maloney (D) ....(202) 225-7944
Thomas J. Manton (D)...........................(202) 225-3965
tmanton@hr.house.gov
John M. McHugh (R)..............................(202) 225-4611
Michael R. McNulty (D) ....(202) 225-5076
Susan Molinari (R)................................(202) 225-3371
molinari@hr.house.gov
Jerrold Nadler (D) ....(202) 225-5635
Major R. Owens (D)...............................(202) 225-6231
Bill Paxon (R) ....(202) 225-5265
Jack Quinn (R) ....(202) 225-3306
Charles B. Rangel (D)............................(202) 225-4365
Charles E. Schumer (D)..........................(202) 225-6616
Jose E. Serrano (D)................................(202) 225-4361
jserrano@hr.house.gov
Louise M. Slaughter (D).........................(202) 225-3615
Gerald B. Solomon (R) ....(202) 225-5614
Edolphus Towns (D)..............................(202) 225-5936
Nydia M. Velazquez (D) ....(202) 225-2361
James T. Walsh (R)................................(202) 225-3701

North Carolina

Thomas C. Ballenger (R) ....(202) 225-2576
cassmail@hr.house.gov
Richard Burr (R) ....(202) 225-2071
Eva Clayton (D) ....(202) 225-3101

Howard Coble (R)..(202) 225-3065
David Funderburk (R)..(202) 225-4531
                                    funnc02@hr.house.gov
W. G. Hefner (D) ....(202) 225-3715
Frederick Heineman (R) ....(202) 225-1784
                                    thechief@hr.house.gov
Walter Jones, Jr. (R) ....(202) 225-3415
Sue Myrick (R)...(202) 225-1976
                                    myrick@hr.house.gov
Charles Rose (D)..(202) 225-2731
                                    crose@hr.house.gov
Charles Hart Taylor (R) ....(202) 225-6401
                                    chtaylor@hr.house.gov
Melvin Watt (D) ....(202) 225-1510
                                    melmail@hr.house.gov

NORTH DAKOTA

Earl Pomeroy (D)...(202) 225-2611
                                    epomeroy@hr.house.gov

OHIO

John Andrew Boehner (R)..................................(202) 225-6205
Sherrod Brown (D)..(202) 225-3401
Steve Chabot (R)...(202) 225-2216
Frank Cremeans (R)...(202) 225-5705
Paul E. Gillmor (R)..(202) 225-6405
Tony P. Hall (D)..(202) 225-6465
David L. Hobson (R)..(202) 225-4324
Martin R. Hoke (R) ....(202) 225-5871
                                    hokemail@hr.house.gov
Marcy Kaptur (D)..(202) 225-4146
John R. Kasich (R)...(202) 225-5355
Steven LaTourette (R) ....(202) 225-5731
Bob Ney (R) ....(202) 225-6265
Michael G. Oxley (R)...(202) 225-2676
Rob Portman (R)..(202) 225-3164
                                    portmail@hr.house.gov
Deborah Pryce (R)...(202) 225-2015
Ralph Regula (R) ....(202) 225-3876
Thomas C. Sawyer (D)..(202) 225-5231
Louis Stokes (D)..(202) 225-7032
James Traficant, Jr. (D).......................................(202) 225-5261

OKLAHOMA

Bill Kent Brewster (D) ....(202) 225-4565
Tom Coburn (R)...(202) 225-2701
Ernest Jim Istook, Jr. (R) ....(202) 225-2132
                                    istook@hr.house.gov
Steve Largent (R)...(202) 225-2211
Frank Lucas (R)..(202) 225-5565
J. C. Watts, Jr. (R) ....(202) 225-6165

OREGON

Jim Bunn (R)...(202) 225-5711
Wes Cooley (R)..(202) 225-6730
Peter A. DeFazio (D)..(202) 225-6416
                                    pdefazio@hr.house.gov
Elizabeth Furse (D)..(202) 225-0855
                                    furseor1@hr.house.gov
Ronald Wyden (D)..(202) 225-4811

PENNSYLVANIA

Robert A. Borski (D)...(202) 225-8251
William Clinger, Jr. (R).......................................(202) 225-5121
William J. Coyne (D) ....(202) 225-2301
Mike Doyle (D) ....(202) 225-2135
Phil English (R)...(202) 225-5406
Chaka Fattah (D) ....(202) 225-4001
Thomas M. Foglietta (D) ....(202) 225-4731
Jon Fox (R)...(202) 225-6111
    jonfox@hr.house.gov
George W. Gekas (R) ....(202) 225-4315
William F. Goodling (R) ....(202) 225-5836
Jim Greenwood (R)..(202) 225-4276
Tim Holden (D) ....(202) 225-5546
Paul E. Kanjorski (D) ....(202) 225-6511
    kanjo@hr.house.gov
Ron Klink (D) ....(202) 225-2565
Joseph M. McDade (R) ....(202) 225-3731
Frank Mascara (D)..(202) 225-4665
Paul McHale (D)...(202) 225-6411
    mchale@hr.house.gov
John P. Murtha (D) ....(202) 225-2065
    murtha@hr.house.gov
Bud Shuster (R)..(202) 225-2431
Robert S. Walker (R) ....(202) 225-2411
    pa16@hr.house.gov
Curt Weldon (R)..(202) 225-2011
    curtpa7@hr.house.gov

RHODE ISLAND

Patrick Kennedy (D) ....(202) 225-4911
John F. Reed (D)..(202) 225-2735

SOUTH CAROLINA

James E. Clyburn (D) ....(202) 225-3315
Lindsey Graham (R)...(202) 225-5301
Bob Inglis (R) ....(202) 225-6030
Mark Sanford (R) ....(202) 225-3176
    sanford@hr.house.gov
Floyd Spence (R)...(202) 225-2452
John M. Spratt, Jr. (D) ....(202) 225-5501
    jspratt@hr.house.gov

SOUTH DAKOTA

Timothy P. Johnson (D) ....(202) 225-2801

TENNESSEE

Ed Bryant (R) ....(202) 225-2811
Robert Clement (D)...(202) 225-4311
John J. Duncan, Jr. (R) ....(202) 225-5435
Harold E. Ford (D) ....(202) 225-3265
Bart Gordon (D)..(202) 225-4231
Van Hilleary (R)..(202) 225-6831
James H. Quillen (R) ....(202) 225-6356
John S. Tanner (D)...(202) 225-4714
Zach Wamp (R)..(202) 225-3271

TEXAS

William Archer (R)..(202) 225-2571
Richard K. Armey (R)...(202) 225-7772
Joseph Barton (R)..(202) 225-2002
    barton06@hr.house.gov

Ken Bentsen (D) ....(202) 225-7508
Henry Bonilla (R) ....(202) 225-4511
John Bryant (D)....................................(202) 225-2231
Jim Chapman (D)..................................(202) 225-3035
jchapman@hr.house.gov
Ronald D. Coleman (D)...........................(202) 225-4831
Larry Combest (R)..................................(202) 225-4005
E. de la Garza (D)..................................(202) 225-2531
Thomas DeLay (R) ....(202) 225-5951
Lloyd Doggett (D) ....(202) 225-4865
doggett@hr.house.gov
Chet Edwards (D)...................................(202) 225-6105
Jack Fields (R) ....(202) 225-4901
Martin Frost (D)....................................(202) 225-3605
frost@hr.house.gov
Peter Geren (D).....................................(202) 225-5071
Henry B. Gonzalez (D)...........................(202) 225-3236
Gene Green (D).....................................(202) 225-1688
ggreen@hr.house.gov
Ralph M. Hall (D)..................................(202) 225-6673
Sheila Jackson-Lee (D) ....(202) 225-3816
Eddie Bernice Johnson (D) ....(202) 225-8885
Sam Johnson (R)....................................(202) 225-4201
samtx03@hr.house.gov
Gregory H. Laughlin (D) ....(202) 225-2831
Solomon P. Ortiz (D) ....(202) 225-7742
Lamar S. Smith (R)................................(202) 225-4236
Charles W. Stenholm (D) ....(202) 225-6605
Steve Stockman (R)................................(202) 225-6565
Frank Tejeda (D) ....(202) 225-1640
William Thornberry (R)...........................(202) 225-3706
Charles Wilson (D) ....(202) 225-2401
cwilson@hr.house.gov

UTAH

James V. Hansen (R) ....(202) 225-0453
William H. Orton (D).............................(202) 225-7751
ortonut3@hr.house.gov
Enid Waldholtz (R) ....(202) 225-3011
enidutah@hr.house.gov

VERMONT

Bernard Sanders (I) ....(202) 225-4115

VIRGINIA

Herbert H. Bateman (R) ....(202) 225-4261
Thomas J. Bliley, Jr. (R) ....(202) 225-2815
Rick Boucher (D) ....(202) 225-3861
ninthnet@hr.house.gov
Thomas Davis (R) ....(202) 225-1492
tomdavis@hr.house.gov
Robert W. Goodlatte (R) ....(202) 225-5431
talk2bob@hr.house.gov
James P. Moran, Jr. (D)...........................(202) 225-4376
Lewis F. Payne, Jr. (D) ....(202) 225-4711
Owen B. Pickett (D) ....(202) 225-4215
opickett@hr.house.gov
Robert C. Scott (D) ....(202) 225-8351
Norman Sisisky (D).................................(202) 225-6365
Frank R. Wolf (R) ....(202) 225-5136

Government

WASHINGTON

Norman D. Dicks (D)..(202) 225-5916
Jennifer Dunn (R) ....(202) 225-7761
     dunnwa08@hr.house.gov
Doc Hastings (R)..(202) 225-5816
James A. McDermott (D)......................................(202) 225-3106
Jack Metcalf (R) ....(202) 225-2605
George Nethercutt (R)..(202) 225-2006
Linda Smith (R) ....(202) 225-3536
     asklinda@hr.house.gov
Randy Tate (R)...(202) 225-8901
     rtate@hr.house.gov
Rick White (R) ....(202) 225-6311
     repwhite@hr.house.gov

WASHINGTON, DC

Eleanor Holmes Norton (D) ....(202) 225-8050

WEST VIRGINIA

Alan B. Mollohan (D) ....(202) 225-4172
Nick Joe Rahall II (D)..(202) 225-3452
Robert E. Wise, Jr. (D) ....(202) 225-2711

WISCONSIN

Thomas M. Barrett (D) ....(202) 225-3571
Steve Gunderson (R) ....(202) 225-5506
Gerald D. Kleczka (D)..(202) 225-4572
Scott Klug (R) ....(202) 225-2906
     badger02@hr.house.gov
Mark Neumann (R) ....(202) 225-3031
     mneumann@hr.house.gov
David R. Obey (D)...(202) 225-3365
Thomas E. Petri (R) ....(202) 225-2476
Toby Roth (R) ....(202) 225-5665
     roth08@hr.house.gov
F. J. Sensenbrenner, Jr. (R) ....(202) 225-5101

WYOMING

Barbara Cubin (R)...(202) 225-2311

For periodic updates of the U.S. House of Representatives e-mail list, send mail to congress@hr.house.gov. You may also retrieve this information through the gopher site at gopher.house.gov or via the World Wide Web at http://www.house.gov.

U.S. Senators

Alabama, Howell T. Heflin (D).........................(202) 224-4124
Alabama, Richard C. Shelby (R)......................(202) 224-5744
Alaska, Frank H. Murkowski (R)......................(202) 224-6665
Alaska, Ted Stevens (R)...................................(202) 224-3004
Arizona, Jon Kyl (R) ....(202) 224-4521
     info@kyl.senate.gov
Arizona, John McCain (R) ....(202) 224-2235
Arkansas, Dale Bumpers (D)............................(202) 224-4843
Arkansas, David Pryor (D)...............................(202) 224-2353
California, Barbara Boxer (D)...........................(202) 224-5161
     senator@boxer.senate.gov
California, Dianne Feinstein (D)......................(202) 224-3841
Colorado, Mark Brown (R)..............................(202) 224-5941
     senator_brown@brown.senate.gov
Colorado, Ben N. Campbell (R)........................(202) 224-4761

Connecticut, Christopher J. Dodd (D)..............(202) 224-2823
        sen_dodd@dodd.senate.gov
Connecticut, Joseph I. Lieberman (D) ....(202) 224-4041
        senator_lieberman@lieberman.senate.gov
Delaware, Joseph R. Biden, Jr. (D) ....(202) 224-5042
        senator@biden.senate.gov
Delaware, William V. Roth, Jr. (R)....................(202) 224-2441
Florida, Robert Graham (D) ....(202) 224-3041
Florida, Connie Mack (R)..................................(202) 224-5274
Georgia, Paul Coverdell (R) ....(202) 224-3643
        senator_coverdell@coverdell.senate.gov
Georgia, Samuel Nunn (D)................................(202) 224-3521
Hawaii, Daniel K. Akaka (D) ....(202) 224-6361
Hawaii, Daniel K. Inouye (D)............................(202) 224-3934
Idaho, Larry E. Craig (R) ....(202) 224-2752
        larry_craig@craig.senate.gov
Idaho, Dirk Kempthorne (R) ....(202) 224-6142
        dirk_kempthorne@kempthorne.senate.gov
Illinois, Carol Moseley-Braun (D) ....(202) 224-2854
        senator@moseley-braun.senate.gov
Illinois, Paul Simon (D) ....(202) 224-2152
        senator@simon.senate.gov
Indiana, Daniel R. Coats (R)..............................(202) 224-5623
Indiana, Richard G. Lugar (R)...........................(202) 224-4814
Iowa, Charles E. Grassley (R) ....(202) 224-3744
        chuck_grassley@grassley.senate.gov
Iowa, Tom Harkin (D) ....(202) 224-3254
        tom_harkin@harkin.senate.gov
Kansas, Robert Dole (R) ....(202) 224-6521
Kansas, Nancy L. Kassebaum (R) ....(202) 224-4774
Kentucky, Wendell H. Ford (D) ....(202) 224-4343
        wendell_ford@ford.senate.gov
Kentucky, Mitch McConnell (R) ....(202) 224-2541
Louisiana, John B. Breaux (D)...........................(202) 224-4623
        senator@breaux.senate.gov
Louisiana, J. Bennett Johnston (D) ....(202) 224-5824
        senator@johnston.senate.gov
Maine, William S. Cohen (R) ....(202) 224-2523
Maine, Olympia Snowe (R)...............................(202) 224-5344
Maryland, Barbara A. Mikulski (D)...................(202) 224-4654
        senator@mikulski.senate.gov
Maryland, Paul S. Sarbanes (D).........................(202) 224-4524
        senator@sarbanes.senate.gov
Massachusetts, Edward M. Kennedy (D) ....(202) 224-4543
        senator@kennedy.senate.gov
Massachusetts, John F. Kerry (D) ....(202) 224-2742
        john_kerry@kerry.senate.gov
Michigan, Spencer Abraham (R) ....(202) 224-4822
Michigan, Carl Levin (D) ....(202) 224-6221
        senator@levin.senate.gov
Minnesota, Rod Grams (R)................................(202) 224-3244
        mail_grams@grams.senate.gov
Minnesota, Paul Wellstone (D) ....(202) 224-5641
        senator@wellstone.senate.gov
Mississippi, Thad Cochran (R) ....(202) 224-5054
Mississippi, Trent Lott (R)................................(202) 224-6253
Missouri, John Ashcroft (R)..............................(202) 224-6154
        john_ashcroft@ashcroft.senate.gov
Missouri, Christopher S. Bond (R)....................(202) 224-5721
Montana, Max Baucus (D).................................(202) 224-2651
        max@baucus.senate.gov

Montana, Conrad R. Burns (R) ....(202) 224-2644
conrad_burns@burns.senate.gov
Nebraska, J. James Exon (D).............................(202) 224-4224
Nebraska, Bob Kerrey (D)..................................(202) 224-6551
bob@kerrey.senate.gov
Nevada, Richard H. Bryan (D) ....(202) 224-6244
Nevada, Harry Reid (D)......................................(202) 224-3542
New Hampshire, Judd Gregg (R).....................(202) 224-3324
mailbox@gregg.senate.gov
New Hampshire, Robert Smith (R)...................(202) 224-2841
opinion@smith.senate.gov
New Jersey, William Bradley (D) ....(202) 224-3224
senator@bradley.senate.gov
New Jersey, Frank R. Lautenberg (D) ....(202) 224-4744
New Mexico, Jeff Bingaman (D) ....(202) 224-5521
senator_bingaman@bingaman.senate.gov
New Mexico, Pete V. Domenici (R)..................(202) 224-6621
senator_domenici@domenici.senate.gov
New York, Alfonse M. D'Amato (R)..................(202) 224-6542
New York, Daniel P. Moynihan (D) ....(202) 224-4451
North Carolina, Leuch Faircloth (R) ....(202) 224-3154
North Carolina, Jesse Helms (R) ....(202) 224-6342
North Dakota, Kent Conrad (D) ....(202) 224-2043
North Dakota, Byron L. Dorgan (D) ....(202) 224-2551
Ohio, Michael DeWine (R)................................(202) 224-2315
senator_dewine@dewine.senate.gov
Ohio, John Glenn (D) ....(202) 224-3353
Oklahoma, James Inhofe (R) ....(202) 224-4721
Oklahoma, Donald Nickles (R) ....(202) 224-5754
Oregon, Mark O. Hatfield (R)...........................(202) 224-3753
Oregon, Seat Open...(202) 224-5244
Pennsylvania, Rick Santorum (R) ....(202) 224-6324
Pennsylvania, Arlen Specter (R) ....(202) 224-4254
Rhode Island, John H. Chafee (R) ....(202) 224-2921
senator_chafee@chafee.senate.gov
Rhode Island, Claiborne Pell (D) ....(202) 224-4642
South Carolina, Ernest F. Hollings (D) ....(202) 224-6121
senator@hollings.senate.gov
South Carolina, Strom Thurmond (R)..............(202) 224-5972
South Dakota, Thomas A. Daschle (D) ....(202) 224-2321
tom_daschle@daschle.senate.gov
South Dakota, Larry Pressler (R) ....(202) 224-5842
larry_pressler@pressler.senate.gov
Tennessee, Bill Frist (R) ....(202) 224-3344
senator_frist@frist.senate.gov
Tennessee, Fred Thompson (R) ....(202) 224-4944
Texas, Phil Gramm (R) ....(202) 224-2934
Texas, Kay Bailey Hutchison (R).......................(202) 224-5922
senator@hutchison.senate.gov
Utah, Robert Bennett (R)...................................(202) 224-5444
Utah, Orrin G. Hatch (R) ....(202) 224-5251
Vermont, James M. Jeffords (R) ....(202) 224-5141
vermont@jeffords.senate.gov
Vermont, Patrick J. Leahy (D) ....(202) 224-4242
senator_leahy@leahy.senate.gov
Virginia, Charles S. Robb (D)............................(202) 224-4024
senator@robb.senate.gov
Virginia, John W. Warner (R).............................(202) 224-2023
senator@warner.senate.gov
Washington, Slade Gorton (R)...........................(202) 224-3441
senator_gorton@gorton.senate.gov

Washington, Patty Murray (D) ....(202) 224-2621
        senator_murray@murray.senate.gov
West Virginia, Robert C. Byrd (D) ....(202) 224-3954
West Virginia, John D. Rockefeller IV (D) ....(202) 224-6472
        senator@rockefeller.senate.gov
Wisconsin, Russell Feingold (D) ....(202) 224-5323
        senator@feingold.senate.gov
Wisconsin, Herbert H. Kohl (D) ....(202) 224-5653
        senator_kohl@kohl.senate.gov
Wyoming, Alan K. Simpson (R) ....(202) 224-3424
Wyoming, Craig Thomas (R) ....(202) 224-6441

*To retrieve periodic updates of the U.S. Senators e-mail list, use the
anonymous account at: ftp.senate.gov:70.*

State Attorneys General

Alabama, Jeff Sessions..(334) 242-7300
Alaska, Charles Cole...(907) 465-3600
Arizona, Grant Woods ....(602) 542-4266
Arkansas, Winston Bryant ....(501) 682-2007
California, Daniel Lungren ....(916) 324-5437
Colorado, Gale Norton ....(303) 866-3052
Connecticut, Richard Blumenthal......................(203) 566-3579
Delaware, Jane Brady..(302) 577-3838
Florida, Robert Butterworth ....(904) 487-1963
Georgia, Michael Bowers ....(404) 656-4585
Hawaii, Robert Marks...(808) 586-1282
Idaho, Al Lance ....(208) 334-2400
Illinois, Jim Ryan ....(312) 814-2503
Indiana, Pamela Fanning Carter ....(317) 232-6201
Iowa, Tom Miller ....(515) 281-3053
Kansas, Carla Stovall...(913) 296-2215
Kentucky, Chris Gorman ....(502) 564-7600
Louisiana, Richard Ieyoub..................................(504) 342-7013
Maine, Andrew Ketterer ....(207) 626-8800
Maryland, Joseph Curran ....(410) 576-6300
Massachusetts, L. Scott Harshbarger.................(617) 727-2200
Michigan, Frank Kelley ....(517) 373-1110
Minnesota, Skip Humphrey ....(612) 296-6196
Mississippi, Mike Moore.....................................(601) 359-3692
Missouri, Jeremiah D. "Jay" Nixon....................(314) 751-3321
Montana, Joseph Mazurek...................................(406) 444-2026
Nebraska, Don Stenberg......................................(402) 471-2682
Nevada, Franky Sue Del Papa.............................(702) 687-4170
New Hampshire, Jeffrey R. Howard....................(603) 271-3658
New Jersey, Deborah Poritz ....(609) 292-4925
New Mexico, Tom Udall.....................................(505) 827-6000
New York, Dennis Vacco.....................................(212) 416-8519
North Carolina, Mike Easley ....(919) 733-3377
North Dakota, Heidi Heitkamp...........................(701) 328-2210
Ohio, Betty Montgomery ....(614) 466-3376
Oklahoma, Drew Edmondson ....(405) 521-3921
Oregon, Theodore R. Kulongoski ....(503) 378-6002
Pennsylvania, Ernest D. Preate, Jr......................(717) 787-3391
Rhode Island, Jeffrey Pine ....(401) 274-4400
South Carolina, Charlie Condon........................(803) 734-3970
South Dakota, Mark Barnett...............................(605) 773-3215
Tennessee, Charles W. Burson ....(615) 741-3491
Texas, Dan Morales ....(512) 463-2191
Utah, Jan Graham ....(801) 538-1326
Vermont, Jeffrey Amestoy ....(802) 828-3171

Virginia, James Gilmore ....(804) 786-2071
Washington, Christine Gregoire ....(206) 753-6200
West Virginia, Darrell V. McGraw, Jr. ....(304) 558-2021
Wisconsin, James E. Doyle ....(608) 266-1221
Wyoming, Joseph Meyer ....(307) 777-7841

State Chambers of Commerce

Alabama..(205) 834-6000
Alaska ....(907) 586-2323
Arizona ....(602) 248-9172
Arkansas ....(501) 374-9225
California..(916) 444-6670
Colorado ....(303) 831-7411
Connecticut..(203) 244-1990
Delaware ....(302) 655-7221
Florida..(904) 425-1200
Georgia..(404) 223-2264
Hawaii..(808) 545-4300
Idaho..(208) 343-1849
Illinois..(312) 983-7100
Indiana..(317) 264-3110
Iowa..(515) 244-6149
Kansas ....(913) 357-6321
Kentucky..(502) 695-4700
Louisiana..(504) 928-5388
Maine..(207) 623-4568
Maryland..(410) 269-0642
Massachusetts ....(508) 548-8500
Michigan..(517) 371-2100
Minnesota..(612) 292-4650
Mississippi..(601) 969-0022
Missouri..(314) 634-3511
Montana ....(406) 442-2405
Nebraska ....(402) 474-4422
Nevada..(702) 786-3030
New Hampshire..(603) 224-5388
New Jersey ....(609) 989-7888
New Mexico ....(505) 842-0644
New York ....(518) 465-7511
North Carolina..(919) 828-0758
North Dakota ....(701) 222-0929
Ohio..(614) 228-4201
Oklahoma ....(405) 424-4003
Oregon ....(503) 588-0050
Pennsylvania..(717) 255-3252
Rhode Island..(401) 272-1400
South Carolina..(803) 799-4601
South Dakota..(605) 224-6161
Tennessee ....(615) 256-5141
Texas ....(512) 472-1594
Utah..(801) 628-1658
Vermont..(802) 223-3443
Virginia..(804) 644-1607
Washington..(206) 357-3362
West Virginia ....(304) 342-1115
Wisconsin ....(608) 258-3400

Employment Agencies

ANCHORAGE, AK

Adams & Assocs.	(907) 561-5161
Alaska Executive Search	(907) 276-5707
Mila	(907) 562-6452

ATLANTA, GA

Paces Personnel	(404) 688-5307
Perimeter Placement	(404) 393-0000
Taurus Personnel Consultants	(404) 951-2461

ATLANTIC CITY, NJ

Snelling Personnel Services	(609) 646-6470

BALTIMORE, MD

Baltimore's Premier Placement & Co.	(410) 337-8480
Don Richard Assocs. of Baltimore	(410) 752-5244
Snelling Personnel Services	(410) 528-9400

BOSTON, MA

Fanning Personnel	(617) 728-4100
Kennison & Assocs.	(617) 478-2888
KNF&T	(617) 227-0677
New Boston Assocs.	(617) 720-0990
Winter, Wyman & Co.	(617) 542-5000

BUFFALO, NY

APA Employment Agency	(716) 874-6760
DCA	(716) 632-1500
Dunhill	(716) 885-3576
The Recruitment Group	(716) 631-3100

CHARLOTTE, NC

Advance Personnel	(704) 364-7886
Morgan Resources	(704) 541-7555
Don Richard Assocs.	(704) 377-6447
Snelling Personnel Services	(704) 525-3652
United Personnel Services	(704) 588-2281

CHICAGO, IL

Banner Personnel Service	(312) 704-6000
Excel Personnel Service	(312) 372-0014
The Richard Michael Group	(312) 558-9199

CINCINNATI, OH

ADOW Personnel	(513) 721-2369
CBS Personnel Services	(513) 651-1111
Tower Personnel	(513) 241-6012

CLEVELAND, OH

Business World Personnel	(216) 461-8959
Champion Personnel System	(216) 781-5900
Dawson Personnel Systems	(216) 771-8100

COLUMBUS, OH

Courtney Services	(614) 575-1770
Dawson Personnel Systems	(614) 228-2461
Robert Half International	(614) 221-9300
Martha Vance & Assocs.	(614) 799-0200

DALLAS, TX

Babich & Assocs.	(214) 361-5735

Human Resources (Employment Agencies)

Personnel One ....(214) 361-6000
Snelling Personnel Services ....(214) 934-9030

DENVER, CO

Command Staffing ....(303) 770-1200
Margaret Hook's Personnel ....(303) 770-2100
Snelling Personnel Services ....(303) 779-3060

DETROIT, MI

#1 Personnel ....(313) 274-4230
Dorothy Day Personnel ....(313) 962-0565

GRAND RAPIDS, MI

Robert Half International ....(616) 454-9444
The Job Shoppe ....(616) 957-1300
Snelling Personnel Services ....(616) 452-2154

GREENVILLE, SC

Adia Personnel Services......................................(803) 271-1360
Paragon Placement ....(803) 579-1999
Personnel Solutions...(803) 585-6300
Snelling Personnel Services ....(803) 268-9300
TRS Total Recruiting Services............................(803) 574-4785

HARRISBURG, PA

The Byrnes Group ....(717) 846-5656
Employment East...(717) 843-0031
Executive Avail-a-Search....................................(717) 291-1871
JFC Staffing Assocs. ....(717) 657-4923

HARTFORD, CT

Allied Personnel...(203) 787-4231
J. Morrissey & Co..(203) 246-9000
New England Personnel ....(203) 525-8616
Robert Half International ....(203) 562-9262
Universal Staffing..(203) 527-8135

HONOLULU, HI

Adia: The Employment People...........................(808) 533-8889
Altres Making Business Simple...........................(808) 591-4900
Employment Specialists.......................................(808) 528-1550
Remedy Intelligent Staffing ....(808) 487-7787

HOUSTON, TX

M. David Lowe Personnel Services....................(713) 784-4226
Skillmaster, the Personnel Resource Group.......(713) 871-5200
Snelling Personnel Services ....(713) 847-1700

INDIANAPOLIS, IN

Century Personnel...(317) 580-8500
Dan Lane Personnel ....(317) 255-9632
The Registry ....(317) 634-1200

KANSAS CITY, KS

Advantage, Cameron & Merrill..........................(913) 338-2134
Morgan Hunter Corporate Search ....(913) 491-3434

KANSAS CITY, MO

Corporate Personnel...(816) 454-4080

LAS VEGAS, NV

AAA Placement Service.......................................(702) 451-3361
Appleone Employment Services ....(702) 734-8110
Eastman Personnel Services ....(702) 228-2813

Eastridge Personnel...(702) 732-8861

MIAMI, FL

Hastings & Hastings...(305) 374-2255
Linda Robins Assocs...(305) 828-8367
Personally Yours...(305) 822-7756

MILWAUKEE, WI

Division 10 Personnel ....(414) 476-8700
Dunhill of Milwaukee...(414) 272-4860
Snelling Personnel Services ....(414) 278-7272

MINNEAPOLIS, MN

Hayden & Assocs. ....(612) 941-6300
Office Consultants...(612) 544-3000
The Recruiting Group..(612) 544-1005

NASHVILLE, TN

Baker & Baker Employment Service ....(615) 824-5253
Darrell Walker Personnel Consultants ....(615) 361-5840
Dianne Holt Personnel...(615) 377-2302
Wood Personnel Services ....(615) 399-0006

NEW ORLEANS, LA

Conrad Consulting Group....................................(504) 592-2606
Delta Personnel ....(504) 561-5884
Snelling Personnel Services ....(504) 529-5781

NEW YORK, NY

A. Taylor...(212) 213-5600
Career Blazers ....(212) 719-3232
Eden Personnel..(212) 685-8600
Rand Assocs..(212) 818-0200
Winston Resources ....(212) 557-5000

NORFOLK, VA

Don Richards Assocs. ....(804) 455-8600
ProTemps ....(804) 490-9617
Reliance Temporary Services ....(804) 424-6464
Snelling Personnel Services ....(804) 497-7500

OKLAHOMA CITY, OK

Personnel Solutions..(405) 946-0404
Snelling Personnel Services ....(405) 848-2606
Susan Frew & Company.......................................(405) 842-6300
Terry Neese Personnel Services.........................(405) 942-8551

ORLANDO, FL

AAA Employment ....(407) 724-4170
Job Specialists..(407) 855-5627
Personnel One ....(407) 422-5800
Snelling Personnel Services ....(407) 788-7300

PHILADELPHIA, PA

American Staffing Resources ....(215) 568-9999
Parker Personnel..(215) 564-2997
Powers Personnel ....(215) 563-5520

PHOENIX, AZ

Professional Placement..(602) 955-0870
Snelling Personnel Services ....(602) 277-1818
Western Human Resources Assocs. ....(602) 279-5301

PITTSBURGH, PA

Allegheny Personnel Services ....(412) 391-2044
GFA Assocs. ....(412) 788-6232
International Business Assocs. ....(412) 281-6263

PORTLAND, OR

Adams & Assocs...(503) 224-5870
APA Employment Agency ....(503) 233-1200
DB Brown and Assocs. ....(503) 224-6860
Office Notes 5..(503) 287-7918

PROVIDENCE, RI

Capitol Personnel ....(401) 438-6067
Services Rendered ....(401) 942-7200
Snelling Personnel Services ....(401) 724-6700
Wholing City Employment Services..................(508) 999-3477

RALEIGH, NC

Creative Staffing Services ....(919) 833-3111
Elite Personnel Services ....(919) 881-9000
Snelling Personnel Services ....(919) 876-0660

SACRAMENTO, CA

Act•1 Personnel Services ....(916) 444-2442
AppleOne ....(916) 483-9180
Cooper & Assocs..(916) 481-8092
Nelson...(916) 648-3611

ST. LOUIS, MO

The Keystone Partnership ....(314) 721-7200
Personnel Partnership......................................(314) 863-6060
The Resource Team ....(314) 436-7980
Snelling Personnel..(314) 862-2727

SALT LAKE CITY, UT

Prince, Perelson and Assocs. ....(801) 532-1000
Professional Recruiters.....................................(801) 268-9940
Snelling Personnel Services ....(801) 268-8444

SAN ANTONIO, TX

Deacon Rawley Personnel Consulting...............(210) 525-1994
Encore Personnel Services.................................(210) 841-5757
Snelling Personnel Services ....(210) 822-8224
Symcox Personnel Consultants.........................(210) 494-6674

SAN DIEGO, CA

Alliance Staffing Assoc. ....(619) 684-3515
The Eastridge Group ....(619) 260-2000
Interim Personnel ....(619) 624-9400
Omni Express..(619) 974-9773

SAN FRANCISCO, CA

Innovations Personnel Services ....(415) 392-4022
Pathways Personnel Agency..............................(415) 391-2060
Stansbury Staffing Consultants.........................(415) 677-0167

SEATTLE, WA

Adams & Assocs...(206) 447-9200
Business Careers...(206) 447-7474
Snelling Personnel Services ....(206) 246-6610

TAMPA, FL

Accord Personnel Services.................................(813) 887-3290

Availability ....(813) 286-8800
Personnel One ....(813) 289-7700
Snelling Personnel Services ....(813) 799-1170

WASHINGTON, DC

Adia Personnel Services.....................................(202) 857-0800
Career Blazers ....(202) 467-4222
Doyle Personnel Services ....(202) 296-2885
Snelling Personnel Services ....(202) 223-3540

WEST PALM BEACH, FL

Career Planners ....(407) 683-8785
David Wood Personnel.......................................(407) 686-4571
Personnel One ....(407) 686-6400
Snelling Personnel Services ....(407) 689-5400

Executive Search Firms

A. T. Kearney, Chicago, IL ....(312) 648-0111
Battalia Winston, New York, NY.......................(212) 308-8080
D. E. Foster Partners, New York, NY ....(212) 872-6232
DHR, Chicago, IL ....(312) 782-1581
Diversified Search Cos., Philadelphia, PA.........(215) 732-6666
Egon Zehnder, New York, NY............................(212) 838-9199
Gilbert Tweed Assocs., New York, NY ....(212) 758-3000
Goodrich & Sherwood, New York, NY ....(212) 697-4131
Gould & McCoy, New York, NY ....(212) 688-8671
Handy HRM, New York, NY ....(212) 557-0400
Heidrick & Struggles, Chicago, IL....................(312) 372-8811
Korn/Ferry, New York, NY ....(212) 687-1834
Lamalie Amrop, New York, NY ....(212) 953-7900
Norman Broadbent, New York, NY ....(212) 953-6990
Paul Ray Berndtson, Fort Worth, TX ....(817) 334-0500
Russell Reynolds, New York, NY ....(212) 351-2000
Sampson, Neill & Wilkins,
  Upper Montclair, NJ.......................................(201) 783-9600
Ward Howell, New York, NY.............................(212) 697-3730
Witt, Keiffer, Ford, Hadelman, Lloyd,
  Oak Brook, IL...(708) 990-1370

National Temporary Employment Agencies

Ablest Service, Clearwater, FL...........................(813) 461-5656
Accountemps Service of Robert Half International
  Menlo Park, CA ....(415) 854-9700
AccuStaff, Virginia Beach, VA ....(804) 431-2004
Adia Services, Menlo Park, CA.........................(415) 324-0696
Alternative Resources, Lincolnshire, IL ....(708) 317-1000
Career Horizons, Woodbury, NY.......................(516) 496-2300
Claims Overload Systems, Los Angeles, CA .....(310) 447-7144
DayStar Temporary Services, Cleveland, OH ...(216) 696-1122
Dunhill Temporary Systems, Woodbury, NY .....(516) 364-8800
Express Personnel Services,
  Oklahoma City, OK...(800) 652-6400
Hooper Holmes, Basking Ridge, NJ ....(908) 953-6250
Interim Services, Ft. Lauderdale, FL ....(305) 938-7600
Kelly Services, Troy, MI ....(313) 362-4444
Labor World of America, Boca Raton, FL.........(407) 997-5000
MacTemps, Cambridge, MA ....(617) 868-6800
Manpower, Milwaukee, WI................................(414) 961-1000
Norrell, Atlanta, GA...(404) 240-3000
Office Specialists, Wakefield, MA ....(617) 246-4900

The Olsten Corp., Westbury, NY......................(516) 832-8200
Pro Staff Personnel Services,
   Minneapolis, MN..(612) 339-2221
Remedy Temporary Services,
   San Juan Capistrano, CA..............................(714) 661-1211
Snelling and Snelling, Dallas, TX.....................(214) 239-7575
Stivers Temporary Personnel, Chicago, IL ....(312) 558-3550
TAC/TEMPS, Newton Upper Falls, MA ....(617) 969-3100
TAD Temporaries, Rochester, NY ....(716) 546-1660
Talent Tree, Houston, TX ....(713) 789-1818
Today's Temporary, Dallas, TX..........................(214) 380-9380
TRC Staffing, Atlanta, GA ....(404) 392-1411
Triad Personnel, Oakbrook Terrace, IL..............(708) 954-0455
Uniforce Services, New Hyde Park, NY............(516) 437-3300
Volt Temporary Services, Orange, CA ....(714) 921-8800
Western Temporary Services,
   Walnut Creek, CA ....(510) 930-5300

Source: List excerpted from the National Association of Temporary
Services Directory. *These companies have at least 20 offices operating
in 10 different states in the U.S. A complete directory of members is
available from the association. Contact: ATS, 119 South Saint Asaph
Street, Alexandria, VA 22314. Phone: (703) 549-6287.*

Outplacement Firms

ATLANTA, GA

Challenger, Gray & Christmas..........................(404) 681-0736
Drake Beam Morin...(404) 671-1500
EnterChange..(404) 604-6000
Lee Hecht Harrison ....(404) 551-2780
Mainstream Access ....(404) 255-4218
The Mulling Group ....(404) 395-3131
Payne Lendman ....(404) 952-1077
People Management ....(404) 396-5244
Right Assocs. ....(404) 392-7299

BALTIMORE, MD

Drake Beam Morin...(410) 494-0960
Fox-Morris Assocs. ....(410) 296-4500
Manchester ....(410) 821-9100
Right Assocs. ....(410) 727-0997
White Ridgely & Assocs. ....(410) 296-1900

BOSTON, MA

Action Management ....(617) 720-0633
Drake Beam Morin...(617) 345-0101
Fitzgerald, Stevens & Ford ....(617) 338-9363
The Keystone Assocs...(617) 742-2779
Lee Hecht Harrison ....(617) 424-1800
Manchester ....(617) 737-9100
Right Assocs. ....(617) 451-2298
Strategic Outsourcing..(617) 261-3555
Stybel, Peabody & Assocs. ....(617) 736-0900

CHARLOTTE, NC

Drake Beam Morin...(704) 522-7416
Fox-Morris Assocs. ....(704) 522-8244
Freiburger & Assocs...(704) 847-0340
Morehead Assocs. ....(704) 522-0776
Right Assocs. ....(704) 342-1795

CHICAGO, IL

Cambridge Outplacement International	(312) 251-0400
Challenger, Gray & Christmas	(312) 332-5790
Clarke, Poynton & Assocs.	(312) 759-7100
D. P. Baiocchi Assocs.	(312) 474-0081
The Derson Group	(312) 663-4179
Drake Beam Morin	(312) 578-4200
Hardy Freeman & Assocs.	(312) 372-6500
Jannotta, Bray & Assocs.	(312) 441-1500
Jarosz Assocs.	(312) 930-0550
The John Joseph Group	(312) 663-4176
Lee Hecht Harrison	(312) 726-1880
Mulligan & Assocs.	(312) 346-9219
Right Assocs.	(312) 606-0096
The Transition Team Network	(312) 609-9700

CINCINNATI, OH

Drake Beam Morin	(513) 671-1999
Promark	(513) 768-6500
Right Assocs.	(513) 733-1313
Schonberg Assocs.	(513) 891-0666

CLEVELAND, OH

American Management Development	(216) 642-8600
Challenger, Gray & Christmas	(216) 243-4477
Disc & Company	(216) 752-1700
Drake Beam Morin	(216) 621-5222
EnterChange	(216) 589-9900
Fox-Morris Assocs.	(216) 524-6565
Hite Executive Outplacement	(216) 461-1600
Louis Thomas Masterson	(216) 356-0804
Patrick•Douglas	(216) 621-1550
Right Assocs.	(216) 621-8640
Russell Rogat Transition Specialists	(216) 591-1511

COLUMBUS, OH

Right Assocs.	(614) 438-2604
Schonberg Assocs.	(614) 436-2022

DALLAS, TX

The Career Control Group	(214) 702-6001
Challenger, Gray & Christmas	(214) 788-1816
Drake Beam Morin	(214) 788-5302
Fox-Morris Assocs.	(214) 404-8044
Human Resource Management	(214) 437-5511
Karli & Assocs.	(214) 644-9489
King Chapman Broussard & Gallagher	(214) 754-0666
Reedie & Co.	(214) 361-5678
Right Assocs.	(214) 239-7374

DENVER, CO

Bennett & Curran Consultants	(303) 691-5626
Drake Beam Morin	(303) 296-9500
Hutchens Resnik & Assocs.	(303) 292-0240
The John Joseph Group	(303) 592-9334
King Chapman Broussard & Gallagher	(303) 892-6530
Right Assocs.	(303) 295-2055
Sunshine Consulting Assocs.	(303) 629-1991

DETROIT, MI

Mainstream Access	(313) 446-6931

GRAND RAPIDS, MI

G. A. Burns & Assocs. ....(616) 372-0290
Jannotta, Bray & Assocs.................................(616) 285-6886
Right Assocs. ....(616) 956-5557
Robertson Lowstuter...(616) 454-6670

HARRISBURG, PA

Career Concepts ....(717) 399-7617
Kranz Assocs. ....(717) 291-5582
Quinlivan & Co. ....(717) 846-7188

HARTFORD, CT

Drake Beam Morin ....(203) 561-1466
Lee Hecht Harrison ....(203) 282-9800
Wilson McLeran...(203) 562-5546

HONOLULU, HI

Mainstream Access..(808) 523-8400
Rudolph Dew & Assocs.....................................(808) 528-4321

HOUSTON, TX

Career Visions..(713) 260-9675
Challenger, Gray & Christmas...........................(713) 789-2499
Dawson & Dawson Consultants ....(713) 784-3197
Drake Beam Morin ....(713) 739-7000
King Chapman Broussard & Gallagher ....(713) 223-7230
Michael D. McKee & Assocs. ....(713) 739-7815
Reedie & Co. ....(713) 968-6590
Right Assocs. ....(713) 439-8585

INDIANAPOLIS, IN

Career Consultants..(317) 639-5601
Right Assocs. ....(317) 469-4255

KANSAS CITY, MO

Drake Beam Morin ....(816) 931-3888
Human Resource Management ....(816) 931-4800

LOS ANGELES, CA

Challenger, Gray & Christmas...........................(310) 445-2388
Drake Beam Morin ....(310) 643-5000
Jannotta, Bray & Assocs...................................(310) 670-5700
Lee Hecht Harrison ....(310) 391-8291
Right Assocs. ....(310) 670-5700
TTG Consultants ....(213) 936-6600

MEMPHIS, TN

Randall Howard..(901) 754-3333
Right Assocs. ....(901) 754-1403

MIAMI, FL

Executive Group...(305) 377-3330
Right Assocs. ....(305) 599-8512

MILWAUKEE, WI

Jannotta, Bray & Assocs...................................(414) 778-0800
Lee Hecht Harrison ....(414) 291-9300
Right Assocs. ....(414) 453-2323

MINNEAPOLIS, MN

Challenger, Gray & Christmas...........................(612) 339-5565
Drake Beam Morin ....(612) 291-8000
Market Share ....(612) 375-9277

The Meredith Co. of Minnesota........................(612) 830-0946
Personnel Decisions...(612) 339-0927
Right Assocs. ....(612) 339-7387

NEW ORLEANS, LA

Drake Beam Morin ....(504) 525-9150

NEW YORK, NY

Arbor Group ....(212) 685-0400
The Ayers Group ....(212) 726-6600
BRG ....(212) 432-9818
Career Relocation Corp. of America ....(212) 661-6868
Challenger, Gray & Christmas...........................(212) 947-4500
Corporate Executive Outplacement ....(212) 832-2300
Drake Beam Morin ....(212) 692-7716
Goodrich & Sherwood..(212) 697-4131
Jannotta, Bray & Assocs......................................(212) 856-5600
King Chapman Broussard & Gallagher ....(212) 687-9688
Lee Hecht Harrison ....(212) 557-0009
Mainstream Access...(212) 922-2130
Manchester ....(212) 867-9100
Mullin & Assocs..(212) 768-3900
Oliver Human Resource Consultants ....(212) 307-5740
Potocki Assocs...(212) 605-0324
Swain & Swain..(212) 953-9100

OKLAHOMA CITY, OK

Joy Reed Belt & Assocs.......................................(405) 842-6336

ORLANDO, FL

The Curtiss Group...(407) 422-4471
Drake Beam Morin ....(407) 855-7800

PHILADELPHIA, PA

Challenger, Gray & Christmas...........................(215) 569-4033
Drake Beam Morin ....(215) 564-3000
Executive Assets Corp...(215) 563-5557
Fox-Morris Assocs. ....(215) 561-6300
Manchester ....(215) 563-7800
Right Assocs. ....(215) 972-7277

PHOENIX, AZ

Drake Beam Morin ....(602) 955-9665
Executive Horizons...(602) 230-1551
Murro Consulting ....(602) 224-5000
Right Assocs. ....(602) 231-9445
Rudolph Dew & Assocs. ....(602) 277-1545

PITTSBURGH, PA

Bizet & Co...(412) 922-5661
Drake Beam Morin ....(412) 765-3410
Fox-Morris Assocs. ....(412) 232-0410
Management Science & Development..............(412) 281-1528
Right Assocs. ....(412) 288-9600

PORTLAND, OR

Drake Beam Morin ....(503) 224-1321
Lee Hecht Harrison ....(503) 221-0241

PROVIDENCE, RI

Right Assocs. ....(401) 331-1729

RALEIGH, NC

Mainstream Access .... (919) 544-4299
Right Assocs. .... (919) 881-2020

SACRAMENTO, CA

Arnold Menn & Assocs. .... (916) 442-8016
Drake Beam Morin .... (916) 649-9585
Right Assocs. .... (916) 565-7412

ST. LOUIS, MO

Challenger, Gray & Christmas........................... (314) 434-4774
Drake Beam Morin .... (314) 576-1122
Human Resource Management Corp................. (314) 962-9400
Right Assocs. .... (314) 576-5600

SALT LAKE CITY, UT

OCM.. (801) 531-6504

SAN ANTONIO, TX

Reedie-York and Assocs .... (512) 794-8286

SAN DIEGO, CA

Executive Horizons... (619) 453-8860
Lee Hecht Harrison... (619) 457-7700
Right Assocs. .... (619) 587-8084

SAN FRANCISCO, CA

De Recat & Assocs.. (415) 433-3987
Drake Beam Morin .... (415) 986-3532
Lee Hecht Harrison... (415) 434-0125
Peller Marion Assocs. .... (415) 296-2559
Power Marketing .... (415) 392-7097
Right Assocs. .... (415) 986-6988
Torchiana Mastrov .... (415) 512-0771
Transitions Management Group .... (415) 981-0202

SEATTLE, WA

Waldron & Co.. (206) 441-4144

TAMPA, FL

The Curtiss Group... (813) 287-5106
Drake Beam Morin .... (813) 281-0225
Executive Group... (813) 870-1230
Right Assocs. .... (813) 572-9810

WASHINGTON, DC

Drake Beam Morin .... (202) 466-3264
Drake Beam Morin .... (202) 466-6090
Jannotta, Bray & Assocs..................................... (202) 508-1100
Manchester .... (202) 659-2555
Q. E. Englerth & Assocs. .... (202) 863-7955
Right Assocs. .... (202) 296-9405

Long Distance/Teleconferencing

American Conferencing ....(800) 852-8852
AT&T Alliance Teleconference ....(800) 544-6363
AT&T, business ....(800) 222-0400
AT&T Classic Teleconference ....(800) 232-1234
AT&T, residential ....(800) 222-0300
Conference Call Service ....(800) 272-5663
Conference Call USA ....(800) 654-0455
Darome Teleconferencing ....(800) 922-1124
MCI, business ....(800) 444-2222
MCI Forum ....(800) 475-4700
MCI, residential...(800) 950-5555
Sprint, business...(800) 877-2000
Sprint Conference Line....................................(800) 366-2663
Sprint, residential ....(800) 877-4646

Magazines

Architectural Digest ....(213) 965-3700
The Atlantic...(617) 536-9500
           mailatl@aol.com
Better Homes and Gardens ....(515) 284-3000
Bon Appétit ....(212) 880-8800
Business Week ....(212) 512-2511
           bwonline@mgh.com
The Cable Guide & Total TV ....(215) 443-9300
Car & Driver ....(212) 767-6095
           caranddriv@aol.com
CompuServe Magazine......................................(614) 457-8600
          cis.edit@compuserve.com
Conde Nast Traveler ....(212) 880-8800
        cnt-feedback@openmarket.com
Consumers Digest ....(312) 275-3590
Cooking Light..(205) 877-6000
           dcrichton@aol.com
Cosmopolitan ....(212) 649-3303
Country..(414) 423-0100
Country Home ....(515) 284-3000
Country Living ....(212) 649-3192
           hacl@hearst.com
Discover ....(212) 633-4400
         letters@discover.com
Ebony ....(312) 322-9200
Elle Top Model ....(212) 767-6000
Entertainment Weekly ....(212) 522-5600
           ew@aol.com
Esquire...(212) 459-7500
          esquire@hearst.com
Essence ....(212) 642-0600
        essenceonline@nyo.com
Family Circle ....(212) 878-8700
Field & Stream ....(212) 719-6000
          field@enews.com
Forbes...(212) 620-2200
        509.6930@mcimail.com
Fortune...(212) 586-1212
       fortune@cis.compuserve.com

Glamour..(212) 880-8800
         letters@glamour.com

Golf	(212) 779-5000
Golf Digest	(203) 373-7000
Good Housekeeping	(212) 649-3531
	hagh@hearst.com
Gourmet	(212) 371-1330
Gentlemen's Quarterly	(212) 880-7901
	gqmag@aol.com
Harper's Bazaar	(212) 903-5000
	bazaar@heasrt.com
Home	(212) 767-5800
Home Mechanix Illustrated	(212) 779-5134
House Beautiful	(212) 903-5100
Hustler	(213) 858-7100
	admin@onprod.com
Internet World	(203) 226-6967
	neubarth@1w.com
Kiplinger's Personal Finance	(202) 887-6400
	feedback@kiplinger.com
Ladies' Home Journal	(212) 953-7070
Life	(212) 522-1212
	lifeedit@life.timeinc.com
Mademoiselle	(212) 880-8800
	mllemag@aol.com
Mature Outlook	(515) 284-3059
McCall's	(212) 878-8700
Modern Maturity	(310) 496-2277
Men's Health	(215) 967-5171
	menshealth@msn.com
Money	(212) 586-1212
	letters@moneymag.com
National Black Monitor	(212) 967-4000
National Geographic	(202) 857-7000
	ngsforum@aol.com
NetGuide	(516) 562-5000
	netmail@netguide.cmp.com
New Woman	(212) 251-1500
	new-woman@wwire.com
The New Yorker	(212) 840-3800
New York Magazine	(212) 880-0700
	76702.2510@compuserve.com
Newsweek	(212) 445-4000
	letters@newsweek.com
Outdoor Life	(212) 687-3000
Parade	(212) 573-7000
Parents	(212) 878-8700
PC Computing	(415) 578-7000
	72241.1724@compuserve.com
PC Magazine	(212) 503-5255
	157.9301@mcimail.com
PC World	(415) 243-0500
	letters@pcworld.com
Penthouse	(201) 874-4300
	phoinfo@aol.com
People Weekly	(212) 522-1212
	74774.1513@compuserve.com
Playboy	(312) 751-8000
	dearpb@playboy.com
Popular Mechanics	(212) 649-3085
	hapm@heasrt.com
Popular Science	(212) 779-5000
	askpopsci@aol.com

Prevention ....(610) 967-5171
Reader's Digest..(212) 953-0030
readersdigest@notes.compuserve.com
Redbook ....(212) 649-3330
harb@heasrt.com
Rolling Stone...(212) 484-1616
rolling-stone@echo.nyc.com
Self ....(212) 880-8800
comments@self.com
Seventeen ....(212) 407-9700
seventeenm@aol.com
Southern Living..(205) 877-6000
Sports Illustrated...(212) 522-1212
si@cis.compuserve.com
Sunset ....(415) 321-3600
openhouse@sunsetpub.com
Taste of Home...(414) 423-0100
Teen Magazine...(310) 854-2222
Time..(212) 522-1212
timeletter@aol.com
Travel & Leisure ....(212) 382-5600
tl404@aol.com
TV Guide...(610) 293-8500
U.S. News & World Report ....(202) 955-2000
71154.1006@compuserve.com
Us..(212) 484-1616
usmag@echo.nyc.com
Vanity Fair ....(212) 880-8800
vfmail@vf.com
Vogue ....(212) 880-8800
voguemail@aol.com
Weight Watchers..(212) 370-0644
Woman's Day...(212) 767-6000
womansday@aol.com
Woman's World ....(201) 569-0006
Working Mother/Working Woman ....(212) 551-9500
YM ....(212) 878-8700

*Source: Oxbridge Communications Standard Periodical Directory on
CD-ROM. To order the CD-ROM, call (800) 955-0231. Note: E-
mail addresses change frequently. Contact the publication for updates
and specific staff addresses.*

Newsletters

Al Hanson's Economic Newsletter ....(218) 367-2404
Alert..(916) 444-6670
AOI Business Viewpoint ....(503) 588-0050
ASA News ....(312) 464-0090
ASIS Dynamics ....(703) 522-5800
Benefits Watch ....(813) 785-2819
Blue Chip Economic Indicators ....(703) 683-4100
Blue Chip Financial Forecasts............................(703) 683-4100
Bootstrappin' Entrepreneur ....(310) 568-9861
Bottom Line Business ....(203) 625-5900
Bureau of Business Practice
    Management Letter ....(203) 442-4365
Business & Acquisition Newsletter....................(713) 783-0100
Business & Economics..(703) 487-4630
Business and the Environment............................(617) 648-8700
Business Mailers Review......................................(202) 723-3397
Business Planning Advisory ....(201) 467-8700

Business Review	(713) 373-3535
Canada's Business Climate	(416) 866-8061
CBI Online	(404) 885-8158
The Cogent Communicator	(602) 574-9353
Consultants' & Contractors' Newsletter	(201) 299-1535
The Co-Op Newsletter	(707) 445-3185
Corporate Financing Week	(212) 224-3233
Corporate Secretary's Guide	(312) 583-8500
Cottage Connection	(312) 472-8116
CounciLine	(416) 961-8663
Currencies & Credit Markets	(612) 895-8511
Customer Service Newsletter	(212) 228-0246
Delphi Report	(617) 247-1025
Dempsey Canadian Letter	(216) 241-1160
The Digest of Municipal and Planning Law	(416) 609-8000
Directory Marketplace	(914) 358-6213
Distribution Center Management	(212) 228-0246
The Distributor's & Wholesaler's Advisor	(212) 228-0246
Don Larson's Business Newsletter	(507) 455-3220
Economic Development from the State Capitals	(703) 549-8606
Economics Update	(404) 521-8788
EDI News	(301) 340-2100
Efficient Auditor	(703) 845-9204
Employers' Human Rights & Equity Report	(416) 609-8000
Endowment Builder	(502) 426-3594
Euromedia Acquisitions	(408) 624-1536
EuroWatch	(215) 784-0941
Executive Compensation Report	(703) 425-1322
Executive Report on Customer Satisfaction	(212) 228-0246
Federal Contracts Report	(202) 452-4200
Fiberoptics Marketing/Intelligence	(401) 849-6771
Financial Update	(404) 521-8269
FTC FOIA Log	(703) 856-2216
FTC WATCH	(202) 434-8222
Futureletter	(905) 404-0405
Georgeson Report	(212) 440-9800
Global Business Technology Report	(510) 977-8685
Goods & Services Bulletin	(617) 727-2834
Government Inventions for Licensing	(703) 487-4630
Grantee's Action Alert Bulletin	(801) 561-1556
High Tech Ceramics News	(203) 853-4266
Jack Kemp's American Entrepreneur	(301) 340-2100
Kiplinger California Letter	(202) 887-6400
Kiplinger Florida Letter	(202) 887-6408
Kiplinger Washington Letter	(202) 887-6400
Leisure Industry Report	(202) 232-7107
Lesko's Info-Power Newsletter	(301) 924-0556
Market Monitor	(216) 623-8964
Mealey's Litigation Report: Intellectual Property	(610) 688-6566
Minnesota Management Review	(612) 625-0843
Minorities in Business Insider	(301) 588-6380
Monthly Product Announcement Data User Services Div.	(301) 457-4100
NAP Forum	(212) 949-5900
National Review of Corporate Acquisitions	(415) 435-2175
On Target—for Individuals Running Small & Midsize Companies	(513) 339-0336
Opportunity New York	(518) 474-6950
PCS News	(301) 340-2100

Personal Report for the Professional Secretary..(703) 548-3885
Perspective..(202) 289-4336
PresentFutures Report ....(703) 538-6181
Privacy & American Business............................(201) 996-1154
Productivity Views: Newsletter of
   Service Quality ....(508) 692-1818
PSI Research Memo ....(503) 479-9464
Quality Management...(203) 442-4365
The Real Entrepreneur...(706) 694-8441
Regional Update..(404) 521-8269
Research News..(512) 471-1616
Resort Management Report ....(804) 230-0736
Safe Money Report..(407) 627-3300
Sales Prospector..(708) 234-6665
SAS Newsletter ....(301) 694-8122
Securities and Federal Corporate Law Report ...(800) 221-9428
Semi Standards Information Alert.......................(415) 964-5111
Sid Cato's Newsletter on Annual Reports.........(616) 344-2286
The Small Business Advisor..................................(516) 295-1323
Small Business Service Bureau Bulletin.............(508) 756-3513
Small Business Wire..(518) 465-7511
Small Business—USA ....(202) 293-8830
Soundview Executive Book Summaries.............(802) 453-4062
Sourcebank ....(708) 961-2161
Stanger Review..(908) 389-3600
The Successful Benefits Communicator ....(312) 335-0037
Supervisory Management ....(212) 903-8075
Supplier Selection and Management Report.....(212) 244-0360
T-Shirt Business Info Mapping Newsletter ....(303) 575-5676
The Take-Charge Assistant...................................(212) 903-8075
Think and Grow Rich Newsletter ....(800) 343-3648
Think Yourself Rich ....(619) 320-7717
Troubled Company Prospector...........................(301) 951-6400
Turnarounds & Workouts.....................................(301) 951-6400
Turnarounds & Workouts—Europe ....(301) 951-6400
Turnarounds & Workouts—Survey.....................(309) 195-1640
Ukrainian Business Digest....................................(203) 221-7450
U.S. Chamber Watch in Legislation and
   Regulation...(202) 463-5533
USSR Business Machine ....(604) 873-4347
Valuation Researcher..(414) 271-8662
Wall Street Transcript ....(212) 747-9500
The Winsor Report...(203) 633-4301

*Source: Oxbridge Communications Standard Periodical Directory on
CD-ROM. To order the CD-ROM, call (800) 955-0231.*

Newspapers

ANCHORAGE, AK
Anchorage Daily News.....................................(907) 257-4200
                      74220.2560@compuserve.com
ATLANTA, GA
Atlanta Constitution..(404) 526-5151
                      constitution@ajc.com

ATLANTIC CITY, NJ
Press of Atlantic City ....(609) 272-7000
                      thepress@acy.digex.net

BALTIMORE, MD

Baltimore Sun..(410) 332-6000
baltsun@clark.net

BOSTON, MA

Boston Globe...(617) 929-2935
letter@globe.com
Boston Herald..(617) 426-3000
heraldedit@delphi.com

BUFFALO, NY

Buffalo News..(716) 849-3434
aw118@freenet.buffalo.edu

CHARLOTTE, NC

The Charlotte Observer.......................................(704) 358-5000
gary.nielson@community.com

CHICAGO, IL

Chicago Sun Times..(312) 321-3000
cary@plink.geis.com
Chicago Tribune..(312) 222-3232
tribletter@aol.com

CINCINNATI, OH

Cincinnati Enquirer..(513) 721-2700
enqedit@aol.com
Cincinnati Post..(513) 352-2000

CLEVELAND, OH

Plain Dealer...(216) 999-5000
ej821@cleveland.freenet.edu

COLUMBUS, OH

Columbus Dispatch ....(614) 461-5000
letters@cd.columbus.oh.us

DALLAS, TX

Dallas Morning News...(214) 977-8222
tdmned@pic.net

DENVER, CO

Denver Post ....(303) 820-1010
Rocky Mountain News...(303) 892-5000
rmn@csn.net

DETROIT, MI

Detroit News..(313) 222-2300
rgiles@detnews.com
Detroit Free Press..(313) 222-6400
business@det-freepress.com

GRAND RAPIDS, MI

Grand Rapids Press..(616) 459-1400

GREENVILLE, SC

Greenville News...(803) 298-4100

HARRISBURG, PA

The Patriot ....(215) 683-7343

HARTFORD, CT

Hartford Courant...(203) 241-6200
courant@pnet.com

HONOLULU, HI

Advertiser ....(808) 525-8000
76322.2016@compuserve.com
Honolulu Star Bulletin......................(808) 525-8640
davids@aloha.net

HOUSTON, TX

Houston Chronicle.............................(713) 220-7171
hci@chron.com
Houston Post ....(713) 840-5600
abramsbiz@aol.com

INDIANAPOLIS, IN

Indianapolis News ....(317) 633-1240
newsedit@aol.com

KANSAS CITY, MO

Kansas City Star ....(816) 234-4141

LAS VEGAS, NV

Las Vegas Review-Journal ....(702) 383-0211

LOS ANGELES, CA

Investor's Business Daily.....................(310) 207-1832
ibdee@ensemble.com
La Opinión ....(213) 622-8332
Los Angeles Times..............................(213) 237-5000
schwadron@news.latimes.com

LOUISVILLE, KY

Courier-Journal...................................(502) 582-4011

MEMPHIS, TN

Commercial Appeal ....(901) 529-2211

MIAMI, FL

Miami Herald ....(305) 350-2111
comments@herald.kri.com

MILWAUKEE, WI

Milwaukee Community Journal ....(414) 265-5300
Milwaukee Sentinel............................(414) 224-2000

MINNEAPOLIS, MN

St. Paul Pioneer Press........................(612) 222-5011
rpress@aol.com
Star Tribune..(612) 673-4000
opinion@startribune.com

NASHVILLE, TN

Nashville Banner................................(615) 259-8817
Tennessean..(615) 259-8817

NEW ORLEANS, LA

Times-Picayune...................................(504) 826-3279
tpmoney@communique.net

NEW YORK, NY

New York Daily News ....(212) 210-2100
New York Post ....(212) 815-8000
New York Times ....(212) 556-1934
letters@nytimes.com
Wall Street Journal..............................(212) 416-2000
Wall Street Journal—Eastern Edition...............(212) 416-2574

Wall Street Journal—Southwest Edition ....(212) 416-2613

NORFOLK, VA

Daily Press...(804) 247-4600
Virginian-Pilot...(804) 446-2000
denj@infi.net

OKLAHOMA CITY, OK

Daily Oklahoman ....(405) 475-3311

ORLANDO, FL

Orlando Sentinel...(407) 420-5000
osopost@aol.com

PHILADELPHIA, PA

Philadelphia Daily News ....(215) 854-5900
Philadelphia Inquirer..(215) 854-2000
editpage@aol.com

PHOENIX, AZ

Arizona Republic..(602) 271-8000
opinions@aol.com
Phoenix Gazette ....(602) 271-8000
phxgazette@aol.com

PITTSBURGH, PA

Pittsburgh Press..(412) 263-1100

PORTLAND, OR

Oregonian...(503) 221-8327
oreeditors@aol.com

PROVIDENCE, RI

Providence Journal ....(401) 277-7000
1q1q89b@prodigy.com

RALEIGH, NC

News & Observer ....(919) 829-4500
frank3@nando.net

SACRAMENTO, CA

Sacramento Bee..(916) 321-1000
sacbedit@netcom.com

ST. LOUIS, MO

St. Louis Post-Dispatch ....(314) 340-8000
advocate@pd.stlnet.com

SALT LAKE CITY, UT

Salt Lake Tribune ....(801) 237-2045
the.editors@sltrib.com

SAN ANTONIO, TX

San Antonio Express-News.....................................(512) 225-7411

SAN DIEGO, CA

San Diego Union-Tribune......................................(619) 299-3131
computerlink@sduniontrib.com

SAN FRANCISCO, CA

San Francisco Chronicle ....(415) 777-1111
chronletters@sfgate.com

San Francisco Examiner ....(415) 777-2424
sfexaminer@aol.com

SEATTLE, WA
Post-Intelligencer ....(206) 448-8000
Seattle Times ....(206) 464-2111
new@seatimes.com

TAMPA, FL
St. Petersburg Times ....(813) 893-8111
comments@sptimes.com
Tampa Tribune...(813) 259-7711
tb0199b@prodigy.com

WASHINGTON, DC
USA Today ....(703) 276-3400
usatoday@clark.net
Washington Post...(202) 334-6000

WEST PALM BEACH, FL
Palm Beach Post ....(407) 820-4100

Source: Oxbridge Communications Standard Periodical Directory on CD-ROM. To order the CD-ROM, call (800) 955-0231. Note: E-mail addresses change frequently. Contact the publication for updates.

Printing Companies

Fifty of the largest companies in the U.S. by total sales:

American Business Products, Atlanta, GA ....(404) 953-8300
American Signature, Greenwich, CT...............(203) 531-1100
Banta, Menasha, WI..(414) 751-7771
Bertelsmann Printing & Manufacturing,
New York, NY...(212) 782-7676
Bowater Communication Papers, Moline, IL ....(309) 797-1389
Bowne, New York, NY ....(212) 924-5500
Brown Printing, Waseca, MN ....(507) 835-2410
Cadmus Communications, Richmond, VA ....(804) 287-5680
Clarke American, San Antonio, TX ....(210) 690-9999
Continental Graphics,
Los Angeles, CA...(213) 938-2511
Data Documents, Omaha, NE...........................(402) 339-0900
Deluxe, St. Paul, MN ....(612) 787-1000
Duplex Products, Sycamore, IL.........................(815) 895-2101
Engraph, Atlanta, GA.......................................(404) 325-0517
Graphic Arts Center, Portland, OR..................(503) 226-2402
Graphic Industries, Atlanta, GA ....(404) 874-3327
Jostens Printing & Publishing Group
Bloomington, MN ....(612) 830-3300
Menasha, Neenah, WI ....(414) 751-1000
Merrill, St. Paul, MN ....(612) 646-4501
New England Business Service, Groton, MA....(508) 448-6111
Perry Printing, Waterloo, WI............................(414) 478-3551
Quad/Graphics, Pewaukee, WI ....(414) 691-9200
R. R. Donnelley & Sons, Chicago, IL ....(312) 326-8000
Reynolds & Reynolds, Dayton, OH..................(513) 443-2000
Ringier America, Itasca, IL ....(708) 285-6000
Sealright, Overland Park, KS............................(913) 344-9000
Shorewood Packaging, New York, NY..............(212) 371-1500
Standard Register, Dayton, OH ....(513) 443-1000
Stevens Graphics, Atlanta, GA.........................(404) 753-1121
Sullivan Graphics, Brentwood, TN ....(615) 377-0377
Systemedia Group, AT&T Global Information
Solutions, Miamisburg, OH............................(513) 439-8200

Taylor Group, North Mankato, MN	(507) 625-2828
Treasure Chest Advertising, Glendora, CA	(909) 592-4449
UARCO, Barrington, IL	(708) 381-2580
United States Banknote, New York, NY	(212) 582-9200
Valassis Communications, Livonia, MI	(313) 591-3000
W. H. Brady, Milwaukee, WI	(414) 358-6600
Wallace Computer Services, Hillside, IL	(708) 449-8600
Webcraft Technologies, North Brunswick, NJ	(908) 297-5100
Western Publishing, Racine, WI	(414) 633-2431
World Color Press, New York, NY	(212) 986-2440

Radio Stations

ANCHORAGE, AK

KATB-FM	(907) 333-5282
KBYR-AM, KNIK-FM	(907) 561-4200
KEAG-FM	(907) 243-3141
KENI-AM, KBFX-FM	(907) 272-7461
KFQD-AM, KWHL-FM	(907) 344-9622
KHAR-AM, KBJR-FM	(907) 522-3422
KKSD-AM, KASH-FM	(907) 522-1515
KLEF-FM	(907) 561-5556
KPXR-FM	(907) 243-3141
KSKA-FM	(907) 561-1161
KYAK-AM, KGOT-FM	(907) 272-5945
KYMG-FM	(907) 272-5945

ATLANTA, GA

WABE-FM	(404) 827-8900
WAEC-AM	(404) 355-8600
WAFS-AM	(404) 888-0920
WAOK-AM, WVEE-FM	(404) 898-8900
WAZX-AM	(404) 436-6171
WCLK-FM	(404) 880-8273
WGKA-AM	(404) 231-1190
WGST-AM, WPCH-FM	(404) 233-0640
WGUN-AM	(404) 491-1010
WIGO-AM	(404) 752-5460
WKHX-AM	(404) 955-0101
WKLS-FM	(404) 325-0960
WNIV-AM	(404) 365-0970
WNNX-FM	(404) 266-0997
WQXI-AM	(404) 261-2970
WRAS-FM	(404) 651-2240
WREK-FM	(404) 894-2468
WRFG-FM	(404) 523-3471
WSB-AM/FM	(404) 897-7000
WYZE-AM	(404) 622-7802
WZGC-FM	(404) 851-9393

ATLANTIC CITY, NJ

WAYV-FM	(609) 484-8444
WFPG-AM/FM	(609) 348-4646
WMGM-AM	(609) 653-1400
WMID-AM/FM	(609) 344-0300
WUSS-AM	(609) 345-7134

BALTIMORE, MD

WBAL-AM, WIYY-FM	(410) 467-3000
WBGR-AM	(410) 367-7773
WBJC-FM	(410) 333-5100

WBMD-AM, WQSR-FM ....(410) 825-1000
WBYQ-FM ....(410) 780-6572
WCAO-AM, WXYV-FM.....................................(410) 653-2200
WCBM-AM ....(410) 356-3003
WEAA-FM ....(410) 319-3564
WITH-AM ....(410) 528-1230
WJFK-AM ....(703) 691-1900
WJHU-FM ....(410) 516-9548
WLIF-FM ....(410) 823-1570
WOLB,-AM WERQ-FM.....................................(410) 332-8200
WPOC-FM ....(410) 366-3693
WRBS-FM ....(410) 247-4100
WSSF-FM ....(410) 466-9272
WWIN-AM/FM ....(410) 332-8200
WWLG-AM ....(410) 576-8860
WWMX-FM ....(410) 825-5400

Boston, MA

WBCN-FM ....(617) 266-1111
WBCS-FM ....(617) 542-0241
WBUR-FM ....(617) 353-2790
WBZ-AM...(617) 787-7000
WCLB-FM ....(617) 375-2100
WECB-AM ....(617) 578-8850
WEEI-AM ....(617) 242-5900
WERS-FM ....(617) 578-8892
WEZE-AM ....(617) 328-0880
WGBH-FM ....(617) 492-2777
WHDH-AM ....(617) 248-5500
WILD-AM ....(617) 427-2222
WJMN-FM ....(617) 290-0009
WMEX-AM, WMJX-FM ....(617) 542-0241
WODS-FM ....(617) 426-2200
WRBB-FM ....(617) 373-4338
WRKO-AM, WBMX-FM ....(617) 236-6800
WROL-AM ....(617) 423-0210
WUMB-FM ....(617) 287-6900
WZLX-FM ....(617) 267-0123

Buffalo, NY

WBEN-AM, WMJQ-FM.....................................(716) 876-0930
WBFO-FM ....(716) 829-2555
WBUF-FM ....(716) 882-4300
WDCX-FM ....(716) 883-3010
WFBF-FM ....(716) 674-8244
WNED-AM/FM ....(716) 845-7000
WGR-AM, WGRF-FM.....................................(716) 881-4555
WHTT-AM/FM...(716) 854-1120
WJYE-FM ....(716) 856-3550
WWKB-AM ....(716) 884-5101
WWWS-AM, WUFX-FM ....(716) 885-1400
WYRK-FM ....(716) 852-7444

Charlotte, NC

WAQS-AM, WAQQ-FM.....................................(704) 399-6195
WBT-AM/FM...(704) 374-3500
WFAE-FM ....(704) 549-9323
WGIV-AM ....(704) 342-2644
WHVN-AM ....(704) 596-1240
WIST-AM...(704) 598-1480
WMXC-FM ....(704) 372-1104

WOGR-AM ....(704) 393-1540
WSOC-FM ....(704) 335-4700

Chicago, IL

WBBM-AM/FM ....(312) 944-6000
WBEZ-FM ....(312) 460-9150
WCRW-AM ....(312) 763-8250
WCRX-FM ....(312) 663-1693
WCYC-FM ....(312) 762-9292
WEDC-AM ....(312) 631-0700
WFMT-FM ....(312) 565-5000
WGCI-AM/FM ....(312) 427-4800
WGN-AM ....(312) 222-4700
WHPK-FM ....(312) 702-8289
WIND-AM ....(312) 751-5560
WJJD-AM, WJMK-FM ....(312) 977-1800
WJPC-AM ....(312) 360-9000
WKKC-FM ....(312) 602-5313
WKQX-FM ....(312) 527-8348
WLIT-FM ....(312) 329-9002
WLS-AM/FM ....(312) 984-0890
WLUW-FM ....(312) 915-6558
WMAQ-AM ....(312) 670-6767
WMBI-AM/FM ....(312) 329-4300
WMVP,-AM WLUP-FM ....(312) 440-5270
WNIB-FM ....(312) 633-9700
WNUA-FM ....(312) 645-9550
WOPA-AM ....(312) 738-1200
WOUI-FM ....(312) 567-3087
WPNT-FM ....(312) 440-3100
WSBC-AM, WXRT-FM ....(312) 282-9722
WSCR-AM ....(312) 777-1700
WUSN-FM ....(312) 649-0099
WWBZ-FM ....(312) 861-8100
WYSY-FM ....(312) 781-7300
WZRD-FM ....(312) 583-4050

Cincinnati, OH

WAKW-FM ....(513) 542-3442
WCIN-AM ....(513) 281-7180
WCKY-AM, WPPT-FM ....(513) 241-6565
WGUC-FM ....(513) 241-8282
WKRQ-FM ....(513) 763-5500
WLW-AM, WEBN-FM ....(513) 621-9326
WRRM-FM ....(513) 241-9898
WSAI-AM ....(513) 241-6565
WTSJ-AM ....(513) 931-8080
WUBE-AM/FM ....(513) 721-1050
WVXU-FM ....(513) 745-3738

Cleveland, OH

WABQ-AM ....(216) 231-8005
WCLV-FM ....(216) 464-0900
WCPN-FM ....(216) 432-3700
WCRF-FM ....(216) 526-1111
WCSB-FM ....(216) 687-3523
WENZ-FM ....(216) 861-0100
WERE-AM, WNCX-FM ....(216) 696-1300
WGAR-FM ....(216) 328-9950
WHK-AM, WMMS-FM ....(216) 781-1420
WJMO,-AM WZAK-FM ....(216) 621-9300

WKNR-AM	(216) 838-1220
WMJI-FM	(216) 623-1105
WQAL-FM	(216) 696-6666
WRDZ-AM	(216) 526-8989
WRMR-AM, WDOK-FM	(216) 696-0123
WRUW-FM	(216) 368-2208
WWWE-AM, WLTF-FM	(216) 696-4444

COLUMBUS, OH

WAHC-FM	(614) 442-2000
WBNS-AM/FM	(614) 460-3850
WCOL-AM/FM	(614) 221-7811
WMNI-AM, WBZX-FM	(614) 481-7800
WNCI-FM	(614) 224-9624
WOSU-AM/FM	(614) 292-9678
WRFD-AM	(614) 885-5342
WTVN-AM, WLVQ-FM	(614) 486-6101
WVKO-AM, WSNY-FM	(614) 451-2191
WWHT-FM	(614) 442-2000

DALLAS, TX

KCBI-FM	(817) 792-3800
KDMX-FM	(214) 688-0641
KERA-FM	(214) 871-1390
KGBS-AM	(214) 526-2580
KGGR-AM	(214) 941-1040
KHVN-AM, KJMZ-FM	(214) 556-8100
KKDA-FM	(214) 263-9911
KLIF-AM	(214) 526-2400
KLUV-FM	(214) 526-9870
KMRT-AM	(214) 630-8531
KNON-FM	(214) 828-9500
KPBC-AM	(214) 445-1700
KRLD-AM	(214) 634-1080
KRRW-FM	(214) 522-0979
KRSM-FM	(214) 363-6491
KSKY-AM	(214) 827-5759
KTCK-AM	(214) 826-8425
KVTT-FM	(214) 351-6655
KYNG-FM	(214) 716-7800
KZPS-FM	(214) 770-7777
WRR-FM	(214) 670-8888

DENVER, CO

KBNO-AM	(303) 292-5266
KBPI-FM	(303) 534-6200
KCFR-FM	(303) 871-9191
KCUV-AM	(303) 861-1156
KDEN-AM	(303) 343-1133
KHOW-AM/FM	(303) 694-6300
KJME-AM	(303) 623-1390
KLZ-AM	(303) 433-5500
KOA-AM, KAZY-FM	(303) 893-3699
KOSI-FM	(303) 696-1714
KPOF-AM	(303) 428-0910
KRZN-AM, KMJI-FM	(303) 741-5654
KUVO-FM	(303) 480-9272
KVOD-FM	(303) 936-3428
KXKL-AM/FM	(303) 832-5665
KYBG-AM	(303) 721-9210
KYGO-AM/FM	(303) 321-0950

Detroit, MI

WCHB-AM, WJZZ-FM	(313) 871-0590
WDET-FM	(313) 577-4146
WDTR-FM	(313) 596-3507
WGPR-FM	(313) 259-8862
WHYT-FM	(313) 871-3030
WJLB-FM	(313) 965-2000
WJR-AM	(313) 875-4440
WKQI-FM	(810) 967-3750
WLLZ-FM	(810) 855-5100
WLQV-AM	(810) 477-4600
WLTI-FM	(810) 354-9100
WMUZ-FM	(313) 272-3434
WNZK-AM	(810) 557-3500
WOMC-FM	(810) 546-9600
WQBH-AM	(313) 965-4500
WQRS-FM	(810) 355-1051
WRIF-FM	(810) 827-1111
WWJ-AM, WJOI-FM	(810) 423-3300
WWWW-AM/FM	(313) 259-4323
WXYT-AM, WMXD-FM	(810) 569-8000
WYCD-FM	(810) 799-0600

Grand Rapids, MI

WBCT-FM	(616) 363-7701
WBYW-FM	(616) 453-3711
WCSG-FM	(616) 942-1500
WCUZ-AM/FM	(616) 451-2551
WFGR-FM	(616) 458-2600
WFUR-AM/FM	(616) 451-9387
WGRD-AM/FM	(616) 459-4111
WGVU-AM	(616) 771-6666
WLAV-AM/FM	(616) 456-5461
WLHT-FM	(616) 451-4800
WODJ-FM	(616) 956-3323
WOOD-AM/FM	(616) 459-1919
WVGR-FM	(313) 764-9210

Greenville, SC

WESC-AM/FM	(803) 242-4660
WFBC-AM/FM	(803) 271-9200
WLFJ-FM	(803) 292-6040
WMUU-AM/FM	(803) 242-6240
WPCI-AM	(803) 370-1490
WPLS-FM	(803) 294-3045
WSSL-AM/FM	(803) 242-1005

Harrisburg, PA

WCMB-AM, WIMX-FM	(717) 763-7020
WHP-AM, WRVV-FM	(717) 540-8800
WITF-FM	(717) 236-6000
WKBO-AM	(717) 540-8800
WTCY-AM, WNNK-FM	(717) 238-1402
WWKL-FM	(717) 541-9515

Hartford, CT

WCCC-AM/FM	(203) 233-4426
WDRC-AM/FM	(203) 243-1115
WHCN-FM	(203) 247-1060
WJMJ-FM	(203) 242-8800
WKSS-FM	(203) 249-9577

WPOP-AM	(203) 666-1411
WRTC-FM	(203) 297-2450
WTIC-AM/FM	(203) 522-1080
WZMX-FM	(203) 677-6700

Honolulu, HI

KAIM-AM/FM	(808) 735-2424
KCCN-AM/FM	(808) 536-2728
KDEO-AM/FM	(808) 671-2851
KGU-AM	(808) 841-7600
KHPR-FM	(808) 955-8821
KHVH-AM, KHHH-FM	(808) 531-4602
KIKI-AM/FM	(808) 531-4602
KINE-FM	(808) 536-2728
KIPO-FM	(808) 955-8821
KISA-AM	(808) 841-4555
KLHT-AM	(808) 524-1040
KNDI-AM	(808) 946-2844
KPOI-FM	(808) 524-7100
KQMQ-AM/FM	(808) 539-9369
KSSK-AM/FM	(808) 841-8300
KUMU-AM/FM	(808) 531-4511
KWAI-AM	(808) 523-3868
KZOO-AM	(808) 593-2880

Houston, TX

KBXX-FM	(713) 623-2108
KCOH-AM	(713) 522-1001
KEYH-AM	(713) 995-8500
KHCB-FM	(713) 520-5200
KHMX-FM	(713) 790-0965
KIKK-AM/FM	(713) 772-4433
KILT-AM/FM	(713) 526-3461
KKBQ-AM	(713) 961-0093
KKRW-FM	(713) 780-0937
KLAT-AM, KLTN-FM	(713) 868-4344
KLDE-FM	(713) 622-5533
KMJQ-FM	(713) 623-0102
KNUZ-AM, KQUE-FM	(713) 523-2581
KODA-FM	(713) 622-1010
KPFT-FM	(713) 526-4000
KPRC-AM	(713) 588-4800
KRBE-AM/FM	(713) 266-1000
KTRH-AM, KLOL-FM	(713) 526-5874
KTRU-FM	(713) 527-4098
KTSU-FM	(713) 527-4354
KUHF-FM	(713) 743-0887
KXYZ-AM	(713) 472-2500
KYOK-AM	(713) 621-1590

Indianapolis, IN

WBDG-FM	(317) 244-9234
WBRI-AM	(317) 255-5484
WDAF-AM, KYYS-FM	(816) 931-6100
WEDM-FM	(317) 899-2000
WFMS-FM	(317) 842-9550
WFYI-FM	(317) 636-2020
WGRL-FM	(317) 842-9550
WHHH-FM	(317) 293-9600
WIBC-AM, WKLR-FM	(317) 844-7200
WICR-FM	(317) 788-3280

WJEL-FM	(317) 259-5278
WNDE-AM, WFBQ-FM	(317) 257-7565
WNTS-AM	(317) 359-5591
WSYW-AM/FM	(317) 271-9799
WTLC-AM/FM	(317) 923-1456
WTPI-FM	(317) 925-1079
WXLW-AM	(317) 293-9600

Kansas City, KS

KFEZ-AM	(913) 341-5552
KMBZ-AM, KLTH-FM	(913) 677-8998
KXTR-FM	(913) 432-1480

Kansas City, MO

KBEQ-AM/FM	(816) 531-2535
KCUR-FM	(816) 235-1551
KFKF-FM	(816) 753-4000
KKFI-FM	(816) 931-3122
KLJC-FM	(816) 331-8700
KMXV-FM	(816) 753-0933
KPRT-AM, KPRS-FM	(816) 763-2040
WDAF-AM, KYYS-FM	(816) 931-6100

Las Vegas, NV

KCEP-FM	(702) 648-4218
KDWN-AM	(702) 385-7212
KEDG-FM	(702) 795-1035
KENO-AM, KOMP-FM	(702) 876-1460
KEVY-FM	(702) 732-7753
KFMS-AM/FM	(702) 732-7753
KILA-AM	(702) 731-5452
KKVV-AM	(702) 731-5588
KLAV-AM	(702) 796-1230
KMTW-AM, KKLZ-FM	(702) 739-9600
KNPR-FM	(702) 456-6695
KNUU-AM	(702) 735-8644
KORK-AM, KXPT-FM	(702) 876-1460
KRLV-FM	(702) 796-4040
KUNV-FM	(702) 739-3877
KXNO-AM, KLUC-FM	(702) 739-9383

Los Angeles, CA

KABC-AM, KLOS-FM	(310) 840-4900
KBIG-FM	(213) 874-7700
KFI-AM, KOST-FM	(213) 385-0101
KFSG-FM	(213) 483-5374
KFWB-AM	(213) 466-9283
KGFJ-AM	(213) 930-9090
KIIS-AM/FM	(213) 466-8381
KKBT-FM	(213) 466-9566
KKGO-FM	(310) 478-5540
KKHJ-AM	(213) 461-9300
KKLA-FM	(818) 956-5552
KLAC-AM, KZLA-FM	(818) 842-0500
KLSX-FM	(213) 383-4222
KMPC-AM	(213) 460-5672
KNX-AM, KCBS-FM	(213) 460-3000
KPFK-FM	(818) 985-2711
KPWR-FM	(818) 953-4200
KRTH-FM	(213) 937-5230
KTNQ-AM, KLVE-FM	(213) 465-3171
KTWV-FM	(213) 466-9283

KUSC-FM	(213) 743-5872
KWKW-AM	(213) 466-8111
KXED-AM	(213) 466-3001
KXEZ-FM	(818) 955-7000
KXLU-FM	(310) 338-2866

Memphis, TN

KWAM-AM, KJMS-FM	(901) 323-0101
WBBP-AM	(901) 278-7878
WDIA-AM, WHRK-FM	(901) 529-4300
WEVL-FM	(901) 528-0560
WHBQ-AM, WGKX-FM	(901) 682-1106
WJCE,-AM WRVR-FM	(901) 767-0104
WKNO-FM	(901) 458-2521
WLOK-AM	(901) 527-9565
WMC-AM/FM	(901) 726-0555
WREC-AM, WEGR-FM	(901) 578-1100
WSMS-FM	(901) 678-3176
WXSS-AM	(901) 272-3004
WYKL-FM	(901) 680-9898

Miami, FL

WAQI-AM, WRTO-FM	(305) 445-4040
WCMQ-AM	(305) 446-3900
WDNA-FM	(305) 662-8889
WEDR-FM	(305) 623-7711
WINZ-AM, WZTA-FM	(305) 654-9494
WIOD-AM, WFLC-FM	(305) 759-4311
WLRN-FM	(305) 995-2204
WMCU-FM	(305) 953-1155
WMRZ-AM, WLYF-FM	(305) 653-8811
WOCN-AM	(305) 649-1450
WPOW-FM	(305) 653-6796
WQAM-AM	(305) 431-6200
WQBA-AM/FM	(305) 441-2073
WSUA-AM	(305) 285-1260
WTMI-FM	(305) 856-9393
WWFE-AM	(305) 642-4422

Milwaukee, WI

WEMP-AM, WMYX-FM	(414) 529-1250
WISN-AM, WLTQ-FM	(414) 342-1111
WKLH-FM	(414) 454-0900
WLUM-FM	(414) 771-1021
WLZR-AM/FM	(414) 453-4130
WMSE-FM	(414) 277-7247
WNOV-AM	(414) 449-9668
WOKY-AM	(414) 545-5920
WQFM-FM	(414) 276-2040
WTMJ-AM, WKTI-FM	(414) 332-9611
WUMW-FM	(414) 229-4664
WVCY-FM	(414) 935-3000
WYMS-FM	(414) 475-8890
WZTR-FM	(414) 964-8300

Minneapolis, MN

KBEM-FM	(612) 627-2833
KFAI-FM	(612) 341-3144
KJJO-AM/FM	(612) 941-5774
KMOJ-FM	(612) 377-0595
KRXX-AM/FM	(612) 452-6200
KTCJ-AM, KTCZ-FM	(612) 339-0000

KTIS-AM/FM	(612) 631-5000
KUOM-AM	(612) 625-3500
WBOB-FM	(612) 333-8118
WCCO-AM	(612) 370-0611
WCTS-AM	(612) 522-7339
WLTE-FM	(612) 339-1029
WWTC-AM	(612) 926-1280

NASHVILLE, TN

WAMB-AM/FM	(615) 889-1960
WENO-AM	(615) 242-4240
WKDA-AM, WKDF-FM	(615) 244-9533
WLAC-AM/FM	(615) 256-0555
WMDB-AM	(615) 255-2876
WNAH-AN	(615) 254-7611
WNAZ-FM	(615) 248-1689
WNQM-AM	(615) 255-1300
WPLN-FM	(615) 862-5810
WRVU-FM	(615) 322-3691
WSIX-FM	(615) 664-2400
WSM-AM/FM	(615) 889-6595
WYFN-AM	(615) 868-4458
WZEZ-FM	(615) 259-0929

NEW ORLEANS, LA

WBOK-AM	(504) 943-4600
WBSN-FM	(504) 286-3600
WBYU-FM	(504) 522-1450
WEZB-FM	(504) 581-7002
WNOE-AM/FM	(504) 529-1212
WQUE-AM/FM	(504) 827-6000
WRNO-FM	(504) 889-2424
WSHO-AM	(504) 527-0800
WSMB-AM	(504) 593-6376
WTIX-AM	(504) 888-9849
WTKL-AM	(504) 834-9587
WTUL-FM	(504) 865-5887
WVOG-AM	(504) 831-6941
WWL-AM, WLMG-FM	(504) 593-6376
WWNO-FM	(504) 286-7000
WWOZ-FM	(504) 568-1239
WYLD-AM/FM	(504) 827-6000

NEW YORK, NY

WABC-AM	(212) 613-3800
WADO-AM	(212) 687-9236
WAXQ-FM	(212) 575-1043
WBAI-FM	(212) 279-0707
WBBR-AM	(212) 318-2000
WCBS-AM/FM	(212) 975-4321
WEVD-FM	(212) 777-7900
WFAN-AM	(718) 706-7690
WFUV-FM	(718) 365-9070
WHCR-FM	(212) 650-7481
WINS-AM	(212) 397-1010
WKCR-FM	(212) 854-5223
WKDM-AM	(212) 594-1380
WKRB-FM	(718) 934-9572
WLIB-AM, WBLS-FM	(212) 661-3344
WLTW-FM	(212) 258-7000
WMCA-AM	(201) 507-5700

WMXV-FM ....(212) 752-3322
WNEW-FM ....(212) 489-1027
WNYC-AM/FM ....(212) 669-7800
WNYE-FM ....(718) 935-4480
WNYU-FM ....(212) 998-1660
WOR-AM ....(212) 642-4500
WPLJ-FM ....(212) 613-8900
WQCD-FM ....(212) 210-2800
WQHT-FM ....(212) 840-0097
WQEW-AM, WQXR-FM ....(212) 633-7600
WRKS-FM ....(212) 642-4300
WSKQ-FM ....(212) 541-9200
WWRL-AM ....(718) 335-1600
WYNY-FM ....(212) 704-3900
WZRC-AM, WXRK-FM ....(212) 935-5170

Norfolk, VA

WCMS-AM/FM ....(804) 424-1050
WHRO-FM ....(804) 489-9476
WNIS-AM ....(804) 640-8500
WNOR-AM/FM ....(804) 336-9900
WNVZ-FM ....(804) 497-1067
WOWI-FM ....(804) 627-5800
WSVY-AM/FM ....(804) 627-5800
WTAR-AM, WLTY-FM ....(804) 671-1000

Oklahoma City, OK

KATT-FM ....(405) 848-0100
KBYE-AM ....(405) 478-2100
KEBC-FM ....(405) 631-7501
KMGL-FM ....(405) 478-5104
KOCC-FM ....(405) 425-5622
KOMA-AM/FM ....(405) 794-4000
KQVC-AM ....(405) 521-1412
KTOK-AM, KJYO-FM ....(405) 840-5271
KTST-FM ....(405) 528-5543
KVSP-AM ....(405) 427-5877
KXXY-AM/FM ....(405) 528-5543
KYIS-FM ....(405) 848-0100
WKY-AM ....(405) 478-2930

Orlando, FL

WDBO-AM, WWKA-FM ....(407) 295-5858
WDIZ-FM ....(407) 682-7676
WHBS-AM ....(407) 671-7023
WHOO-AM, WHTQ-FM ....(407) 295-3990
WMFE-FM ....(407) 273-2300
WMMO-FM ....(407) 422-9890
WOMX-AM/FM ....(407) 629-5105
WONQ-AM ....(407) 830-0800
WUCF-FM ....(407) 823-3689
WWNZ-AM ....(407) 299-7400

Philadelphia, PA

KYW-AM, WMMR-FM ....(215) 238-4700
WBEB-FM ....(610) 667-8400
WDAS-AM/FM ....(215) 581-2100
WFLN-FM ....(215) 482-6000
WHAT-AM ....(215) 581-5161
WHYY-FM ....(215) 351-9200
WIOQ-FM ....(610) 667-8100
WIP-AM ....(215) 922-5000

WJJZ-FM	(610) 667-3939
WKDU-FM	(215) 895-5920
WOGL-AM/FM	(610) 668-5800
WPEB-FM	(215) 386-3800
WPEN-AM, WMGK-FM	(610) 667-8500
WPHY-AM	(610) 941-9560
WTEL-AM, WXTU-FM	(610) 667-2870
WURD-AM	(215) 533-8900
WUSL-FM	(215) 483-8900
WWDB-FM	(610) 668-4400
WXPN-FM	(215) 898-6677
WYSP-FM	(610) 668-9460
WYXR-FM	(610) 668-0750
WZZD-AM	(610) 828-6965

Phoenix, AZ

KASA-AM	(602) 276-4241
KCWW-AM, KNIX-FM	(602) 966-6236
KESZ-FM	(602) 207-9999
KFLR-FM	(602) 978-0903
KFYI-AM	(602) 258-6161
KHEP-AM	(602) 234-1280
KIDR-AM, KPSN-FM	(602) 279-5577
KJJJ-FM	(602) 834-5627
KOOL-AM/FM	(602) 956-9696
KOY-AM, KYOT-FM	(602) 258-8181
KPHX-AM	(602) 257-1351
KSUN-AM	(602) 252-0030
KTAR-AM, KKLT-FM	(602) 274-6200
KVVA-AM	(602) 266-2005
KYOT-AM, KZON-FM	(602) 258-8181

Pittsburgh, PA

KDKA-AM	(412) 575-2525
KQV-AM	(412) 562-5900
WBZZ-FM	(412) 381-8100
WDUQ-FM	(412) 434-6030
WDVE-FM	(412) 937-1441
WEEP-AM, WDSY-FM	(412) 471-9950
WJAS-AM, WSHH-FM	(412) 531-4800
WLTJ-FM	(412) 922-9290
WORD-FM	(412) 937-1500
WPIT-AM/FM	(412) 281-1900
WPTS-FM	(412) 648-7990
WQED-FM	(412) 622-1436
WRCT-FM	(412) 621-9728
WTAE-AM, WVTY-FM	(412) 731-1250
WWSW-AM/FM	(412) 323-5300
WXRB-FM	(412) 471-9950
WYEP-FM	(412) 362-9937
WYJZ-AM, WAMO-FM	(412) 471-2181

Portland, OR

KBBT-AM, KUFO-FM	(503) 222-1011
KBNP-AM	(503) 223-6769
KBOO-FM	(503) 231-8032
KBPS-AM/FM	(503) 280-5828
KBVM-FM	(503) 283-7455
KEX-AM, KKRZ-FM	(503) 225-1190
KGON-FM	(503) 223-1441
KINK-AM/FM	(503) 226-5080

KKEY-AM..(503) 222-1150
KKSN-FM...(503) 226-9791
KOPB-FM...(503) 293-1905
KPDQ-AM/FM..(503) 231-7800
KRRC-FM...(503) 771-2180
KUPL-AM/FM..(503) 297-3311
KWJJ-AM/FM ....(503) 228-4393
KXL-AM/FM..(503) 231-0750
KXYQ-AM/FM..(503) 226-6731

Providence, RI

WALE-AM ....(401) 521-0990
WBRU-FM ....(401) 272-9550
WDOM-FM ....(401) 865-2460
WHIM-AM ....(401) 941-4700
WHJJ-AM, WHJY-FM...............................(401) 438-6110
WLKW-AM, WWLI-FM.............................(401) 433-4200
WPRO-AM/FM..(401) 433-4200
WRCP-AM...(401) 273-7000
WRIB-AM ....(401) 434-0406
WWBB-FM ....(401) 431-1000

Raleigh, NC

WCLY-AM..(919) 821-1550
WCPE-FM..(919) 556-5178
WKIX-AM, WYLT-FM...............................(919) 851-2711
WKNC-FM...(919) 515-2401
WLLE-AM..(919) 833-3874
WPJL-AM..(919) 834-6401
WPTF-AM, WQDR-FM..............................(919) 876-0674
WRAL-FM..(919) 890-6101
WSHA-FM...(919) 546-8432

Sacramento, CA

KCTC-AM, KYMX-FM...............................(916) 441-5272
KFBK-AM, KGBY-FM................................(916) 929-5325
KHTK-AM, KRAK-FM...............................(916) 923-9200
KJAY-AM...(916) 371-5101
KNCI-FM ....(916) 923-9200
KQPT-FM..(916) 635-1005
KSAC-AM..(916) 446-2294
KSEG-FM..(916) 446-5769
KSMJ-AM..(916) 920-1025
KWOD-FM...(916) 448-5000
KXOA-AM/FM..(916) 923-6800
KXPR-FM ....(916) 485-5977

St. Louis, MO

KASP-AM, WKBQ-FM...............................(314) 644-1380
KATZ-AM, KMJM-FM...............................(314) 361-1108
KDHX-FM..(314) 664-3955
KEZK-FM..(314) 727-2160
KMOX-AM, KLOU-FM..............................(314) 621-2345
KRJY-FM...(314) 781-9600
KSD-AM/FM..(314) 531-0000
KSTL-AM...(314) 621-5785
KWMU-FM..(314) 553-5968
KXEN-AM..(314) 436-6550
KXOK-AM..(314) 727-0808
KYKY-FM..(314) 531-9898
WEW-AM..(314) 862-8181
WRTH-AM, WYIL-FM..............................(314) 436-1600

Salt Lake City, UT

KALL-AM, KODJ-FM	(801) 533-0102
KBZN-FM	(801) 364-9836
KCNR-AM, KLZX-FM	(801) 485-6700
KDYL-AM, KSFI-FM	(801) 524-2600
KISN-AM/FM	(801) 262-9797
KRCL-FM	(801) 363-1818
KSL-AM	(801) 575-7600
KSOP-AM/FM	(801) 972-1043
KTKK-AM	(801) 264-8250
KUER-FM	(801) 581-6625
KVRI-FM	(801) 485-6700
KXRK-FM	(801) 521-9696
KZHT-AM, KBER-FM	(801) 322-3311

San Antonio, TX

KCHL-AM	(210) 333-0050
KCOR-AM, KROM-FM	(210) 246-1350
KEDA-AM	(210) 226-5254
KENS-AM	(210) 366-5000
KHBL-AM	(210) 226-6444
KISS-FM	(210) 646-0105
KKYX-AM, KCYY-FM	(210) 615-5400
KONO-AM	(210) 340-1234
KPAC-FM	(210) 614-8977
KQXT-FM	(210) 736-9700
KRTU-FM	(210) 736-8159
KSLR-AM	(210) 344-8481
KSJL-FM	(210) 271-9600
KSTX-FM	(210) 614-8977
KSYM-FM	(210) 733-2793
KTSA-AM, KTFM-FM	(210) 599-5500
KXTN-AM/FM	(210) 829-1075
KZEP-AM/FM	(210) 226-6444
KZXS-AM	(210) 736-9700
WOAI-AM, KAJA-FM	(210) 736-9700

San Diego, CA

KBZS-FM	(619) 452-9595
KCBQ-AM/FM	(619) 286-1170
KFMB-AM/FM	(619) 292-7600
KFSD-FM	(619) 239-9091
KIFM-FM	(619) 587-9800
KIOZ-FM	(619) 560-5464
KJQY-FM	(619) 560-1037
KKLQ-AM/FM	(619) 565-6006
KPBS-FM	(619) 594-8100
KPOP-AM, KGB-FM	(619) 292-1360
KSDO-AM, KCLX-FM	(619) 278-1130
KSDS-FM	(619) 234-1062
KSON-AM/FM	(619) 299-1240
KURS-AM	(619) 425-2132
KYXY-FM	(619) 571-7600

San Francisco, CA

KABL-FM	(415) 788-5225
KALW-FM	(415) 695-5740
KCBS-AM, KRQR-FM	(415) 765-4000
KDFC-FM	(415) 788-2022
KEAR-FM	(415) 626-3010
KEST-AM	(415) 978-5378

KFAX-AM	(501) 713-1100
KFRC-AM/FM	(415) 986-6100
KGO-AM	(415) 954-8100
KIOI-FM	(415) 956-5101
KIQI-AM	(415) 695-1010
KITS-FM	(415) 512-1053
KKHI-AM/FM	(415) 986-2151
KKSF-FM	(415) 788-2022
KMEL-FM	(415) 391-1061
KOFY-AM	(415) 821-2020
KOIT-AM/FM	(415) 777-0965
KPOO-FM	(415) 346-5373
KQED-FM	(415) 553-2129
KSAN-FM	(415) 291-0202
KSFO-AM, KYA-FM	(415) 398-5600
KSRY-AM/FM	(415) 512-9999
KUSF-FM	(415) 386-5873

Seattle, WA

KBLE-AM	(206) 324-2000
KCMU-FM	(206) 543-5541
KEZX-AM/FM	(206) 441-3699
KGNW-AM	(206) 443-8200
KING-AM/FM	(206) 448-3666
KIRO-AM/FM	(206) 728-7777
KISW-FM	(206) 285-7625
KIXI-AM	(206) 454-1540
KJR-AM, KLTX-FM	(206) 285-2295
KKDZ-AM	(206) 382-1250
KMPS-AM/FM	(206) 443-9400
KMTT-AM/FM	(206) 233-1037
KNDD-FM	(206) 622-3251
KOMO-AM	(206) 443-4010
KPLU-FM	(206) 535-7758
KPRM-FM	(206) 649-0106
KUBE-FM	(206) 285-2295
KULL-AM	(206) 649-0106
KUOW-FM	(206) 543-2710
KVI-AM, KPLZ-FM	(206) 223-5700
KXRX-FM	(206) 283-5979
KZOK-AM/FM	(206) 281-5600

Tampa, FL

WAMA-AM	(813) 875-0086
WBVM-FM	(813) 289-8040
WDAE-AM, WUSA-FM	(813) 289-0455
WFLA-AM, WFLZ-FM	(813) 839-9393
WMNF-FM	(813) 238-8001
WMTX-AM	(813) 536-9600
WQBN-AM	(813) 281-0013
WRBQ-FM	(813) 287-1047
WTIS-AM	(813) 576-2234
WTMP-AM	(813) 620-1300
WUSF-FM	(813) 974-4890

Washington, DC

WAMU-FM	(202) 885-1030
WDCU-FM	(202) 282-7588
WETA-FM	(703) 998-2790
WGMS-FM	(301) 468-1800
WHUR-FM	(202) 806-3500

WJZE-FM	(202) 722-1000
WKYS-FM	(202) 686-9300
WMAL-AM, WRQX-FM	(202) 686-3100
WMZQ-FM	(202) 362-8330
WOL-AM	(202) 675-4800
WPFW-FM	(202) 783-3100
WTOP-AM, WASH-FM	(202) 895-5000
WUST-AM	(703) 532-0400
WWDC-AM/FM	(301) 587-7100
WWRC-AM, WGAY-FM	(301) 587-4900
WYCB-AM	(202) 737-6400

WEST PALM BEACH, FL

WBZT-AM, WIRK-FM	(407) 965-9211
WEAT-AM/FM	(407) 965-5500
WJNO-AM, WRLX-FM	(407) 838-4300
WOEQ-AM	(407) 687-9350
WXEL-FM	(407) 737-8000

Stock Photo Companies

American Stock Photography, Hollywood, CA	(213) 469-3900
Animals Animals/Earth Scenes, Chatham, NY	(518) 392-5500
Art Resource, New York, NY	(212) 505-8700
Black Star, New York, NY	(212) 679-3288
Bruce Coleman Photo Library, New York, NY	(212) 979-6252
Camerique International, Blue Bell, PA	(610) 272-4000
Compix Photo Agency, Miami, FL	(305) 576-0102
Comstock, New York, NY	(212) 353-8600
Design Conceptions, New York, NY	(212) 254-1688
Devaney Stock Photos, Huntington, NY	(516) 673-4477
Ewing Galloway, Rockville Centre, NY	(516) 764-8620
Fotos International, Studio City, CA	(818) 508-6400
FPG International, New York, NY	(212) 777-4210
Gamma Liaison, New York, NY	(212) 447-2525
Hillstrom Stock Photo, Chicago, IL	(312) 775-4090
The Image Works, Woodstock, NY	(914) 246-8800
Impact Visuals Photo & Graphics, New York, NY	(212) 683-9688
Index Stock Photography, New York, NY	(212) 929-4644
Joan Kramer and Assocs., Los Angeles, CA	(310) 446-1866
Harold M. Lambert Studios, Philadelphia, PA	(215) 885-3355
LGI Photo Agency, New York, NY	(212) 736-4602
Medichrome, New York, NY	(212) 679-8480
Nawrocki Stock Photo, Chicago, IL	(312) 427-8625
Photri, Falls Church, VA	(703) 931-8600
Retna, New York, NY	(212) 255-0622
Rex USA, New York, NY	(212) 586-4432
Sharpshooters, Miami, FL	(305) 666-1266
Southern Stock Photo Agency, Ft. Lauderdale, FL	(800) 486-7118
The Stock Market, New York, NY	(212) 684-7878
The Stock Shop, New York, NY	(212) 679-8480
Superstock, Jacksonville, FL	(904) 565-0066
Tom Stack & Assocs., Colorado Springs, CO	(719) 570-1000
U.S. Naval Institute, Annapolis, MD	(410) 268-6110
Visuals Unlimited, East Swanzey, NH	(603) 352-6436
West Stock, Seattle, WA	(206) 728-7726

Westlight, Los Angeles, CA..............................(310) 820-7077

Television Stations

ANCHORAGE, AK
KAKM (PBS) ....(907) 563-7070
KDMD ....(907) 344-7817
KIMO (ABC) ....(907) 561-1313
KTBY (FOX) ....(907) 274-0404
KTUU (NBC) ....(907) 257-0202
KTVA (CBS) ....(907) 562-3456
KYES...(907) 248-5937

ATLANTA, GA
WAGA (FOX) ....(404) 875-5555
WATL ....(404) 881-3600
WGNX (CBS)...(404) 325-4646
WPBA (PBS) ....(404) 827-8900
WSB (ABC) ....(404) 897-7000
WTBS..(404) 827-1717
WVEU ....(404) 325-6929
WXIA (NBC)..(404) 892-1611

ATLANTIC CITY, NJ
WWAC..(609) 344-6800

BALTIMORE, MD
WBAL (CBS)..(410) 467-3000
WBFF (FOX) ....(410) 467-4545
WJZ (ABC) ....(410) 466-0013
WMAR (NBC) ....(410) 377-2222
WNUV ....(410) 462-5400

BOSTON, MA
WABU ....(617) 787-6868
WBZ (CBS)..(617) 787-7000
WCVB (ABC) ....(617) 449-0400
WFXT (FOX) ....(617) 326-8825
WGBH (PBS)..(617) 492-2777
WHDH (NBC) ....(617) 725-0777
WLVI ....(617) 265-5656
WSBK ....(617) 783-3838

BUFFALO, NY
WGRZ (NBC)..(716) 856-1414
WIVB (CBS) ....(716) 874-4410
WKBW (ABC)..(716) 845-6100
WNED (PBS) ....(716) 845-7000
WNYB (REL) ....(716) 875-4919
WUTV (FOX)..(716) 773-7531

CHARLOTTE, NC
WBTV (CBS)..(704) 374-3500
WCCB (FOX) ....(704) 372-1800
WCNC (NBC)...(704) 329-3636
WSOC (ABC) ....(704) 335-4999
WTVI (ABC)...(704) 372-2442

CHICAGO, IL
WBBM (CBS) ....(312) 944-6000
WCFC (REL) ....(312) 433-3838
WCIU (SPN) ....(312) 663-0260

WFLD (FOX) ....(312) 565-5532
WGN ....(312) 528-2311
WLS (ABC) ....(312) 750-7777
WMAQ (NBC) ....(312) 836-5555
WPWR ....(312) 276-5050
WSNS (SPN) ....(312) 929-1200
WTTW (PBS) ....(312) 583-5000
WYCC (PBS) ....(312) 838-4853

CINCINNATI, OH

WCET (PBS) ....(513) 381-4033
WCPO (CBS) ....(513) 721-9900
WKRC (ABC) ....(513) 763-5500
WLWT (NBC) ....(513) 352-5000
WSTR ....(513) 641-4400
WXIX (FOX) ....(513) 772-1919

CLEVELAND, OH

WEWS (ABC) ....(216) 431-5555
WJW (FOX) ....(216) 431-8888
WKYC (NBC) ....(216) 344-3333
WOLO (CBS) ....(216) 771-1943
WVIZ (PBS) ....(216) 398-2800

COLUMBUS, OH

WBNS (CBS) ....(614) 460-3700
WCMH (NBC) ....(614) 263-4444
WOSU (PBS) ....(614) 292-9678
WSYX (ABC) ....(614) 481-6666
WTTE (FOX) ....(614) 895-2800

DALLAS, TX

KDAF...(214) 634-8833
KDFI ....(214) 637-2727
KDFW (FOX)...................................(214) 720-4444
KDTX (REL) ....(214) 313-1333
KERA (PBS) ....(214) 871-1390
KFWD (SPN) ....(214) 255-5200
KTVT (CBS) ....(817) 451-1111
KTXA ....(214) 743-2100
KXAS (NBC) ....(817) 536-5555
KXTX ....(214) 521-3900
WFAA (ABC)...................................(214) 748-9631

DENVER, CO

KCEC (UNI) ....(303) 235-0049
KCNC (CBS) ....(303) 861-4444
KDVR (FOX)....................................(303) 595-3131
KMGH (ABC) ....(303) 832-7777
KRMA (PBS) ....(303) 892-6666
KTVD ....(303) 792-2020
KUBD (SPN) ....(303) 751-5959
KUSA (NBC) ....(303) 871-9999
KWBI (REL).....................................(303) 697-5924
KWGN ....(303) 740-2222

DETROIT, MI

WDIV (NBC)....................................(313) 222-0444
WJBK (FOX).....................................(810) 557-2000
WKBD ....(810) 350-5050
WTVS (PBS) ....(313) 873-7200
WWJ (CBS) ....(313) 259-8862

WXON ....(313) 355-2020
WXYZ (ABC) ....(313) 827-7777

Grand Rapids, MI

WGVU (PBS) ....(616) 771-6666
WLLA (REL) ....(616) 345-6421
WOOD (NBC) ....(616) 456-8888
WOTV (ABC) ....(616) 968-9341
WWMT (CBS) ....(616) 388-3333
WXMI (FOX) ....(616) 364-8722
WZZM (ABC) ....(616) 785-1313

Greenville, SC

WGGS (REL)....................................(803) 244-1616
WYFF (NBC) ....(803) 242-4404

Harrisburg, PA

WGAL (NBC) ....(717) 393-5851
WHP (CBS) ....(717) 238-2100
WHTM (ABC) ....(717) 236-2727
WITF (PBS) ....(717) 236-6000
WLYH (CBS) ....(717) 228-1500
WPMT (FOX) ....(717) 843-0043

Hartford, CT

WEDH (PBS) ....(203) 278-5310
WFSB (CBS) ....(203) 728-3333
WTIC (FOX) ....(203) 527-6161
WTNH (ABC)....................................(203) 784-8888
WVIT (NBC).....................................(203) 521-3030

Honolulu, HI

KBFD ....(808) 521-8066
KFVE...(808) 847-3246
KGMB (CBS)....................................(808) 973-5462
KHET (PBS)......................................(808) 955-7878
KHNL ....(808) 847-3246
KHON (NBC) ....(808) 531-8585
KIKU...(808) 847-2021
KITV (NBC) ....(808) 545-4444
KOBN ....(808) 254-5826
KWHE ....(808) 538-1414

Houston, TX

KETH (REL) ....(713) 561-5828
KHOU (CBS).....................................(713) 526-1111
KHTV..(713) 781-3939
KLTJ..(713) 212-1077
KPRC (NBC) ....(713) 771-4631
KRIV (FOX) ....(713) 626-2610
KTRK (ABC) ....(713) 666-0713
KTXH ....(713) 661-2020
KUHT (PBS) ....(713) 748-8888

Indianapolis, IN

WFYI (PBS) ....(317) 636-2020
WHMB ....(317) 773-5050
WISH (CBS) ....(317) 932-8888
WRTV (ABC).....................................(317) 635-9788
WTHR (NBC) ....(317) 636-1313
WTTV...(317) 782-4444
WXIN (FOX) ....(317) 632-5900

Kansas City, KS

KCTV (CBS)	(913) 677-5555
KSMO	(913) 621-6262
KYFC (REL)	(913) 262-1700

Kansas City, MO

KCPT (PBS)	(816) 756-3580
KMBC (ABC)	(816) 221-9999
KSHB (FOX)	(816) 753-4141
WDAF (NBC)	(816) 753-4567

Las Vegas, NV

KFBT	(702) 873-0033
KLAS (CBS)	(702) 792-8888
KLVX (PBS)	(702) 737-1010
KRLR	(702) 382-2121
KTVN (ABC)	(702) 876-1313
KVBC (NBC)	(702) 642-3333
KVVU (FOX)	(702) 435-5555

Los Angeles, CA

KABC (ABC)	(310) 557-7777
KCAL	(213) 467-9999
KCBS (CBS)	(213) 460-3000
KCET (PBS)	(213) 666-6500
KCOP	(213) 851-1000
KLCS (PBS)	(213) 625-6958
KMET	(213) 469-5638
KMEX (UNI)	(310) 216-3434
KNBC (NBC)	(818) 840-4444
KTLA	(213) 460-5500
KTTV (FOX)	(213) 856-1000
KWHY (SPN)	(213) 466-5441

Memphis, TN

WHBQ (ABC)	(901) 320-1313
WKNO (PBS)	(901) 458-2521
WLMT	(901) 346-3030
WMC (NBC)	(901) 726-0555
WPTY (FOX)	(901) 278-2424
WREG (CBS)	(901) 577-0100

Miami, FL

WBFS	(305) 621-3333
WCTD	(305) 670-3535
WDZL	(305) 925-3939
WFOR (CBS)	(305) 593-0606
WHFT (REL)	(305) 962-1700
WLRN (PBS)	(305) 995-2204
WLTV (UNI)	(305) 470-2323
WPBT (PBS)	(305) 949-8321
WPLG (ABC)	(305) 576-1010
WSVN (FOX)	(305) 751-6692
WTVJ (NBC)	(305) 379-4444

Milwaukee, WI

WCGV	(414) 442-7050
WDJT (CBS)	(414) 271-5800
WISN (ABC)	(414) 342-8812
WITI (FOX)	(414) 355-6666
WMVS (PBS)	(414) 271-1036
WMVT (PBS)	(414) 271-1036

WTMJ (NBC) ....(414) 332-9611
WVCY (REL) ....(414) 935-3000
WVTV ....(414) 442-7050

Minneapolis, MN

KARE (NBC) ....(612) 546-1111
KITN (FOX) ....(612) 424-2929
KLGT ....(612) 646-2300
KMSP ....(612) 944-9999
KSTP (ABC) ....(612) 646-5555
KTCA (PBS) ....(612) 222-1717
WCCO (CBS) ....(612) 339-4444

Nashville, TN

WDCN (PBS) ....(615) 259-9325
WKRN (ABC) ....(615) 248-7222
WSMV (NBC) ....(615) 353-4444
WTVF (CBS) ....(615) 244-5000
WXMT ....(615) 256-3030
WZTV (FOX) ....(615) 244-1717

New Orleans, LA

WDSU (NBC) ....(504) 527-0666
WGNO ....(504) 581-2600
WLAE (PBS) ....(504) 866-7411
WNOL (FOX) ....(504) 525-3838
WVUE (ABC) ....(504) 486-6161
WWL (CBS) ....(504) 529-4444
WYES (PBS) ....(504) 486-5511

New York, NY

WABC (ABC) ....(212) 456-7777
WCBS (CBS) ....(212) 975-4321
WNBC (NBC) ....(212) 664-4444
WNET (PBS) ....(212) 560-2000
WNYC (PBS) ....(212) 669-7800
WNYE (PBS) ....(718) 935-4480
WNYW (FOX) ....(212) 452-5555
WPIX ....(212) 949-1100
WWOR ....(201) 348-0009

Norfolk, VA

WAVY (NBC) ....(804) 393-1010
WGNT ....(804) 393-2501
WHRO (PBS) ....(804) 489-9476
WTKR (CBS) ....(804) 446-1000
WTVZ (FOX) ....(804) 622-3333
WVEC (ABC) ....(804) 625-1313

Oklahoma City, OK

KETA (PBS) ....(405) 848-8501
KFOR (NBC) ....(405) 424-4444
KOCB ....(405) 478-3434
KOCO (ABC) ....(405) 478-3000
KOKH (FOX) ....(405) 843-2525
KSBI (REL) ....(405) 631-7335
KTBO (REL) ....(405) 848-1414
KTLC (FOX) ....(405) 478-4300
KWTV (CBS) ....(405) 843-6641

Orlando, FL

WBSF ....(407) 254-4343

WCPX (CBS)	(407) 291-6000
WESH (NBC)	(904) 226-2222
WFTV (ABC)	(407) 841-9000
WIRB	(407) 725-0056
WMFE (PBS)	(407) 273-2300
WOFL (FOX)	(407) 644-3535

PHILADELPHIA, PA

KYW (NBC)	(215) 238-4700
WCAU (CBS)	(215) 668-5510
WGBS	(215) 563-5757
WPHL	(215) 878-1700
WPVI (ABC)	(215) 878-9700
WTXF (FOX)	(215) 925-2929
WYBE (PBS)	(215) 483-3900

PHOENIX, AZ

KAET (PBS)	(602) 965-3506
KNXV (ABC)	(602) 243-4151
KPAZ (REL)	(602) 273-1477
KPHO (CBS)	(602) 264-1000
KPNX (NBC)	(602) 257-1212
KSAC (FOX)	(602) 257-1234
KTVK	(602) 263-3333
KTVW (UNI)	(602) 243-3333
KUTP	(602) 268-4500

PITTSBURGH, PA

KDKA (CBS)	(412) 575-2200
WNEU	(412) 531-6365
WPGH (FOX)	(412) 931-5300
WPTT	(412) 856-9010
WPXI (NBC)	(412) 237-1100
WQED (PBS)	(412) 622-1300
WQEX (PBS)	(412) 622-1550
WTAE (ABC)	(412) 242-4300

PORTLAND, OR

KATU (ABC)	(503) 231-4222
KGW (NBC)	(503) 226-5000
KNMT	(503) 252-0792
KOIN (CBS)	(503) 464-0600
KOPB (PBS)	(503) 244-9900
KPTV	(503) 222-9921

PROVIDENCE, RI

WJAR (NBC)	(401) 455-9100
WLNE (ABC)	(401) 453-8000
WNAC (FOX)	(508) 252-9711
WOST	(401) 455-0162
WPRI (CBS)	(401) 438-7200
WSBE (PBS)	(401) 277-3636

RALEIGH, NC

WLFL (FOX)	(919) 872-9535
WRAL (CBS)	(919) 821-8555
WRDC (NBC)	(919) 876-0674
WTVD (ABC)	(919) 683-1111

SACRAMENTO, CA

KCMY	(916) 443-2929
KCRA (NBC)	(916) 446-3333

KFTL (REL) ....(510) 632-5385
KOVR (CBS) ....(916) 374-1313
KRBK ....(916) 929-0300
KSCH ....(916) 635-5858
KTXL (FOX) ....(916) 454-4422
KVIE (PBS) ....(916) 929-5843
KXTV (ABC) ....(916) 441-2345

St. Louis, MO

KDNL (FOX) ....(314) 436-3030
KETC (PBS) ....(314) 725-2460
KMOV (CBS) ....(314) 621-4444
KNLC (REL) ....(314) 436-2424
KPLR...(314) 367-7211
KSDK (NBC) ....(314) 421-5055
KTVI (ABC) ....(314) 647-2222

Salt Lake City, UT

KJZZ..(801) 537-1414
KSL (NBC) ....(801) 575-5555
KSTU (FOX) ....(801) 532-1300
KTVX (ABC) ....(801) 975-4444
KUED (PBS) ....(801) 581-7777
KUTV (CBS) ....(801) 973-3000

San Antonio, TX

KABB...(210) 366-1129
KENS (CBS) ....(210) 366-5000
KHCE (SPN) ....(210) 496-2323
KLRN (PBS)...(210) 270-9000
KMOL (NBC) ....(210) 226-4444
KSAT (ABC) ....(210) 351-1200
KVDA (SPN) ....(210) 340-8860
KWEX (UNI) ....(210) 227-4141

San Diego, CA

KFMB (CBS) ....(619) 571-8888
KGTV (ABC) ....(619) 237-1010
KNSD (NBC) ....(619) 279-3939
KPBS (PBS)...(619) 594-1515
KTTY ....(619) 575-6969
KUSI ....(619) 571-5151
XETV (SPN) ....(619) 279-6666
XEWT (SPN) ....(619) 528-1212

San Francisco, CA

KBHK ....(415) 249-4444
KCNS ....(415) 863-3800
KDTV (UNI) ....(415) 641-1400
KGO (ABC)...(415) 954-7777
KICU ....(408) 298-3636
KLXV (REL)...(408) 264-6565
KNTV (ABC) ....(408) 286-1111
KOFY...(415) 821-2020
KPIX (CBS) ....(415) 362-5550
KQED (PBS) ....(415) 864-2000
KRON (NBC) ....(415) 441-4444
KSTS (SPN)...(408) 435-8848
KTEH (PBS) ....(408) 437-5454
KTSF...(415) 468-2626
KTVU (FOX) ....(510) 834-1212

Media/Communications

SEATTLE, WA

KCTS (PBS)	(206) 728-6463
KING (NBC)	(206) 448-5555
KIRO	(206) 728-7777
KOMO (ABC)	(206) 443-4000
KSTW (CBS)	(206) 441-7945
KTZZ	(206) 282-2202

TAMPA, FL

WBSV	(813) 379-0062
WEDU (PBS)	(813) 254-9338
WFLA (NBC)	(813) 228-8888
WFTS (ABC	(813) 623-2828
WTOG	(813) 576-4444
WTSP (CBS)	(813) 577-1010
WTTA	(813) 684-3838
WTVT (FOX)	(813) 876-1313
WUSF (PBS)	(813) 974-4000
WWSB (ABC)	(813) 923-8840

WASHINGTON, DC

WDCA	(301) 986-9322
WETA (PBS)	(703) 998-2600
WFTY	(301) 230-1550
WHMM (PBS)	(202) 636-5600
WJLA (ABC)	(202) 364-7777
WMDO (SPN)	(301) 589-4800
WRC (NBC)	(202) 885-4000
WTTG (FOX)	(202) 244-5151
WUSA (CBS)	(202) 895-5999

WEST PALM BEACH, FL

WFLX (FOX)	(407) 845-2929
WPBF (ABC)	(407) 694-2525
WPEC (CBS)	(407) 844-1212
WPTV (NBC)	(407) 655-5455
WTCE	(407) 489-2701
WTVX	(407) 464-3434
WXEL (PBS)	(407) 737-8000

Videotaping/Editing Studios

ANCHORAGE, AK

Action Video Productions	(907) 277-8115
Media Production Assocs	(907) 277-4444
Sally B. Blackford Video	(907) 338-7288

ATLANTA, GA

Dan Sperling Video & Film	(404) 339-8595
Executive Visions	(404) 416-6100
SPI Visual Comms. Group	(404) 451-7000
Video Services	(404) 242-8911

BALTIMORE, MD

Advanced Video Systems	(410) 363-3680
Cooper Productions	(410) 880-4144
Hocus Focus Productions	(410) 832-5740
Producers Video	(410) 523-7520

BOSTON, MA

Adler Assocs	(617) 439-4441
Rampion Visual Productions	(617) 574-9601

Robert Gilmore Assocs..(617) 536-0700
Video/Visual..(617) 527-7800

BUFFALO, NY

The Advertising Center ....(716) 874-5155
Astral Comms..(716) 823-5703
BCMK Recording Studios.......................................(716) 877-2265
Videoccasions ....(716) 877-7129

CHARLOTTE, NC

Allstarr Video Productions....................................(704) 554-0905
CIN Services..(704) 847-8507
Studio South..(704) 525-0296
Taylored Video Services ....(704) 366-0404

CHICAGO, IL

Golan Productions...(312) 274-3456
Karl Productions ....(708) 782-5553
Motivation Media..(312) 836-1100

CINCINNATI, OH

Aztec Video Productions ....(513) 481-5004
Impact Video Productions......................................(513) 681-9191
On Location Video Productions ....(513) 241-2227
Paradigm Comm. Group..(513) 381-7100

CLEVELAND, OH

Am Tech Video ....(216) 676-0441
Avid Comms...(216) 266-7551
Media Dimensions...(216) 875-5739
MRI Video Productions...(216) 696-1122

COLUMBUS, OH

Platinum Productions ....(614) 888-4181
Shaw Video...(614) 457-4477
Vanguard Video Productions..................................(614) 436-4610

DALLAS, TX

Kaleidoscope Video Productions..........................(214) 340-3997
On Video ....(214) 406-9292
Thornhill Productions...(214) 556-0766
Video Editor...(214) 788-4988
You Make the Edit...(214) 340-4022

DENVER, CO

Broadcast One Teleproductions ....(303) 698-1145
Business Video Productions...................................(303) 799-3900
Rocky Mountain Audio/Video Productions ......(303) 730-1100
Transtar Productions..(303) 695-4207

DETROIT, MI

Color Bars..(810) 778-2277
MVP Comms. ....(810) 588-7600
RTI Visual Comms. ....(810) 442-2525

GRAND RAPIDS, MI

Great Lakes Video Services....................................(616) 454-2002
Motion Picture Makers...(616) 949-5744

GREENVILLE, SC

Action Video Productions......................................(803) 297-8865
American Image Makers ....(803) 271-1509
Spectrum South..(803) 232-7369

TVP Productions ....(803) 239-0566

Harrisburg, PA

Action Video Productions....................................(717) 560-0605
Images Unlimited ....(717) 293-7170
JPL Video Productions ....(717) 558-8048
On Camera ....(717) 274-2927

Hartford, CT

MediaVision Productions ....(203) 249-2424
Penfield Productions..(203) 548-0112

Honolulu, HI

Mystical Sounds & Video Productions ....(808) 737-0269
Noel Enterprises ....(808) 941-5255
Post Production Service ....(808) 593-2939
Tri-Star Video Data Services................................(808) 682-1525

Houston, TX

Astro Audio Visual..(713) 528-7119
Olivier Video Productions....................................(713) 621-8596
Studio W Productions ....(713) 377-6300
Texas Premiere Productions ....(713) 873-0000

Indianapolis, IN

Better Way Video Productions.............................(317) 882-3762
Bill Donella's Videos & Such...............................(317) 252-4317

Kansas City, KS

Central Video Services...(913) 648-1525
Colortech Video Services.....................................(913) 451-3919

Kansas City, MO

Double Exposure..(816) 474-5522
Video Post..(816) 531-1225

Las Vegas, NV

Goodwyn Production Group ....(702) 363-7710
Laguna Productions ....(702) 731-5600
Productions Plus ....(702) 876-1520
Tellestarr Video Productions ....(702) 376-1736

Los Angeles, CA

Bill White Productions..(213) 934-1412
Business Video Productions.................................(818) 240-4040
Heart & Soul Design Comms. ....(310) 671-1794
ITV Productions ....(800) 310-8433
McCune Video ....(800) 486-7686

Memphis, TN

DAT Teleproductions ....(901) 525-2621
Dragonwyck Teleproductions ....(901) 272-0611
Motion Moments Video ....(901) 366-4321
Studio M Productions..(901) 385-1711

Miami, FL

Broadcast Quality Incorporated ....(305) 665-5416
Multivision Video & Film ....(305) 662-6011

Milwaukee, WI

Marx Communications...(414) 351-5060
Taylor Video ....(414) 778-0362
Video Wisconsin..(414) 785-6680

MINNEAPOLIS, MN

Big City Productions ....(612) 452-1108
Mediatrend Communications ....(612) 944-1961
Precision Tapes ....(612) 333-9111
ProMedia Productions ....(612) 631-3681
Take 1 Productions ....(612) 831-7757

NASHVILLE, TN

Cummings Video & Film ....(615) 385-4400
Fox Video Production House ....(615) 872-8656
Tyler Productions..(615) 385-2244
VMI (Video Music International) ....(615) 256-4321

NEW ORLEANS, LA

Communications Unlimited ....(612) 561-1704
Pinnacle Video Productions..............................(612) 888-3332
Real Productions...(612) 646-9472

NEW YORK, NY

Ace Video ....(212) 206-1475
ANS International Video....................................(212) 366-1733
USA Studios...(212) 989-6400
Video Portfolios Productions............................(212) 725-3505

NORFOLK, VA

Advance Video..(804) 425-1234
Allied Video ....(804) 424-9757
Creative Edge ....(804) 420-3605
E. L. Hamm & Assocs. ....(804) 497-5000

OKLAHOMA CITY, OK

Action Production Group ....(405) 943-2247
Garman Audio/Video Productions....................(405) 842-3230
Premier Video Productions...............................(405) 454-6880
The Production Room..(405) 840-2100

ORLANDO, FL

Image Technical Services. ....(407) 843-0043
Omni World Productions..................................(407) 281-9087
Video Production Center (PCV) ....(407) 834-8667

PHILADELPHIA, PA

CSR Productions ....(610) 668-6353
FMP Visual Comms..(215) 763-3400
Sound Image ....(215) 355-6055
WCL Comms...(609) 881-6480

PHOENIX, AZ

EastWest Media Productions.............................(602) 319-4066
Video Media Productions ....(602) 966-6545

PITTSBURGH, PA

Comstock Video ....(412) 271-8273
JR Productions...(412) 821-1000
R.E.S. Video Productions ....(412) 788-0220
Video Tone Productions ....(412) 269-0080

PORTLAND, OR

Aardvark Video Productions.............................(503) 282-5411
Alternative Video Productions ....(503) 777-1203
Cinemagic Studios...(503) 233-2141
Limelight Video Productions ....(503) 242-0506

Media/Communications

PROVIDENCE, RI

Creative Comms...(401) 434-3291
Universal Video Productions ....(401) 463-6660

RALEIGH, NC

Gaughan Video Productions ....(919) 477-5779
MVP Video Productions....................................(919) 933-6463
Myriad Media Designs.......................................(919) 836-8004
North State Video Productions.........................(919) 682-7153

SACRAMENTO, CA

ATV Video Center..(916) 635-1205
Bill Rase Productions ....(916) 929-9181
Capitol Video Center ....(916) 447-5050
Dynasty Video Productions ....(916) 424-3797
KCSO TV Video ....(209) 578-1900

ST. LOUIS, MO

Innervision Studios...(314) 569-2500
Mercury Productions ....(314) 647-8044
St. Louis Studio Services....................................(314) 968-2626

SALT LAKE CITY, UT

Arrow America Video ....(801) 485-7000
Channel 3 Video Productions............................(801) 265-1335
Gekko Productions ....(800) 214-3550
The World of Video & Film...............................(801) 359-5120

SAN ANTONIO, TX

Alamo Video Services ....(210) 657-5585
Hoffman Reporting and Video Services ....(210) 736-3555
Integral Presentations..(210) 697-8334

SAN DIEGO, CA

Bob Hoffman Video Productions ....(619) 576-0046
Clockwork Studios ....(619) 578-8433
Lightning Corporation ....(619) 565-6494
Perfect Image Video...(619) 292-0818

SAN FRANCISCO, CA

Creative Television and Video Productions ......(415) 897-0049
Frontier Productions..(415) 837-1755
Highlight Productions ....(415) 989-9134
McCune Video ....(415) 641-1111
SVT Video...(415) 882-7205

SEATTLE, WA

A+ Video Productions..(206) 622-8316
Lon Gibby Productions ....(206) 624-4268
ProVideo Productions...(206) 622-6700
Video Now Productions Services.......................(206) 623-5965

TAMPA, FL

AVS Video Productions.......................................(813) 935-1898
Business Video Productions................................(813) 289-2744
CPN Television ....(813) 530-5000
Edit Suites...(813) 254-3321

WASHINGTON, DC

Associated Producers..(202) 347-4700
Commercial Video Services ....(703) 506-9115
Public Production Group ....(202) 898-1808
PVS Media Center ....(202) 775-0894

West Palm Beach, FL

Avanti Video Productions ....(407) 684-9426
Exclusive Video Productions ....(407) 641-4252
Gold Coast Video Productions...........................(407) 798-3129
Multi Image Group ....(407) 659-0332

Libraries

Anchorage, AK, Anchorage Municipal
Libraries...(907) 343-2975
Atlanta, GA, Atlanta-Fulton Public Library.....(404) 730-1700
Atlantic City, NJ, Atlantic City Public Library (609) 345-2269
Baltimore, MD, Enoch Pratt Free Library..........(410) 396-5430
Boston, MA, Boston Public Library...................(617) 536-5400
Buffalo, NY, Buffalo & Erie County Public
Library...(716) 858-8900
Charlotte, NC, Public Library of Charlotte &
Mecklenburg County.....................................(704) 336-2725
Chicago, IL, Chicago Public Library...................(312) 747-4999
Cincinnati, OH, Public Library of Cincinnati &
Hamilton County ....(513) 369-6900
Cleveland, OH, Cleveland Public Library.........(216) 623-2800
Columbus, OH, Columbus Public Library ....(614) 231-2793
Dallas, TX, Johnson J. Eric Public Library......(214) 670-1400
Denver, CO, Denver Public Library ....(303) 640-6200
Detroit, MI, Detroit Public Library...................(313) 833-1000
Grand Rapids, MI, Grand Rapids Public
Library...(616) 456-3600
Greenville, SC, Greenville County Library ......(803) 242-5000
Harrisburg, PA, Dauphin Cty. Library System...(717) 234-4961
Hartford, CT, Hartford Public Library ....(203) 293-6000
Houston, TX. Houston Public Library...............(713) 236-1313
Indianapolis, IN, Indianapolis-Marion County
Public Library...(317) 269-1700
Kansas City, KS, Public Library System.............(913) 551-3280
Kansas City, MO, Kansas City Public Library ...(816) 221-2685
Las Vegas, NV, Las Vegas–Clark County
Library District...(702) 382-3493
Los Angeles, CA, Los Angeles Public Library...(213) 612-3200
Memphis, TN, Memphis/Shelby County
Public Library...(901) 725-8855
Miami, FL, Miami-Dade Public Library.............(305) 375-2665
Milwaukee, WI, Milwaukee Public Library ....(414) 286-3000
Minneapolis, MN, Minneapolis
Public Library...(612) 372-6500
Nashville, TN, West Ben Public Library of
Nashville & Davidson County.......................(615) 862-5800
New Orleans, LA, New Orleans Library............(504) 596-2550
New York, NY, New York Public Library..........(212) 930-0800
Norfolk, VA, Norfolk Public Library ....(804) 441-2887
Oklahoma City, OK, Metropolitan Library of
Oklahoma County ....(405) 235-0571
Orlando, FL, Orange County Library System....(407) 425-4694
Philadelphia, PA, Free Library of Phila. ....(215) 686-5322
Phoenix, AZ, Phoenix Public Library................(602) 262-4636
Pittsburgh, PA, Carnegie Library ....(412) 622-3100
Portland, OR, Multnomah County Library ....(503) 248-5123
Providence, RI, Providence Public Library.......(401) 455-8000
Raleigh, NC, Wake County Public Libraries.....(919) 250-1200
Sacramento, CA, Sacramento Public Library....(916) 264-2770
St. Louis, MO, St. Louis Public Library.............(314) 241-2288
Salt Lake City, UT, Salt Lake City Public
Library...(801) 524-8200
San Antonio, TX, San Antonio Library............(210) 207-7790
San Diego, CA, San Diego Public Library ....(619) 236-5800
San Francisco, CA, San Francisco Public
Library...(415) 557-4400

Seattle, WA, Seattle Public Library ....(206) 386-4100
Tampa, FL, Tampa-Hillsborough Public
   Library ....(813) 273-3652
Washington, DC, Martin Luther King
   Memorial Library ....(202) 727-1111
West Palm Beach, FL, Palm Beach County
   Public Library System ....(407) 233-2600

Restaurants

ANCHORAGE, AK

Aladdin's Fine Mediterranean & American Cuisine,
   4240 Old Seward Hwy., Suite 20 ....(907) 561-2373
Bombay House,
   Eagle River Shopping Center........................(907) 696-6055
Club 26 Restaurant,
   611 W. Ninth Ave ....(907) 279-8043
Crow's Nest, Fifth Ave. & K St ....(907) 276-6000
The Flying Machine Restaurant,
   4800 Spenard Rd ....(907) 243-2300
Harry's Restaurant & Bar,
   101 W. Benson Blvd ....(907) 561-5317
Jens' Restaurant, 701 W. 36th Ave. ....(907) 561-5367
Maharaja's, 328 G St. ....(907) 272-2233
Mesa Grill Restaurant,
   720 W. Fifth Ave. ....(907) 278-3433
Mexico in Alaska Restaurant,
   7305 Old Seward Hwy. ....(907) 349-1528
O'Malley's on the Green,
   3651 O'Malley Rd...(907) 522-3322
Simon & Seafort's Saloon & Grill,
   420 L St...(907) 274-3502
Tempura Kitchen,
   3826 Spenard Rd. ....(907) 277-2741
Top of the World,
   500 W. Third Ave...(907) 265-7111

ATLANTA, GA

103 West, 103 W. Paces Ferry Rd. ....(404) 233-5993
The 1848 House Restaurant, 780 S. Cobb Dr...(404) 428-1848
Abruzzi Ristorante, 2355 Peachtree Rd., NE.....(404) 261-8186
Acacia, Doubletree Hotel, 7 Concourse Pkwy ..(404) 395-3900
The Bistro at Andrews Square,
   56 E. Andrews Dr., NW ....(404) 231-5733
Canoe,
   4199 Paces Ferry Rd. NW ....(404) 432-2663
Chopstix, 4279 Roswell Rd...............................(404) 255-4868
City Grill, 50 Hurt Plaza ....(404) 524-2489
Florencia, Grand Hotel,
   75 14th St. ....(404) 881-9898
La Grotta, 2637 Peachtree Rd., NE...................(404) 231-1368
The Hedgerose Heights Inn,
   490 E. Paces Ferry Rd. ....(404) 233-7673
Nakato Japanese Restaurant,
   1776 Cheshire Bridge Rd. ....(404) 873-6582
Nikolai's Roof, 225 Courtland St.......................(404) 221-6362
Pano's & Paul's,
   1232 W. Paces Ferry Rd..................................(404) 261-3662
Ray's on the River, 6700 Powers Ferry Rd. ....(404) 955-1187
Ruth's Chris Steak House,
   950 E. Paces Ferry Rd. ....(404) 365-0660

Miscellaneous

Savannah Fish Company,
The Westin Peachtree Plaza Hotel at
Peachtree St. and International Blvd. ....(404) 589-7456

ATLANTIC CITY, NJ

12 South, 12 S. Indiana Ave. ....(609) 345-1212
Angeloni's II, 2400 Arctic Ave ....(609) 344-7875
Captain Young's Seafood Emporium,
The Shops on Ocean One, The Boardwalk...(609) 344-2001
Dock's Oyster House, 2405 Atlantic Ave. ....(609) 345-0092
Frisanco's Ristorante, 3426 Atlantic Ave. ....(609) 345-0606
Hunan Chinese Restaurant,
2323 Atlantic Ave. ....(609) 348-5946
Italian Bistro,
The Shops on Ocean One, The Boardwalk...(609) 345-8799
Knife and Fork Inn,
Atlantic and Pacific Aves...............................(609) 344-1133
McGettigan's Saloon, 440 N. Albany Ave. ....(609) 344-3030
Orsatti's, 24 S. North Carolina Ave...................(609) 347-7667
Scannicchio's, 119 S. California Ave. ....(609) 348-6378
Tucci's Ristorante, 1219 Pacific Ave.................(609) 348-4060

BALTIMORE, MD

Berry & Elliot's, 300 Light St............................(410) 528-1234
The Chart House, Pier 4, 601 E. Pratt St..........(410) 539-6616
City Lights, Harborplace, Light St. Pavilion,
301 S. Light St...(410) 244-8811
Fishery Restaurant, 1717 Eastern.....................(410) 327-9340
Kobe Teppan & Sushi, 1023 N. Charles St. ......(410) 685-0780
Lista's, 1637 Thames St....................................(410) 327-0040
M. Gettier Restaurant, 505 S. Broadway ....(410) 732-1151
Mai Thai Restaurant, 1032 Light St..................(410) 539-5611
Marconi's, 106 W. Saratoga St. ....(410) 727-9522
Mughal Garden Restaurant and Bar,
920 N. Charles St. ....(410) 547-0001
Piccolo's at Fell's Point, 1629 Thames St ....(410) 522-6600
Pier 500 Restaurant, 500 Harbor View Dr. ....(410) 625-0500
Prime Rib, 1101 N. Calvert St...........................(410) 539-1804
Ruth's Chris Steak House, 600 Water St...........(410) 783-0033
Taverna Athena, Harborplace, 201 Pratt St......(410) 547-8900
Tony Cheng's Szechuan, 801 N. Charles St. .....(410) 539-6666

BOSTON, MA

Aujourd'Hui, 200 Boylston St............................(617) 338-4400
The Bay Tower, 60 State St. ....(617) 723-1666
Biba, 272 Boylston St. ....(617) 426-7878
The Café Budapest, 90 Exeter St ....(617) 266-1979
The Capital Grille, 359 Newbury St. ....(617) 262-8900
The Chart House Restaurant, 60 Long Wharf ..(617) 227-1576
L'Espalier, 30 Gloucester St...............................(617) 262-3023
Harborside Grill, 101 Harborside Dr.................(617) 568-1234
Jimmy's Harborside Restaurant,
242-248 Northern Ave. ....(617) 423-1000
Julien, 250 Franklin St. ....(617) 451-1900
Kyoto Japanese Steakhouse & Sushi Bar,
201 Stuart St..(617) 542-1166
Mamma Maria, 3 N. Square ....(617) 523-0077
The Ritz-Carlton Dining Room,
15 Arlington St...(617) 536-5700
Seasons, 9 Blackstone St. N ....(617) 523-3600

Buffalo, NY

Coachman's Inn, 10350 Main St. ....(716) 759-6852
Daffodil's, 930 Maple Rd. ....(716) 688-5413
The Friar's Table, 301 Cleveland Dr. ....(716) 833-5554
Justine's, 120 Church St. ....(716) 845-5100
The Park Lane,
    1360 Delaware Ave. at Gates Circle ....(716) 883-3344
Pranzo, 4243 Genesee St. ....(716) 634-2300
The Red Coach Inn, 2 Buffalo Ave. ....(800) 282-1459
Rue Franklin West, 341 Franklin St. ....(716) 852-4416
Salvatore's Italian Gardens, 6461 Transit Rd. ...(716) 683-7990
Taste of India, 484 Elmwood Ave. ....(716) 881-3141

Charlotte, NC

The 30th Edition, 301 S. Tryon St.,
    2 First Union Tower ....(704) 372-7778
La Bibliotheque, 1901 Roxborough Rd. ....(704) 365-5000
Bistro 100, NationsBank Corporate Center ......(704) 344-0515
Carpe Diem Restaurant, 431 S. Tryon St. ....(704) 377-7976
Castaldi's, 311 East Blvd. ....(704) 333-6999
The Fishmarket Restaurant,
    6631 Morrison Blvd. ....(704) 365-0883
Grapevine Cafe, 540-B Brandywine Rd. ....(704) 523-5600
Hereford Barn Steakhouse, 4320 N. I-85 ....(704) 596-0854
The Lamplighter Restaurant,
    1065 E. Morehead St. ....(704) 372-5343
Lone Star Steakhouse & Saloon,
    5033 South Blvd. ....(704) 523-2388
Mangione's Ristorante, 1524 East Blvd. ....(704) 334-4417
McNinch House Restaurant,
    511 N. Church St. ....(704) 332-6159
Nickyo's Uptown Dance Club and Karaoke Bar,
    731 Providence Rd. ....(704) 375-4737
La Paz Restaurant, 523 Fenton Pl. ....(704) 372-4168
Providence Cafe, 110 Perrin Pl. ....(704) 376-2008
The Silver Cricket, 4705 South Blvd.
    at Woodlawn Rd. ....(704) 525-0061
The Townhouse Restaurant,
    1011 Providence Rd. ....(704) 335-1546

Chicago, IL

Ambria, 2300 N. Lincoln Park W ....(312) 472-5959
Berghof, 17 W. Adams St. ....(312) 427-3170
Café Ba-Ba-Reeba!, 2024 N. Halsted St. ....(312) 935-5000
Carson's, the Place for Ribs, 612 N. Wells St. ....(312) 280-9200
Charlie Trotter's, 816 W. Armitage ....(312) 248-6228
Chicago Chop House, 60 W. Ontario St. ....(312) 787-7100
Frontera Grill, 445 N. Clark St ....(312) 661-1434
Hong Min Restaurant, 221 W. Cermak Rd. ......(312) 842-5026
Klay Oven Restaurant, 414 N. Orleans St. ....(312) 527-3999
Morton's of Chicago, 1050 N. State St. ....(312) 266-4820
Old Carolina Crab House,
    465 E. Illinois St. at North Pier ....(312) 321-8400
Papagus Greek Taverna, 600 N. State St. ....(312) 642-8450
The Pump Room, 1301 N. State Pkwy. ....(312) 266-0360
Ron of Japan, 230 E. Ontario St. ....(312) 644-6500
Scoozi, 410 W. Huron St. ....(312) 943-5900
Shaw's Crab House, 21 E. Hubbard St. ....(312) 527-2722
Trattoria No. 10, 10 N. Dearborn ....(312) 984-1718
Tuttaposto, 646 N. Franklin St. ....(312) 943-6262

Miscellaneous

CINCINNATI, OH

Blue Cactus Grill, 7340 Kingsgate Way.............(513) 779-6826
Celestial Restaurant, 1071 Celestial St. ....(513) 241-4455
Champs Italian Chop House, 151 W. Fifth St...(513) 579-1234
Funky's Blackstone Grille, 455 Delta Ave. ....(513) 321-0010
Lenhardt's Restaurant, 151 W. McMillan St. ....(513) 281-3600
Longhorn Steaks, 713 Vine St. ....(513) 421-9696
Maisonette, 114 E. Sixth St. ....(513) 721-2260
McKenna's,
    4501 Eastgate Blvd. ....(513) 752-4400
Morton's of Chicago, 28 W. Fourth St..............(513) 241-4104
La Normandie Grill, 118 E. Sixth St................(513) 721-2761
The Palace, The Cincinnatian Hotel,
    601 Vine St...(513) 381-3000
Petersens Restaurants, 1111 St. Gregory St.......(513) 651-4777
Prima Vista, 810 Matson Pl...............................(513) 251-6467
The Restaurant at the Phoenix, 812 Race St.   (513) 721-8901
Seafood 32 Restaurant, Regal Cincinnati Hotel,
    141 W. Sixth St. ....(513) 352-2160
Tandoor India Restaurant,
    8702 Market Place Ln. ....(513) 793-7484
Viva Barcelonas, Fourth & Race Sts.................(513) 333-0003
The Waterfront, 14 Pete Rose Pier....................(606) 581-1414
Wong Kee Restaurant, 909 Vine St. ....(513) 651-3858

CLEVELAND, OH

Art's Seafood, 16404 Euclid Ave. ....(216) 681-2787
Barnacle Bill's Crab House, 14810 Detroit........(216) 521-2722
Cabin Restaurant, 35 E. Garfield Rd. ....(216) 562-9171
David's, 127 Public Sq.......................................(216) 696-9200
Hunan Gourmet of Tower City,
    230 Huron Rd...(216) 621-2829
Jim's Steak House, 1800 Scranton Rd. ....(216) 241-6343
Morton's of Chicago, 230 Huron Rd. ....(216) 621-6200
Nautica Queen, 1153 Main Ave. ....(216) 696-8888
Pavilion Restaurant, 5300 Rockside Rd.............(216) 524-0700
Piccolo Mondo, 1352 W. Sixth St. ....(216) 241-1300
Sawmill's All-American Steak House,
    2401 Cleveland Rd. W ....(419) 433-3800
Sundial Restaurant & Lounge,
    17000 Bagley Rd. ....(216) 243-5200

COLUMBUS, OH

55 at Crosswoods, 55 Hutchinson Ave..............(614) 846-5555
Cantina del Rio, 2290 Ayers Dr........................(614) 864-2447
Christophers, 77 S. High St. ....(614) 224-4100
The Clarmont, 684 S. High St. ....(614) 443-1125
Ding Ho Restaurant, 3741 W. Broad St.............(614) 276-4395
Fifty-Five on the Boulevard Seafood Restaurant,
    55 Nationwide Blvd...(614) 228-5555
Hoster Brewing Co., 550 S. High St.................(614) 228-6066
Houlihan's, 6240 Busch Blvd. ....(614) 431-1852
Japanese Steak House, 479 N. High St.............(614) 228-3030
Lindey's Restaurant, 169 E. Beck St. ....(614) 228-4343
Longhorn Steakhouse, 6630 Sawmill Rd...........(614) 766-6640
Morton's of Chicago, 2 Nationwide Plaza ....(614) 464-4442
The Old Swiss House, 961 S. High St...............(614) 444-0131
The Refectory, 1092 Bethel Rd..........................(614) 451-9774
Sapporo Wind, 6188 Cleveland Ave. ....(614) 895-7575
Spain Restaurant, 3777 Sullivan Ave................(614) 272-6363
Tamarack at 1105, 1105 Schrock Rd. ....(614) 846-0519

Tony's Italian Ristorante, 16 W. Beck St. ....(614) 224-8669

DALLAS, TX

Al Dente Café, 1920 Greenville ....(214) 821-6054
Café Pacific, 24 Highland Pk. Village................(214) 526-1170
Dakota's, 600 N. Akard ....(214) 740-4001
Enchilada's Restaurant, 7050 Greenville Ave. ..(214) 363-8969
Enigma, 2515 McKinney Ave. at Fairmont.......(214) 953-1111
Hofstetter's, 3840 W. Northwest Hwy., #400.....(214) 358-7660
India Palace, 12817 Preston Rd. ....(214) 392-0190
Kathleen's Art Café, 4424 Lovers Ln.................(214) 691-2355
Landry's Seafood House Restaurant,
　　306 N. Market St..(214) 698-1010
Lawry's The Prime Rib, 3008 Maple Ave. ....(214) 521-7777
Ming Garden, 1442 Preston Forest Sq...............(214) 239-1022
Pappadeaux Seafood Kitchen,
　　3520 Oak Lawn Ave...(214) 521-4700
Pappasito's Cantina, 10433 Lombardy Ln. ....(214) 350-1970
Patrizio, 25 Highland Pk. Village......................(214) 522-7878
Pierre's by the Lake, 3430 Shore Crest Dr. ....(214) 358-2379
Royal 88 Seafood Restaurant,
　　400 N. Greenville, #11 ....(214) 907-8868
Royal Tokyo, 7525 Greenville Ave....................(214) 368-3304
Ruggeri's Ristorante, 2911 Routh St..................(214) 871-7377
St. Martin's, Wine Bistro,
　　3020 Greenville Ave. ....(214) 826-0940
Texas Land and Cattle Company,
　　17390 Preston Rd. ....(214) 248-2424

DENVER, CO

Augusta, 1672 Lawrence St.................................(303) 572-7222
The Broker, 821 17th Ave ....(303) 292-5065
The Buckhorn Exchange, 1000 Osage St ....(303) 534-9505
Centennial Restaurant, 7800 E. Tufts Ave ....(303) 771-1776
The Chart House Restaurant, 25908 Genesee Trail Rd,
　　Lookout Mountain..(303) 526-9813
Cliff Young's, 700 E. 17th Ave ....(303) 831-8900
Denver Buffalo Company, 1109 Lincoln ....(303) 832-0880
European Café, 1515 Market St..........................(303) 825-6555
Imperial Chinese Seafood, 1 Broadway ....(303) 698-2800
Marina Landing, 8101 E. Bellview Ave ....(303) 770-4741
Morton's of Chicago, 900 Auraria Pkwy............(303) 825-3353
Normandy, 1515 Madison ....(303) 321-3311
Palace Arms, 321 17th St....................................(303) 297-3111
Rosso's, 3203 Quebec ....(303) 321-3333
Strings, 1700 Humboldt St..................................(303) 831-7310
Tante Louise, 4900 E. Colfax Ave ....(303) 355-4488
Tuscany, 4150 E. Mississippi...............................(303) 782-9300
The Wellshire Inn, 3333 S. Colorado Blvd.......(303) 759-3333
Zenith American Grill, 1750 Lawrence St........(303) 820-2800

DETROIT, MI

71 Riverside West Fine Dining,
　　71 Riverside Dr., W...(519) 971-0828
Atrium Café, 850 Tower Dr. ....(810) 879-6612
Café Cortina, 30715 W. Ten Mile Rd...............(810) 474-3033
Casa Bianca, 345 Victoria ....(519) 253-5218
Crumpets, 2601 W. Big Beaver Rd....................(810) 643-2211
Early American Room/Ten Eyck Tavern,
　　20310 Oakwood Blvd. ....(313) 271-2700

The Golden Mushroom,
  18100 W. Ten Mile Rd. ....(810) 559-4230
The Grill, 300 Town Center Dr. ....(313) 441-2000
Joe Muer Seafood, 2000 Gratiot ....(313) 567-1088
Lelli's Inn, 7618 Woodward Ave.......................(313) 871-1590
Mario's Restaurant, 4222 Second......................(313) 832-1616
Musashi, 2000 Town Center, Suite 98...............(810) 358-1911
Opus One, 565 E. Larned ....(313) 961-7766
Park Terrace, Windsor Hilton,
  277 Riverside Dr., W ....(519) 973-4225
The Rattlesnake Club, 300 River Pl..................(313) 567-4400
St. Regis Room, 3071 W. Grand Blvd. ....(313) 873-0127
Stewart's Restaurant, 4265 Woodward Ave.......(313) 832-3200
Van Dyke Place, 649 Van Dyke ....(313) 821-2620
The Whitney, 4421 Woodward Ave. ....(313) 832-5700

GRAND RAPIDS, MI

1913 Room, 187 Monroe, NW ....(616) 776-6426
Cygnus, 187 Monroe, NW ....(616) 776-6425
Gibson's Restaurant, 1033 Lake Dr., SE ....(616) 774-8535
Hoffman House, 4101 28th St., SE....................(616) 949-3880
Holly's Landing Restaurant, 270 Ann St., NE ..(616) 363-7748
Hong Kong Inn, 121 Monroe Center................(616) 451-3835
Johnny Noto's Italian Ristorante,
  4259 Lake Michigan Dr., NW.......................(616) 791-0092
Schnitzelbank Restaurant,
  342 Jefferson Ave., SE ....(616) 459-9527
Sigees Restaurant & Lounge,
  4041 Cascade, SE...(616) 949-8800
The Spinnaker Restaurant, 4747 28th St., SE ..(616) 957-0100

GREENVILLE, SC

The 858, 18 E. North St. ....(803) 242-8887
Anita's Mexican Restaurant, 101 Alice Ave. ....(803) 963-3855
Austin's,
  Greenville-Spartanburg Airport Marriott......(803) 297-0300
Caliente Grille, 321 Haywood Rd. ....(803) 288-5013
Crescent City Grille, 106 N. Main St. ....(803) 235-2500
Magnolia's Bar & Grill, 7136 Asheville Hwy. ...(803) 578-5530
Nippon Center Yagoto, 500 Congaree Rd. ....(803) 288-8471
The Open Hearth,
  2801 Wade Hampton Blvd...........................(803) 244-2665
The Pelican, 3795 E. North St. ....(803) 292-5256
Peppino's Italian Restaurant,
  219-C W. Antrim Dr. ....(803) 271-4860
Peter David's Fine Dining, 921 Grove Rd. ....(803) 242-0404
Seven Oaks Restaurant, 104 Broadus Ave.........(803) 232-1895
Stax's Peppermill, 30 Orchard Park Dr. ....(803) 288-9320
Tahoe South, 1 College St. ....(803) 370-1195

HARRISBURG, PA

The Arches Restaurant,
  4125 N. Front St...(717) 233-5891
Ashley's, 4650 Lindle Rd...................................(717) 564-5511
Bangkok Wok, Gateway Sq................................(717) 795-7292
Garden Grille Restaurant, Exit 28, I-81 ....(717) 469-0661

HARTFORD, CT

Blacksmith's Tavern, 2300 Main St. ....(203) 659-0366
Carbone's Ristorante, 588 Franklin Ave.............(203) 296-9646
Costa Del Sol Restaurante,
  901 Wethersfield Ave. ....(203) 296-1714

Mezzanotte, 50 Union Pl....................................(203) 278-1212
Pierpont's Restaurant, 1 Haynes St. ....(203) 246-7500

HONOLULU, HI

Azul, 92-1001 Olani St. ....(808) 679-0079
Bali-by-the-Sea, 2005 Kalia Rd.........................(808) 941-2254
Cascada, 440 Olohana St. ....(808) 943-0202
Castagnola's Italian Lanai,
    1920 Ala Moana Blvd. ....(808) 949-6277
Golden Dragon, 2005 Kalia Rd..........................(808) 946-5336
Hakone, 100 Holomoana St...............................(808) 956-1111
The Hanohano Room, 2255 Kalakaua Ave.......(808) 922-4422
Hula Hut Showroom, 286 Beachwalk ....(808) 923-8411
John Dominis Restaurant, 43 Ahui St..............(808) 523-0955
Kincaid's Fish, Chop & Steak House,
    1050 Ala Moana Blvd. ....(808) 591-2005
Lotus Moon Restaurant, 120 Kaiulani Ave. ......(808) 922-5811
La Mer, 2199 Kalia Rd. ....(808) 923-2311
Parc Café, 2233 Helumoa Rd.............................(808) 921-7272
The Secret, 2552 Kalakaua Ave.........................(808) 922-6611
Sergio's Italian Restaurant, 445 Nohonani St. ..(808) 926-3388
Singha Thai Cuisine, 1910 Ala Moana Blvd. ...(808) 941-2898
Surf Room, 2259 Kalakaua Ave. ....(808) 931-7194
Takanawa Sushi Bar & Restaurant,
    100 Holomoana St.......................................(808) 956-1111
Tony Roma's, a Place for Ribs,
    1972 Kalakaua Ave......................................(808) 942-2121
Village Steak & Seafood, 2005 Kalia Rd. ....(808) 949-4321

HOUSTON, TX

Bistro Lancaster, 701 Texas Ave. ....(713) 228-9502
Brennan's, 3300 Smith St...................................(713) 522-9711
Confederate House, 2925 Wesleyan St..............(713) 622-1936
Damian's, 3011 Smith St....................................(713) 522-0439
Dong Ting, 611 Stuart St. ....(713) 527-0005
La Griglia, 2002 W. Gray St. ....(713) 526-4700
Hunan, 1800 Post Oak Blvd. ....(713) 965-0808
Maxim's, 3755 Richmond Ave...........................(713) 877-8899
Post Oak Grill, 1415 S. Post Oak Ln.................(713) 993-9966
La Réserve, 4 Riverway ....(713) 871-8181
River Oaks Grill, 2630 Westheimer Rd.............(713) 520-1738
Rivoli, 5636 Richmond Ave...............................(713) 789-1900
Rotisserie for Beef and Bird, 2200 Wilcrest Dr..(713) 977-9524
Vargo's, 2401 Fondren Rd. ....(713) 782-3888

INDIANAPOLIS, IN

Acapulco Joe's Mexican Restaurant,
    365 N. Illinois St. ....(317) 637-5160
Chancellor's Restaurant,
    850 W. Michigan St.....................................(317) 269-9000
Daruma Japanese Restaurant,
    3508 W. 86th St...(317) 875-9727
Del Frisco's Restaurant, 55 Monument Circle...(317) 687-8888
Durbin's, 7202 E. 21st St....................................(317) 352-1231
Eagle's Nest Restaurant, 1 S. Capitol Ave.........(317) 632-1234
Ellington's, 110 W. Washington St. ....(317) 236-1800
Fifth Quarter Steakhouse, 82nd St. &
    Allisonville Rd...(317) 577-9840
Iron Skillet Restaurant, 2489 W. 30th St. ....(317) 923-6353
Keystone Grill, 8650 Keystone Crossing ....(317) 848-5202

The Majestic Restaurant,
47 S. Pennsylvania St. ....(317) 636-5418
Marker Restaurant, 2544 Executive Dr..............(317) 381-6146
New Orleans House, 8845 Township Line Rd...(317) 872-9670
Norman's at Union Station, Union Station......(317) 269-2545
Pesto, An Italian Trattoria,
303 N. Alabama St. ....(317) 269-0715
Rick's Café Américain, Union Station..............(317) 634-6666
St. Elmo Steak House, 127 S. Illinois St. ....(317) 635-0636
Steak and Ale, 4830 W. 38th St. ....(317) 298-4400
Teller's Cage, 1 Indiana Sq................................(317) 266-5211

Kansas City, MO

The American Restaurant, 25th & Grand ....(816) 426-1133
Café Allegro, 1815 W. 39th St ....(816) 561-3663
Cascone's Restaurant and Lounge,
3733 N. Oak ....(816) 454-7977
Colony Steakhouse and Lobster Pot,
8821 State Line...(816) 333-5500
EBT Restaurant, 1310 Carondelet ....(816) 942-8870
Fedora Café And Bar, 210 W. 47th...................(816) 561-6565
Hereford House, 20th & Main...........................(816) 842-1080
Italian Gardens, 1110 Baltimore ....(816) 221-9311
The Majestic Steakhouse, 931 Broadway ....(816) 471-8484
Margarita's, 2829 Southwest Blvd......................(816) 931-4849
Parkway 600, 600 Ward Pkwy ....(816) 931-6600
The Peppercorn Duck Club, 2345 McGee St ...(816) 421-1234
Red Dragon House, 312 W. Eighth....................(816) 221-1388
The Rooftop Restaurant at the Ritz-Carlton,
401 Ward Pkwy. ....(816) 756-1500
Savoy Grill, Ninth & Central............................(816) 842-3890
Starker's Restaurant, 200 Nichols Rd. ....(816) 753-3565

Las Vegas, NV

Alpine Village Inn/Rathskeller,
3003 Paradise Rd. ....(702) 734-6888
André's, 401 S Sixth St......................................(702) 385-5016
Chin's, 3200 Las Vegas Blvd., S ....(702) 733-8899
Cipriani, 2790 E. Flamingo Rd. ....(702) 369-6711
Empress Court, 3570 Las Vegas Blvd., S............(702) 731-7110
Marrakech, 3900 Paradise Rd............................(702) 737-5611
Palm Restaurant, 3500 Las Vegas Blvd., S.........(702) 732-7256
Pegasus, 375 E. Harmon Ave. ....(702) 796-3300
Spago, 3500 Las Vegas Blvd., S........................(702) 369-6300

Los Angeles, CA

Azalea, 120 S. Los Angeles St............................(213) 253-9235
Brandy's, 3540 S. Figueroa St............................(213) 748-4141
Cardini, 930 Wilshire Blvd. ....(213) 227-3464
Checkers, 535 S. Grand Ave...............................(213) 624-0000
Engine Co. No. 28, 644 S Figueroa St...............(213) 624-6996
Epicentre, 200 S. Hill St. ....(213) 621-4455
Garden Grill, 120 S. Los Angeles St. ....(213) 629-1200
Grand Café, 251 S. Olive St. ....(213) 356-4155
McCormick & Schmick's, 633 W. Fifth St........(213) 629-1929
Mon Kee's Restaurant, 679 N. Spring St. ....(213) 628-6717
Pacific Dining Car, 1310 W. Sixth St................(213) 483-6000
Palm Terrace, 1020 S. Figueroa St. ....(213) 748-1291
The Sonora Café, 445 S. Figueroa St. ....(213) 857-1800
Stepps on the Court, 330 S. Hope St. ....(213) 626-0900
Tokyo Kaikan, 225 S. San Pedro St...................(213) 489-1333

Top of Five Grill, 404 S. Figueroa St. ....(213) 624-1000
Water Grill, 544 S. Grand Ave. ....(213) 891-0900

MEMPHIS, TN

Anderton's Seafood Restaurant & Oyster Bar,
   1901 Madison Ave. ....:...(901) 726-4010
The Butcher Shop Steakhouse,
   101 S. Front St. ....(901) 521-0856
Chez Phillippe, 149 Union Ave. ....(901) 529-4188
Dux, 149 Union Ave. ....(901) 529-4199
Justine's, 919 Coward Pl. ....(901) 527-9973
King's Palace Café, 162 Beale St. ....(901) 521-1851
Landry's Seafood House, 263 Wagner Pl. ....(901) 526-1966
Maxwell's, 948 S. Cooper St. ....(901) 725-1009
Owen Brennan's Restaurant,
   6150 Poplar Ave. ....(901) 761-0990
Paulette's, 2110 Madison Ave. ....(901) 726-5128
Sekisui of Japan, 50 Humphrey's Blvd. ....(901) 747-0001

MIAMI, FL

Alfredo the Original of Rome,
   4833 Collins Ave. ....(305) 532-3600
The Backstage Restaurant, 640 Ocean Dr. ....(305) 673-6181
Brasserie Le Coze, 2901 Florida Ave. ....(305) 444-9697
Café Savoy, 455 Ocean Dr. ....(305) 532-0200
The Forge, 432 Arthur Godfrey Rd. ....(305) 538-8533
House of India, 22 Merrick Way ....(305) 444-2348
Joe's Stone Crab Restaurant,
   227 Biscayne St. ....(305) 673-0365
Kampai Japanese Restaurant,
   801 S. Bayshore Dr. ....(305) 358-0511
La Paloma Restaurant, 10999 Biscayne Blvd. .....(305) 891-0505
Le Café Royal, 5800 Blue Lagoon Dr. ....(305) 264-4888
Portobello, 136 Collins Ave ....(305) 531-5535
Los Ranchos of Bayside, 401 Biscayne Blvd. ......(305) 375-8188
Ristorante La Bussola, 264 Giralda Ave. ....(305) 445-8783
Rodeo Grill, 2121 Ponce de Leon Blvd. ....(305) 447-6336
Rusty Pelican, 3201 Rickenbacker Cswy. ....(305) 361-3818
Shula's Steak House, Don Shula's
   Hotel & Golf Club ....(305) 822-2324
The Steak and Poodle Lounge,
   4441 Collins Ave. ....(305) 538-2000
Thai Toni, 890 Washington Ave. ....(305) 538-8424
Two Dragons, 350 Ocean Dr. ....(305) 361-2021

MILWAUKEE, WI

333 An American Restaurant,
   333 W. Kilbourn Ave. ....(414) 276-1234
The Anchorage,
   4700 N. Port Washington Rd. ....(414) 962-4710
Benson's Steakhouse, 509 W. Wisconsin Ave. ..(414) 271-7250
Boder's on the River, 11919 N. River Rd. ....(414) 242-0335
Cork & Cleaver, 5311 S. Howell Ave. ....(414) 481-2400
The English Room, 424 E. Wisconsin Ave. ....(414) 273-8222
Giovanni's Restaurant, 1683 N. Van Buren St. ..(414) 291-5600
Grenadier's, 747 N. Broadway ....(414) 276-0747
Harold's Restaurant, 4747 S. Howell Ave. ....(414) 481-8000
John Ernst Café, 600 E. Ogden Ave. ....(414) 273-1878
Main Street Bistro, 340 Main St. ....(414) 637-4340
Nantucket Shores, 924 E. Juneau Ave. ....(414) 278-8660
Pieces of Eight, 550 N. Harbor Dr. ....(414) 271-0597

Polaris Revolving Restaurant and Lounge,
   333 W. Kilbourn Ave.............................(414) 276-1234
Siam Restaurant, 314 W. Juneau Ave...............(414) 272-4933
Szechwan House, 330 E. Kilbourn Ave. ....(414) 272-1688
Third Street Pier Restaurant,
   1110 N. Old World Third St.........................(414) 272-0330
Top of the Plaza, 111 E. Wisconsin Ave. ....(414) 271-5333
Toy's Chinatown Restaurant,
   830 Old World Third St................................(414) 271-5166

MINNEAPOLIS, MN

Anthony's Wharf, 201 Main St., SE.................(612) 378-7058
Basil's Restaurant, 710 Marquette Ave ....(612) 376-7404
Figlio, 3001 Hennepin Ave ....(612) 822-1688
Goodfellow's, 800 Nicollet Mall ....(612) 332-4800
Ichiban Japanese Steakhouse,
   1333 Nicollet Mall ....(612) 339-0540
Jax Cafe, 1928 University Ave., NE ....(612) 789-7297
J. D. Hoyt's, 301 Washington Ave., N..............(612) 338-1560
Manny's Steakhouse, 1300 Nicollet Mall ....(612) 339-9900
Murray's Restaurant, 26 S. Sixth St..................(612) 339-0909
Ping's Szechuan Bar & Grill,
   1401 Nicollet Ave.......................................(612) 874-9404
Sawatdee Thai Restaurant,
   607 Washington Ave. ....(612) 338-6451

NASHVILLE, TN

Antonio's of Nashville,
   7097 Old Harding Rd. ....(615) 646-9166
Arthur's, 1001 Broadway ....(615) 255-1494
Belle Meade Brasserie, 101 Page Rd. ....(615) 356-5450
Capitol Grille,
   231 Sixth Ave., N...(615) 244-3121
Demetri's, 3415 West End Ave. ....(615) 385-1929
F. Scott's, 2210 Crestmoor ....(615) 269-5861
Jimmy Kelly's Restaurant, 217 Louise Ave. ....(615) 329-4349
Kobe Steaks Japanese Restaurant,
   210 25th Ave., N...(615) 327-9081
The Merchants, 401 Broadway ....(615) 254-1892
Mére Bulles, 152 Second Ave., N. ....(615) 256-1946
Mozzarella's Café, 2817 West End Ave. ....(615) 327-9610
Pinnacle, Crowne Plaza, 623 Union St. ....(615) 259-2000
The Prime Cut Steakhouse,
   170 Second Ave., N..(615) 242-3083
Valentino's, 1907 West End Ave........................(615) 327-0148

NEW ORLEANS, LA

Andrea's Restaurant, 3100 19th St. ....(504) 834-8583
Bayou Ridge Café, 437 Esplanade ....(504) 949-9912
Bella Luna, 914 N. Peters....................................(504) 529-1583
Brennan's Restaurant, 417 Royal St...................(504) 525-9713
Café Lafayette, Bourbon Orleans Hotel,
   717 Orleans St. ....(504) 523-2222
Crescent City Steak House,
   1001 N. Broad St. ....(504) 821-3271
K-Paul's Louisiana Kitchen, 416 Chartres St.....(504) 596-2530
Kristal Seafood Cajun Café at Jackson Brewery,
   600 Decatur St..(504) 522-0336
Mike Anderson's Seafood Restaurant and Oyster Bar,
   215 Bourbon St...(504) 524-3884

Patout's Cajun Cabin Restaurant,
501 Bourbon St...(504) 529-4256
Ruth's Chris Steak House, 711 N. Broad St ......(504) 486-0810
Shogun Japanese Restaurant,
2325 Veterans Blvd...(504) 833-7477

New York, NY

21 Club, 21 W. 52nd St.......................................(212) 582-7200
Arizona 206 and Café, 206 E. 60th St. ....(212) 838-0440
Carnegie Deli, 854 Seventh Ave. ....(212) 757-2245
Golden Unicorn, 18 E. Broadway ....(212) 941-0911
Gotham Bar and Grill, 12 E. 12th St. ....(212) 620-4020
Jojo, 160 E. 64th St. ....(212) 223-5656
Le Bernardin, 155 W. 51st St..............................(212) 489-1515
Le Cirque, 58 E. 65th St. ....(212) 794-9292
Lutèce, 249 E. 50th St...(212) 752-2225
Montrachet, 239 W. Broadway ....(212) 219-2777
Palio, 151 W. 51st St..(212) 245-4850
Palm Restaurant, 837 Second Ave.....................(212) 687-2953
Pétrossian, 182 W. 58th St..................................(212) 245-2214
Restaurant Aquavit, 13 W. 54th St. ....(212) 307-7311
Rosa Mexicano, 1063 First Ave. ....(212) 753-7407
The Russian Tea Room, 150 W. 57th St. ....(212) 265-0947
The Sea Grill, 19 W. 49th St................................(212) 246-9201
Tribeca Grill, 375 Greenwich St.........................(212) 941-3900
Union Square Café, 21 E. 16th St. ....(212) 243-4020

Norfolk, VA

Antiquities, Norfolk Airport Hilton..................(804) 466-8000
Captain George's Seafood Restaurant,
1956 Laskin Rd. ....(804) 428-3494
Captain John's Seafood Company,
4616 Virginia Beach Blvd...............................(804) 499-7755
Duck In Waterfront Restaurant,
Shore Dr. at Lynhaven Inlet...........................(804) 481-0201
Freemason Abbey, 209 W. Freemason ....(804) 622-3966
La Galleria Ristorante, 120 College Pl ....(804) 623-3939
Henry's Seafood Restaurant, 3319 Shore Dr......(804) 481-7300
Lynnhaven Fish House Restaurant,
Shore Dr. and Starfish Rd. ....(804) 481-0003
Magnolia Steak,
Corner of Colley Ave. & Princess Anne Rd. (804) 625-0400
Nawab, 888 N. Military Hwy. ....(804) 455-8080
Phillips Waterside, 333 Waterside Dr. ....(804) 627-6600
Il Porto Ristorante, 333 Waterside Dr. ....(804) 627-4400
Rudee's on the Inlet, 227 Mediterranean Ave...(804) 425-1777
Shine Shine Palace, 333 Waterside Dr. ....(804) 623-0778
Ships Cabin, 4110 E. Ocean View Ave. ....(804) 362-4659

Oklahoma City, OK

Bellini's, 63rd and Pennsylvania ....(405) 848-1065
Cattlemen's Steakhouse, 1309 S. Agnew ....(405) 236-0416
Don Serapio's, 11109 N. May ....(405) 755-1664
Eagle's Nest, 5900 Mosteller Dr. ....(405) 840-5655
Molly Murphy's House of Fine Repute,
I-40 & Meridian ....(405) 942-8588
Outback Steakhouse, I-240 & Penn ....(405) 686-0918
Pearls Oyster Bar, 928 NW 63rd.......................(405) 848-8008
Texanna Red's, Reno & Meridian.......................(405) 947-8665
Trappers Fishcamp & Grill, Reno & Meridian..(405) 943-9111

The Waterford Dining Room,
6300 Waterford Blvd. ....(405) 848-4782

ORLANDO, FL

Arthur's 27, 1900 Buena Vista Dr. ....(407) 827-3450
Chalet Suzanne Restaurant & Inn,
3800 Chalet Suzanne Dr..............................(813) 676-6011
Christini's Ristorante Italiano,
7600 Dr., Phillips Blvd. ....(407) 345-8770
Le Cordon Bleu, 537 W. Fairbanks Ave. ....(407) 647-7575
Dux, The Peabody Hotel Orlando,
9801 International Dr....................................(407) 352-4000
Gran Cru Restaurant, 1500 Sand Lake Rd........(800) 231-7883
Hemingway's, Hyatt Regency Grand Cypress,
1 Grand Cypress Blvd..................................(407) 239-1234
Lando's, 60 S. Ivanhoe Blvd..............................(407) 425-4455
Maison & Jardin Restaurant,
430 Wymore Rd. ....(407) 862-4410
Ming Court Restaurant,
9188 International Dr....................................(407) 351-9988
Park Plaza Gardens, 319 S. Park Ave.................(407) 645-2475
Parramore House Cafe, 625 Main St. ....(407) 876-5666
Passage to India, 5532 International Dr.............(407) 351-3456
Ran-Getsu of Tokyo, 8400 International Dr......(407) 345-0044
Ruth's Chris Steak House, 999 Douglas Ave.....(407) 682-6444
Tuscany's Ristorante, Marriott's Orlando World Center,
1 World Center Dr..(407) 239-4200

PHILADELPHIA, PA

Artful Dodger Beef & Ale House,
400-402 S. Second St. ....(215) 922-7880
Bistro Romano, 120 Lombard St........................(215) 925-8880
Blue Moon Jazz Club & Restaurant,
Fourth St. bet. Market & Chestnut Sts. ....(215) 413-2272
Bookbinders 15th St. Seafood House,
215 S. 15th St..(215) 545-1137
City Tavern, Second & Walnut St. ....(215) 413-1443
Cutter's Grand Café, 2005 Market St................(215) 851-6262
Deux Cheminees, 1221 Locust St......................(215) 790-0200
Dickens Inn,
Second St. bet. Pine & Lombard St...............(215) 928-9307
DiNardo's Famous Crabs, 312 Race St...............(215) 925-5115
The Garden, 1617 Spruce St ....(215) 546-4455
The Happy Rooster, 118 S 16th St....................(215) 563-1481
Jack's Firehouse, 2130 Fairmount Ave. ....(215) 232-9000
London Grill, 2301 Fairmount Ave. ....(215) 978-4545
Palm Restaurant, 200 S Broad St.......................(215) 546-7256
Rembrandt's Restaurant and Bar,
23rd & Aspen Sts. ....(215) 763-2228
Rib-It, 1709 Walnut St......................................(215) 568-1555
Rock Lobster,
Pier 13-15 on Christopher Columbus Blvd. ..(215) 627-7625
Sala Thai, 700-02 S. Fifth St. ....(215) 922-4990
San Marco, 27 City Line Ave. ....(610) 664-7844
Susanna Foo, 1512 Walnut St...........................(215) 545-2666
Tang Yean, 220 N. Tenth St. ....(215) 925-3993

PHOENIX, AZ

Christopher's and The Bistro,
2398 E. Camelback Rd. ....(602) 957-3214

Different Pointe of View,
    11111 N. Seventh St. ....(602) 863-0912
Durant's Restaurant, 2611 N. Central Ave........(602) 264-5967
The Fish Market Restaurant,
    1720 E. Camelback Rd. ....(602) 277-3474
New Mandarin Delight, 5380 N. Seventh St....(602) 274-5204
Oscar Taylor, Butcher, Bakery & Bar,
    2420 E. Camelback Rd. ....(602) 956-5705
Pink Pepper Cuisine of Thailand,
    245 E. Bell Rd...(602) 548-1333
Pointe in Tyme Restaurant,
    11111 N. Seventh St. ....(602) 866-6348
Ristorante Pronto, 3950 E. Campbell Ave. ....(602) 956-4049
Rusty Pelican Restaurant,
    9801-A N. Black Canyon Fwy. ....(602) 944-9646
Stockyards Restaurant,
    5001 E. Washington St..................................(602) 273-7378
Vincent Guerithault on Camelback,
    3930 E. Camelback Rd. ....(602) 224-0225

PITTSBURGH, PA

Baum Vivant, 5102 Baum Blvd........................(412) 682-2620
Benkovitz Seafoods, 23rd & Smallman St.........(412) 263-3016
Cafe Azure, 317 S. Craig St. ....(412) 681-3533
Carmassi's Tuscany Grill, 711 Penn Ave. ....(412) 281-6644
Frenchy's, 136 Sixth St.....................................(412) 261-6476
Georgine's, 164 Ft. Couch Rd. ....(412) 833-5300
Hyeholde Restaurant, Coraopolis Hts. Rd.........(412) 264-3116
Kleiner Deutschmann, 643 Pittsburgh St. ....(412) 274-5022
LeMont Restaurant, 1114 Grandview Ave........(412) 431-3100
Liang's Hunan Chinese Restaurant,
    1001 Liberty Ave. ....(412) 471-1688
Louis Tambellini's Restaurant,
    860 Saw Mill Run Blvd. ....(412) 481-1118
Mallorca Restaurant, 2228 E. Carson St............(412) 488-1818
Montemurro's Restaurant, 1822 Main St...........(412) 781-6800
Morton's of Chicago, 625 Liberty Ave..............(412) 261-7141
Original Oyster House, 20 Market Sq ....(412) 566-7925
Ruth's Chris Steak House, 6 PPG Pl ....(412) 391-4800
Samurai Steak and Seafood House,
    2100 Greentree Rd. ....(412) 276-2100
Top of the Triangle, 600 Grant St. ....(412) 471-4100

PORTLAND, OR

Alessandro's Fine Italian Restaurant & Lounge,
    301 SW Morrison St......................................(503) 222-3900
Atwater's Restaurant & Lounge,
    111 SW Fifth Ave..(503) 275-3600
L'Auberge Restaurant,
    2601 NW Vaughn St.....................................(503) 223-3302
B. Moloch/The Heathman Bakery & Pub,
    901 SW Salmon St..(503) 227-5700
Benihana, 9205 SW Cascade Ave. ....(503) 643-4016
Bush Garden Restaurant,
    900 SW Morrison St......................................(503) 226-7181
Cascade Dining Room at Timberline Lodge......(503) 231-7979
Cityside Restaurant, 310 SW Lincoln St...........(503) 221-0450
Genoa, 2832 SE Belmont St. ....(503) 238-1464
The Heathman Restaurant & Bar,
    1009 SW Broadway ....(503) 241-4100

Henry Ford's Restaurant,
9589 SW Barbur Blvd.....................................(503) 245-2434
The London Grill, 309 SW Broadway...............(503) 295-4110
Maxi's Seafood Restaurant & Lounge,
909 N. Hayden Island Dr............................(503) 283-4466
The Olive Garden Italian Resturant,
11650 SW Canyon Rd. ....(503) 644-0607
Red Lion Grille, 1225 N. Thunderbird..............(503) 235-8311
Salty's on the Columbia,
3839 NE Marine Dr......................................(503) 288-4444
Wilf's Restaurant & Piano Bar,
800 NW Sixth Ave.......................................(503) 223-0070
Zefiro Restaurant, 500 NW 21st Ave. ....(503) 226-3394

PROVIDENCE, RI

Agora, 1 W. Exchange St. ....(401) 598-8000
Barnsider's Mile & A Quarter,
375 S. Main St..(401) 351-7300
Bluepoint Oyster Bar & Restaurant,
99 N. Main St...(401) 272-6145
Capital Grille, 1 Cookson Pl.............................(401) 521-5600
Capriccio, 2 Pine St...(401) 421-1320
Carrie's Seafood Bar & Grill,
1035 Douglas Ave.......................................(401) 831-0066
The Gatehouse, 4 Richmond St. ....(401) 521-9229
Hemenway's Seafood Grille & Oyster Bar,
1 Old Stone Sq ....(401) 351-8570
Montana, 272 Thayer St. ....(401) 273-7427
New Japan Restaurant, 145 Washington St. .....(401) 351-0300
New Rivers Restaurant, 7 Steeple St.................(401) 751-0350
Pot au Feu, 44 Custom House ....(401) 273-8953
Rue de l'espoir, 99 Hope St...............................(401) 751-8890

RALEIGH, NC

42nd Street Oyster Bar
508 West Jones St.......................................(919) 831-2811
The Angus Barn,
Raleigh-Durham Hwy. at Airport Rd.............(919) 787-3505
Capital City Club, 411 Fayetteville St. Mall.....(919) 832-5526
The Carriage Club at the Plantation Inn,
6401 Capital Blvd.......................................(919) 876-1411
Carvers Creek, 2711 Capital Blvd. ....(919) 872-2300
The Fox & Hound, 107 Edinburgh S.. ....(919) 380-0080
Kanki Japanese House of Steaks,
4500 Old Wake Forest Rd. ....(919) 876-4157
Tartine's French Restaurant,
1110 Navaho Dr. ....(919) 790-0091
Winston's Grille, 6401 Falls of the Neuse Rd....(919) 790-0700

SACRAMENTO, CA

Chanterelle, 1300 H St. ....(916) 442-0451
Chinois East/West, 2232 Fair Oaks Blvd. ....(916) 648-1961
The Firehouse, 1112 2nd St. ....(916) 442-4772
Frank Fat's, 806 L St...(916) 442-7092
Ming Palace, 3405 Watt....................................(916) 489-9350
Pilothouse, 1000 Front St..................................(916) 441-4440
Terrace Grill, 544 Pavilions Ln ....(916) 920-3800
Tower Café, Land Pk. & Broadway...................(916) 441-0222

ST. LOUIS, MO

Al's Restaurant, 1200 N. 1st St..........................(314) 421-6399
Café de France, 410 Olive St. ....(314) 231-2204

DeMenil Restaurant, 3352 DeMenil Pl. ....(314) 771-5829
Dierdorf & Hart's, 1820 Market St. ....(314) 421-1772
Gianpeppe's, 2126 Marconi Ave ....(314) 772-3303
Harry's Restaurant and Bar, 2144 Market St. ....(314) 421-6969
Hunter's Hollow Inn & Restaurant,
   Washington & Front St................................(314) 458-3326
J. F. Sanfilippo's, 705 N. Broadway ....(314) 621-7213
Kreis' Restaurant, 535 S. Lindbergh ....(314) 993-0735
Lombardo's Trattoria, 201 S. 20th....................(314) 621-0666
Morton's of Chicago, 7822 Bonhomme ....(314) 725-4008
Robata of Japan, 111 Westport Plaza.................(314) 434-1007
Ruth's Chris Steak House, 101 S. 11th St.........(314) 241-7711
Sidney Street Café, 2000 Sidney St...................(314) 771-5777
Tango Grill, 255 N. Union ....(314) 361-4399

Salt Lake City, UT

Allie's Pantry, 75 S. West Temple ....(801) 531-0800
Bangkok Thai, 1400 S. Foothill Dr....................(801) 582-8424
Diamond Lil's, 1528 W. North Temple..............(801) 533-0547
Eibo's Mesquite Broiler, 300 Trolley Sq ....(801) 531-7788
Ferrantelli Ristorante Italiano,
   300 Trolley Sq...(801) 531-8228
JW's, 75 S. West Temple ....(801) 531-0800
Kwan's Downtown Chinese Restaurant,
   139 E. Sout Temple ....(801) 328-8369
Log Haven, 4 miles up Millcreek Canyon ....(801) 272-8255
Market Street Grill, 48 Market St. ....(801) 322-4668
Maxi's, 255 S. West Temple ....(801) 328-2000
The Mexican Keyhole and La Cantina,
   Snowbird Ski and Summer Resort ....(801) 521-6040
Mikado Japanese Restaurant,
   67 W. 100 South ....(801) 328-0929
Ocean's Restaurant, 4760 S. 900 East...............(801) 261-0115
Le Parisien, 417 S. 300 East ....(801) 364-5223
Peppercorn Steakhouse, 343 E. 500 South........(801) 328-4545
The Roof Restaurant, 15 E. South Temple........(801) 539-1911
Room at the Top, 150 W. 500 South ....(801) 532-3344
Santa Fe Restaurant,
   2100 Emigration Canyon ....(801) 582-5888

San Antonio, TX

Anaqua Grill, 555 S. Alamo............................(210) 229-1000
Boudro's, A Texas Bistro,
   421 E. Commerce St......................................(210) 224-8484
Chez Ardid, 1919 San Pedro Ave. ....(210) 732-3203
L'Etoile, 6106 Broadway St................................(210) 826-4551
Fig Tree Restaurant, 515 Villita St....................(210) 224-1976
Fujiya Japanese Garden,
   4315 Fredericksburg Rd. ....(210) 734-3551
Polo's at the Fairmount, 401 S. Alamo..............(210) 224-8800
Ruffino's, 9802 Colonnade Blvd. ....(210) 641-6100

San Diego, CA

Azzura Point, Loews Coronado Bay Resort,
   4000 Coronado Bay Rd. ....(619) 424-4000
Baci's, 1955 Morena Blvd..................................(619) 275-2094
Beyond, 618 Fifth Ave. ....(619) 238-2328
Dakota Grill & Spirits, 901 Fifth Ave. ....(619) 234-5554
Dobson's Bar & Restaurant,
   956 Broadway Circle.................................(619) 231-6771
The Grant Grill, 326 Broadway ....(619) 239-6806

Humphrey's La Jolla Grill, 3299 Holiday Ct. ....(619) 587-0056
Marius, Le Meridien San Diego at Coronado,
    2000 Second St...(619) 435-3000
Miguel's Point Loma, 2912 Shelter Island Dr. ....(619) 224-2401
Mille Fleurs, 6009 Paseo Delicias.......................(619) 756-3085
Trattoria La Strada, Cucina Toscana,
    702 Fifth Ave. ....(619) 239-3400

San Francisco, CA

Acquerello, 1722 Sacramento St. at Van Ness..(415) 567-5432
Bardelli's Restaurant,
    243 O'Farrell St. ....(415) 982-0243
Big Four Restaurant, 1075 California St............(415) 771-1140
Carnelian Room, 555 California St. ....(415) 433-7500
City of Paris Restaurant and Bar,
    101 Shannon Alley..(415) 441-4442
Cypress Club, 500 Jackson St...........................(415) 296-8555
Dante's Italian Seafood Restaurant,
    Pier 39 (Fisherman's Wharf) ....(415) 421-5778
Ernie's Restaurant, 847 Montgomery St. ....(415) 397-5969
Garden Court, 2 New Montgomery St. ....(415) 546-5010
Imperial Palace, 919 Grant Ave........................(415) 982-8889
Iron Horse Restaurant, 19 Maiden Ln. ....(415) 362-8133
Kyo-Ya, New Montgomery St. at Jessie ....(415) 392-8600
Morton's of Chicago, 404 Post St. ....(415) 986-5830
Park Grill, 333 Battery St..................................(415) 296-2933
Tommy Toy's Cuisine Chinoise,
    655 Montgomery St.......................................(415) 397-4888
Venticello, 1257 Taylor St. ....(415) 922-2545
Vertigo Restaurant and Bar,
    600 Montgomery St. ....(415) 433-7250
Victor's, Westin St. Francis & 335 Powell St ....(415) 956-7777
Wu Kong Restaurant, 101 Spear St. ....(415) 957-9300

Seattle, WA

Anthony's Home Port Shilshole Bay,
    6135 Seaview Ave., W ....(206) 783-0780
Asgard, At the Top of the Hilton,
    Sixth & University ....(206) 624-0500
Campagne, 86 Pine St.......................................(206) 728-2800
Canlis Restaurant, 2576 Aurora Ave., N...........(206) 283-3313
Chandler's Crabhouse & Fresh Fish Market,
    901 Fairview Ave., N......................................(206) 223-2722
Chez Shea, 94 Pike St. ....(206) 467-9990
The Cloud Room, 1619 Ninth Ave...................(206) 682-0100
F. X. McRory's Steak, Chop & Oyster House,
    419 Occidental Ave. S ....(206) 623-4800
Ivar's Acres of Clams, Pier 54, Waterfront ....(206) 624-6852
Japanese Cuisine Tatsumi,
    4214 University Way......................................(206) 548-9319
Linyen Restaurant & Cocktail Lounge,
    424 Seventh Ave. S..(206) 622-8181
Metropolitan Grill, Second & Marion ....(206) 624-3287
The Palm Court, 1900 Fifth Ave. ....(206) 728-1000
Pescatore, 5300 34th NW ....(206) 784-1733
Ponti Seafood Grill, 3014 Third Ave., N ....(206) 284-3000
Ray's Boathouse, 6049 Seaview NW ....(206) 789-3770
Umberto's Ristorante,
    1001 Fourth Ave., Suite 50 ....(206) 621-0575

TAMPA, FL

Armani's, Hyatt Regency Westshore,
  6200 Courtney Campbell Cswy ....(813) 281-9165
Bern's Steak House,
  1208 S. Howard Ave..(813) 251-2421
Café Creole, 1330 E. Ninth Ave........................(813) 247-6283
The Castaways,
  7720 Courtney Campbell Causeway ....(813) 281-0770
The Colonnade Restaurant,
  3401 Bayshore Blvd. ....(813) 839-7558
Columbia Restaurant, 2117 E. Seventh Ave.....(813) 248-4961
Donatello, 232 North Dale Mabry Hwy. ....(813) 875-6660
Lauro Ristorante Italiano,
  3915 Henderson Blvd ....(813) 281-2100
Rusty Pelican, 2425 Rocky Point Dr ....(813) 281-1943
Samurai Japanese Steak House,
  1901 13th St. ....(813) 248-5829
Shula's Steak House, Sheraton Grand Hotel.....(813) 286-4400
Valencia Gardens,
  811 W. Kennedy Blvd.....................................(813) 253-3773
Westshore Grille, Tampa Marriott Westshore ...(813) 287-2555

WASHINGTON, DC

101 Royal Steakhouse, 480 King St..................(703) 549-6080
1789 Restaurant, 1226 36th St., NW ....(202) 965-1789
America Restaurant, Union Station,
  50 Massachusetts Ave., NE ....(202) 682-9555
Café Pierre, 480 L'Enfant Plaza, SW.................(202) 646-4433
Celadon, 1331 Pennsylvania Ave., NW............(202) 393-2000
La Chaumiere, 2813 M St., NW.......................(202) 338-1784
Coeur de Lion, 926 Massachusetts Ave., NW ...(202) 638-5200
Filomena Ristorante,
  1063 Wisconsin Ave., NW.............................(202) 338-8800
Galileo, 1110 21st St., NW..............................(202) 293-7191
Hunan Chinatown, 624 H St., NW ....(202) 783-5858
Jean-Louis Chaumiére,
  2650 Virginia Ave., NW ....(202) 298-4488
Lafayette Restaurant, 16th and H St., NW ....(202) 638-6600
Market Inn, 200 E St., SW ....(202) 554-2100
Montpelier, 15th & M St., NW.........................(202) 862-1600
Nicholas, 1127 Connecticut Ave., NW ....(202) 347-8900
The Occidental Grill,
  1475 Pennsylvania Ave., NW ....(202) 783-1475
Paolo's, 1305 Wisconsin Ave., NW ....(202) 333-7353
Petitto's Ristorante d'Italia,
  2653 Connecticut Ave., NW ....(202) 667-5350
Red Sage, 605 14th St., NW............................(202) 638-4444
Signature Room, 525 New Jersey Ave., NW.....(202) 628-2100
Willard Room, 1401 Pennsylvania Ave., NW...(202) 637-7440

WEST PALM BEACH, FL

Atlantis Country Club, 190 Atlantis Blvd. ....(407) 965-7700
Bohemian Garden, 5450 Lake Worth Rd..........(407) 968-4111
Café Chardonnay,
  PGA Blvd. and Military Trail ....(407) 627-2662
Café du Parc, 612 N Federal Hwy. Lake Park....(407) 845-0529
India Garden Restaurant, 7504 S. Dixie Hwy. ..(407) 586-9579
Morton's of Chicago, 777 S. Flagler Dr.............(407) 835-9664
Orchids of Siam, 3027 Forest Hill Blvd............(407) 969-2444
Toucan's Top of the Dock,
  201 Fisherman's Wharf.................................(407) 465-1334

Miscellaneous

Stadiums/Arenas/Convention Centers

ANCHORAGE, AK

Alaska Center for the Performing Arts.............(907) 263-2900
Sullivan Arena ....(907) 279-0618

ATLANTA, GA

Atlanta Civic Center ....(404) 523-6275
Atlanta Fulton County Stadium ....(404) 522-1967
Fox Theatre ....(404) 881-2100
Georgia Dome..(404) 223-9200
Georgia World Congress Center ....(404) 223-4000
The Omni ....(404) 681-2100

ATLANTIC CITY, NJ

Atlantic City Convention Center ....(609) 348-7001
Caesar's Atlantic City ....(609) 343-2535

BALTIMORE, MD

Baltimore Arena...(410) 347-2020
Baltimore Convention Center ....(410) 659-7000
Lyric Opera House ....(410) 685-5086
Oriole Park at Camden Yards.............................(410) 576-0300
USAir Arena ....(301) 808-3030

BOSTON, MA

Bayside Exposition Center ....(617) 825-5151
Berklee Performance Center ....(617) 262-4998
Fenway Park...(617) 267-9440
John B. Hynes Convention Center ....(617) 954-2000
New Boston Garden Corporation ....(617) 227-3200
World Trade Center..(617) 439-5000

BUFFALO, NY

Buffalo Convention Center...............................(716) 855-5555
Kleinhans Music Hall..(716) 883-3560

CHARLOTTE, NC

Blockbuster Pavilion..(704) 549-1292
Bonnie E. Cone University Center....................(704) 547-2267
Charlotte Auditorium ....(704) 357-4700
Charlotte Convention Center ....(704) 332-5051
Independence Arena ....(704) 372-3600
North Carolina Performing Arts Center ....(704) 333-4686
Ovens Auditorium...(704) 372-3600

CHICAGO, IL

Arie Crown Theatre..(312) 791-6516
Auditorium Theatre ....(312) 341-2395
Comiskey Park..(312) 924-1000
McCormick Place Complex ....(312) 791-7500
Rosemont Horizon..(708) 635-6601
U.I.C. Pavilion ....(312) 413-5700
United Center ....(312) 451-5519
Wrigley Field..(312) 404-4076

CINCINNATI, OH

Cincinnati Gardens...(513) 631-7793
Cincinnati Music Hall...(513) 621-1919
Memorial Hall ....(513) 241-6924
Myrl Shoemaker Center.....................................(513) 556-2170
Ohio Center for the Arts ....(513) 241-3344

Riverfront Coliseum ....(513) 241-8500
Riverfront Stadium...(513) 352-5400

CLEVELAND, OH

Cleveland Convention Center ....(216) 348-2211
Cleveland Stadium ....(216) 696-2700
CSU Convocation Center .... (216) 687-9292
Gateway Arena..(216) 420-2000
International Exposition Center ....(216) 676-6000
Playhouse Square Center...................................(216) 771-4444

COLUMBUS, OH

Columbus Convention Center...........................(614) 221-6700
Franklin County Veterans Memorial ....(614) 221-4341
Ohio Exposition Center ....(614) 644-4000

DALLAS, TX

Coca-Cola Starplex Amphitheater....................(214) 421-1111
Dallas Convention Center ....(214) 939-2700
Dallas Market Center/Market Hall ....(214) 748-1023
Majestic Theatre...(214) 880-0137
McFarlin Memorial Auditorium ....(214) 768-3129
Music Hall Fair Park..(214) 565-1116
Reunion Arena ....(214) 939-2770

DENVER, CO

Auraria Event Center...(303) 556-3437
Boettcher Concert Hall......................................(303) 640-2862
Buell Theatre ....(303) 640-2862
Denver Coliseum ....(303) 640-2637
McNichols Sports Arena....................................(303) 640-7300
Mile High Stadium...(303) 458-4850
National Western Complex ....(303) 297-1166

DETROIT, MI

Cobo Arena ....(313) 567-6000
The Fox Theatre...(313) 965-7100
Joe Louis Arena ....(313) 396-7600
Pontiac Silverdome ....(810) 858-7358
Tiger Stadium ....(313) 962-4000

GRAND RAPIDS, MI

Ford Fieldhouse...(616) 771-3990
Grand Center ....(616) 456-3922
Wings Stadium ....(616) 345-1125

GREENVILLE, SC

Greenville Memorial Auditorium......................(803) 241-3800
Greenville Municipal Stadium...........................(803) 299-3456
Knights Stadium ....(803) 548-8051

HARTFORD, CT

Hartford Civic Center..(203) 249-6333
Lincoln Theater...(203) 768-4536
New Haven Veterans Memorial Coliseum ....(203) 772-4200

HONOLULU, HI

Aloha Stadium ....(808) 486-9500
Neal S. Blaisdell Center.....................................(808) 527-5400

HOUSTON, TX

Astrodome USA..(713) 799-9731
George R. Brown Convention Center...............(713) 853-8000

Miscellaneous

Houston Arena Theatre ....(713) 988-2381
Jesse H. Jones Hall for the Performing Arts ......(713) 853-8000
Music Hall ....(713) 247-2592
Sam Houston Coliseum......................................(713) 247-2592
The Summit..(713) 627-9470
Tower Theater Operating Company ....(713) 439-5774
Wortham Theatre Center ....(713) 237-1439

INDIANAPOLIS, IN

Indiana Convention Center & Hoosier Dome..(317) 262-3410
Indiana State Fairgrounds Event Center ....(317) 927-7501
Market Square Arena ....(317) 639-6411

KANSAS CITY, MO

Arrowhead Stadium ....(816) 921-3600
Kauffman Stadium..(816) 921-2200
Kemper Arena/American Royal Center ....(816) 274-6711

LAS VEGAS, NV

Cashman Field Center.......................................(702) 386-7100
MGM Grand...(702) 891-2800
Performing Arts Center.....................................(702) 895-4712
Sands Expo & Convention Center....................(702) 733-5556
Thomas and Mack Center..................................(702) 895-3727

LOS ANGELES, CA

Dodger Stadium..(213) 224-1351
Greek Theatre ....(213) 665-5857
Los Angeles Sports Arena/Memorial Coliseum.(213) 748-6136
Music Center of L.A. County ....(213) 972-7200
Shrine Auditorium & Exposition Center..........(213) 748-5116

MEMPHIS, TN

Memphis Cook Convention Center...................(901) 576-1200
Mid-South Coliseum ....(901) 274-3982
The Pyramid Arena...(901) 521-9675

MIAMI, FL

Dade County Auditorium ....(305) 547-5414
Golden Panther Arena.......................................(305) 348-3258
James L. Knight Center/Convention Center.....(305) 372-0277
Joe Robbie Stadium...(305) 623-6100
Miami Arena ....(305) 530-4400

MILWAUKEE, WI

Bradley Center..(414) 227-0400
Milwaukee County Stadium..............................(414) 933-4114
Milwaukee Exposition Center...........................(414) 271-4000

MINNEAPOLIS, MN

Hubert H. Humphrey Metrodome ....(612) 332-0386
Orchestra Hall ....(612) 371-5600
St. Paul Civic Center ....(612) 224-7361
Target Center...(612) 673-1350

NASHVILLE, TN

Gentry Complex...(615) 320-3173
Grand Ole Opry House ....(615) 889-7502
Nashville Municipal Auditorium......................(615) 862-6392
Tennessee Performing Arts Center ....(615) 741-7975

NEW ORLEANS, LA

Louisiana Superdome ....(504) 587-3663

New Orleans Cultural Center ....(504) 565-7470
Saenger Performing Arts Center......................(504) 525-1052
Tad Gormley Stadium/Alerion Field.................(504) 482-4888
UNO Lakefront Arena ....(504) 286-7171

NEW YORK, NY

Brooklyn Center for the Performing Arts..........(718) 951-5296
Carnegie Hall ....(212) 903-9601
Lincoln Center/Avery Fisher Hall ....(212) 875-5000
Madison Square Garden ....(212) 465-6200
Radio City Music Hall......................................(212) 632-4000
USTA National Tennis Center.........................(718) 592-8000
Yankee Stadium ....(718) 579-4440

NORFOLK, VA

Hampton Coliseum ....(804) 838-5650
Norfolk Scope...(804) 441-2764
Pavilion/Virginia Beach Convention Center ....(804) 428-8000

OKLAHOMA CITY, OK

Civic Center Music Hall ....(405) 297-2584
Myriad Convention Center................................(405) 297-3300
State Fair of Oklahoma ....(405) 948-6700

ORLANDO, FL

Ocean Center/Daytona Beach ....(904) 254-4500
Orange County Convention Center.................(407) 345-9800
Orlando Centroplex ....(407) 849-2000
Tupperware Convention Center ....(407) 826-4475
University of Central Florida Arena.................(407) 823-3070

PHILADELPHIA, PA

Academy of Music of Philadelphia ....(215) 893-1935
Philadelphia Civic Center................................(215) 823-5655
The Spectrum ....(215) 336-3600

PHOENIX, AZ

America West Arena..(602) 379-2000
Arizona Veterans Memorial Coliseum ....(602) 252-6771
Blockbuster Desert Sky Pavilion ....(602) 254-7200
Phoenix Civic Plaza/Municipal Stadium ....(602) 262-6225

PITTSBURGH, PA

A. J. Palumbo Center ....(412) 434-6058
Benedum Center for the Performing Arts ....(412) 456-2600
David L. Lawrence Convention Center ....(412) 565-6000
Heinz Hall for the Performing Arts ....(412) 392-4843
Pittsburgh Civic Arena ....(412) 642-1800
Three Rivers Stadium.......................................(412) 321-9411

PORTLAND, OR

Oregon Arena..(503) 235-8771
Oregon Convention Center..............................(503) 235-7575
Portland Center for the Performing Arts...........(503) 248-4335
Portland Memorial Coliseum ....(503) 235-8771

PROVIDENCE, RI

Providence Civic Center...................................(401) 331-0700
Providence Performing Arts Center ....(401) 421-2997
Roberts Auditorium..(401) 456-8194

RALEIGH, NC

J. S. Dorton Arena...(919) 733-2626

Raleigh Civic Center Complex..........................(919) 755-6011

SACRAMENTO, CA
ARCO Arena ....(916) 928-0000
Sacramento Community Center ....(916) 449-5291

ST. LOUIS, MO
Cervantes Convention/Exhibition Center ....(314) 342-5036
St. Louis Arena...(314) 644-0909

SALT LAKE CITY, UT
Delta Center ....(801) 325-2000
Jon M. Huntsman Center...................................(801) 581-5155

SAN ANTONIO, TX
Alamodome ....(210) 207-3602
Freeman Coliseum ....(210) 226-1177
Majestic Theatre...(210) 226-5700
Municipal Auditorium ....(210) 299-8515
San Antonio Convention Facilities...................(210) 299-8500

SAN DIEGO, CA
Open Air Theatre..(619) 594-6529
San Diego Concourse ....(619) 236-6500
San Diego Jack Murphy Stadium......................(619) 525-8266
San Diego Sports Arena....................................(619) 224-4171

SAN FRANCISCO, CA
Civic Auditorium ....(415) 974-4000
Cow Palace ....(415) 469-6000
Nob Hill Masonic Center ....(415) 776-7014
Oakland Alameda County Coliseum.................(510) 569-2121
San Francisco War Memorial............................(415) 621-6600
San Jose Arena ....(408) 999-5727

SEATTLE, WA
HEC Edmundson Pavilion ....(206) 543-2246
The Kingdome ....(206) 296-3151
Paramount Theatre..(206) 682-1414
Seattle Center...(206) 684-7202

TAMPA, FL
Bayfront Center/Mahaffey Theatre...................(813) 892-5798
Florida State Fairgrounds...................................(813) 621-7821
Sun Dome ....(813) 974-3111
Tampa Bay Lightning Arena ....(813) 229-2658
Tampa Bay Performing Arts Center...................(813) 222-1010
Tampa Stadium...(813) 870-3060
ThunderDome ....(813) 825-3100

WASHINGTON, DC
Charles E. Smith Center ....(202) 994-6650
D.C. Armory..(202) 547-9077
DAR Constitution Hall ....(202) 628-4780
John F. Kennedy Center ....(202) 416-8711
Lisner Auditorium ....(202) 994-6800
RFK Stadium ....(202) 547-9077
Washington Convention Center ....(202) 789-1600

WEST PALM BEACH, FL
Palm Beach Polo & Country Club Stadium......(407) 793-1440
West Palm Beach Auditorium............................(407) 683-6010

Credit Card Companies

All American Express lost or stolen ....(800) 992-3404
American Express...(800) 528-4800
American Express Gold Card...........................(800) 327-2177
Corporate American Express............................(800) 528-2122
Diners Club...(800) 234-6377
Discover ....(800) 347-2683
MasterCard ....(800) 826-2181
Optima...(800) 635-5955
Transmedia...(800) 422-5090
Visa ....(800) 336-8472

Credit Cards/Airline-Affiliated

American (Citibank) ....(800) 950-5114
America West (Bank of America) ....(800) 243-7762
Continental (Marine Midland)........................(800) 874-2100
Northwest (First Bank) ....(800) 360-2900
TWA (European-American Bank) ....(800) 322-8921
United (First National).....................................(800) 537-7783
USAir (NationsBank)..(800) 732-9194

Mutual Funds

AARP Investment Program ....(800) 322-2282
ABT Family of Funds ....(800) 553-7838
Acorn Investment Trust ....(800) 922-6769
Addison Group..(800) 526-6397
Advance Capital I Group..................................(800) 345-4783
Advantage Funds...(800) 241-2039
AIM Family of Funds...(800) 347-1919
Alger Group..(800) 992-3863
Alliance Capital Group......................................(800) 227-4618
American Funds Group ....(800) 421-4120
American Growth Fund ....(800) 525-2406
American Heritage Group..................................(800) 828-5050
American National Funds Group ....(800) 231-4639
American Pension Investors Trust ....(800) 544-6060
AmSouth Funds..(800) 451-8379
Amway Mutual Fund..(800) 346-2670
Analytic Optioned Equity Fund.......................(800) 374-2633
Babson Fund Group..(800) 422-2766
Bailard Biehl & Kaiser Group...........................(800) 882-8383
Baird Mutual Funds ....(800) 792-2473
Baron Asset Fund ....(800) 992-2766
Bartlett Mutual Funds ....(800) 800-4612
Benham Group ....(800) 331-8331
Berger Group ....(800) 333-1001
Berwyn Group..(800) 824-2249
William Blair Mutual Funds...............................(800) 742-7272
Blanchard Group of Funds ....(800) 922-7771
Brandywine Funds ....(800) 656-3017
Bull & Bear Group ....(800) 847-4200
Burnham Group..(800) 874-3863
Calvert Group..(800) 368-2748
Capstone Group ....(800) 262-6631
Cardinal Group..(800) 848-7734
Carillon Group ....(800) 999-1840
Century Shares Trust ....(800) 321-1928
CGM Group ....(800) 345-4048
Clipper Fund..(800) 776-5033

Colonial Group	(800) 248-2828
Columbia Funds	(800) 547-1707
Common Sense Trust	(800) 544-5445
Compass Capital Group	(800) 451-8371
Composite Group of Funds	(800) 543-8072
Conn. Mutual Investment Accts.	(800) 234-5606
Copley Fund	(800) 424-8570
Cowen Funds	(800) 221-5616
Crabbe Huson Funds	(800) 541-9732
Dean Witter Funds	(800) 869-3863
Delaware Group	(800) 523-4640
Dodge & Cox Group	(415) 434-0311
Dreman Mutual Group	(800) 533-1608
Dreyfus Group	(800) 645-6561
Eaton Vance Group	(800) 225-6265
EBI Funds	(800) 554-1156
Eclipse Financial Asset Group	(800) 872-2710
Enterprise Group	(800) 432-4320
Evergreen Funds	(800) 235-0064
FAM Value Fund	(800) 932-3271
Farm Bureau Mutual Funds	(800) 247-4170
Federated Funds	(800) 245-5040
Fidelity Advisor Funds	(800) 522-7297
Fidelity Group	(800) 544-8888
Fiduciary Group	(800) 338-1579
First Eagle Funds	(800) 451-3623
First Investors Group	(800) 423-4026
First Prairie Funds	(800) 346-3621
First Union Funds	(800) 326-3241
Flag Investors Funds	(800) 767-3524
Flex-funds	(800) 325-3539
Fortis Funds	(800) 800-2638
Fortress Investment Funds	(800) 245-5051
Founders Funds	(800) 525-2440
FPA Funds	(800) 982-4372
Franklin Group of Funds	(800) 342-5236
Fremont Mutual Funds	(800) 548-4539
FundTrust Group	(800) 344-9033
G.T. Global Group of Funds	(800) 824-1580
Gabelli Funds	(800) 422-3554
Galaxy Funds	(800) 628-0414
GAM Funds	(800) 426-4685
Gateway Group	(800) 354-6339
General Securities	(800) 331-4923
Gintel Group	(800) 243-5808
GIT Investment Funds	(800) 336-3063
Gradison-McDonald Mutual Funds	(800) 869-5999
Greenspring Fund	(800) 366-3863
Guardian Group	(800) 221-3253
Harbor Funds	(800) 422-1050
Harris Insight Funds	(800) 982-8782
Heartland Funds	(800) 432-7856
Heritage Family of Funds	(800) 421-4184
HighMark Group	(800) 433-6884
Wayne Hummer Group	(800) 621-4477
IAA Trust	(309) 557-3222
IAI Funds	(800) 945-3863
Idex Group	(800) 851-9777
IDS Group	(800) 328-8300
Invesco Family of Funds	(800) 525-8085
Investors Research Fund	(800) 732-1733

Janus Group ....(800) 525-8983
Jefferson Pilot Group..(800) 458-4498
John Hancock Mutual Funds ....(800) 225-5291
Kaufmann Fund..(800) 237-0132
Kemper Funds...(800) 621-1048
Keystone Group...(800) 343-2898
Kidder Family of Funds.......................................(800) 854-2505
Kleinwort Benson Group ....(800) 453-8888
Landmark Funds ....(800) 846-5300
Laurel Funds ....(800) 548-2868
Legg Mason Family of Funds..............................(800) 822-5544
Lexington Group..(800) 526-0056
Liberty Family of Funds ....(800) 245-5051
Lindner Group...(314) 727-5305
Longleaf Partners Funds ....(800) 445-9469
Lord Abbett Family of Funds ....(800) 874-3733
Mackenzie/Ivy Group of Funds ....(800) 456-5111
MainStay Funds..(800) 522-4202
Mairs & Power Funds...(612) 222-8478
Managers Funds ....(800) 835-3879
Mariner Fund Group ....(800) 634-2536
Mathers Fund...(800) 962-3863
Maxus Funds ....(800) 446-2987
Mentor Series Trust ....(800) 825-5353
Merger Fund ....(800) 343-8959
Meridian Fund ....(800) 446-6662
Merrill Lynch Group ....(800) 637-3863
Merriman Funds ....(800) 423-4893
MetLife-State Street Group ....(800) 882-3302
MFS Family of Funds..(800) 654-0266
Midwest Group ....(800) 543-8721
MIM Mutual Funds ....(800) 233-1240
MIMLIC Funds...(800) 443-3677
Monetta Funds...(800) 666-3882
Morgan Keegan Group ....(800) 366-7426
MSB Fund ....(212) 551-1920
Mutual Benefit Funds ....(800) 559-5535
Mutual Series Fund...(800) 553-3014
National Industries Fund.....................................(800) 367-7814
Nationwide Funds...(800) 848-0920
Neuberger & Berman Group...............................(800) 877-9700
New Alternatives Fund ....(800) 423-8383
New England Fund Group....................................(800) 225-7670
Nicholas Group ....(414) 272-6113
Nomura Pacific Basin Fund.................................(800) 833-0018
North American Funds ....(800) 872-8037
Northeast Investors Group..................................(800) 225-6704
Oberweis Emerging Growth Fund.....................(800) 323-6166
Olympic Trust ....(800) 346-7301
Oppenheimer Funds ....(800) 525-7048
Overland Express Funds ....(800) 552-9612
Pacific Horizon Funds..(800) 332-3863
PaineWebber Mutual Funds ....(800) 647-1568
Parnassus Funds ....(800) 999-3505
Pasadena Group...(800) 882-2855
Pax World Fund..(800) 767-1729
PBHG Funds ....(800) 433-0051
William Penn Funds ....(800) 523-8440
Permanent Portfolio Family of Funds ....(800) 531-5142
Philadephia Fund...(800) 749-9933
Phoenix Funds ....(800) 243-4361

Pierpont Funds...(800) 521-5412
Pilgrim Group ....(800) 334-3444
Pioneer Group ....(800) 225-6292
Piper Jaffray Group ....(800) 866-7778
PRA Real Estate Securities Fund.....................(800) 435-1405
Premier Funds ....(800) 242-8671
Principal Preservation Portfolios.....................(800) 826-4600
Princor Family of Mutual Funds......................(800) 451-5447
Prudential Mutual Funds ....(800) 225-1852
Putnam Mutual Funds ....(800) 225-1581
Quantitative Group of Funds ....(800) 331-1244
Quest for Value Funds ....(800) 232-3863
Quest Group ....(800) 221-4268
Reich & Tang Group..(800) 221-3079
Reynolds Funds..(800) 338-1579
Rightime Group..(800) 242-1421
Robertson Stephens Investment Trust..............(800) 766-3863
Rodney Square Funds ....(800) 336-9970
Royce Funds..(800) 221-4268
RSI Retirement Trust ....(800) 772-3615
Rushmore Group ....(800) 343-3355
Safeco Mutual Funds ....(800) 426-6730
Salomon Brothers Group..................................(800) 725-6666
SBSF Group ....(800) 422-7273
Schafer Value Fund ....(800) 343-0481
Schroder Capital Funds....................................(800) 344-8332
Scudder Funds..(800) 535-2726
Seafirst Retirement Funds ....(800) 323-9919
Security Group ....(800) 888-2461
Selected Funds ....(800) 243-1575
Seligman Group..(800) 221-2783
Sentinel Group ....(800) 282-3863
Sentry Group ....(800) 533-7827
Sequoia Fund ....(212) 245-5280
Sierra Trust Funds..(800) 222-5852
SIFE Trust Fund ....(800) 524-7433
Sit Group ....(800) 332-5580
Skyline Group...(800) 458-5222
Smith Barney Shearson Group ....(800) 451-2010
SoGen Funds ....(800) 334-2143
Sound Shore Fund ....(800) 551-1980
Stagecoach Funds ....(800) 222-8222
State Bond Group...(800) 328-4735
State Street Research Group.............................(800) 562-0032
SteinRoe Mutual Funds....................................(800) 338-2550
Stratton Group ....(800) 634-5726
Strong Funds..(800) 368-1030
SunAmerica Funds ....(800) 858-8850
T. Rowe Price Funds ....(800) 638-5660
Templeton Group ....(800) 292-9293
Thomson Fund Group......................................(800) 227-7337
Tocqueville Trust ....(800) 697-3863
Tower Mutual Funds..(800) 999-0124
Transamerica Funds ....(800) 343-6840
Twentieth Century Family of Funds ....(800) 345-2021
United Group ....(800) 366-5465
United Services Funds.......................................(800) 873-8637
USAA Group ....(800) 382-8722
UST Master Funds..(800) 233-1136
Value Line Mutual Funds ....(800) 223-0818
Van Eck Funds ....(800) 544-4653

Van Kampen Merritt Family of Funds ....(800) 225-2222
Vanguard Group ....(800) 662-7447
Venture Advisers Funds...............................(800) 279-0279
Vista Mutual Funds....................................(800) 972-9274
Voyageur Funds..(800) 553-1243
Warburg Pincus Funds................................(800) 257-5614
Wasatch Advisors Funds ....(800) 551-1700
Weitz Funds ....(800) 232-4161
Weston Portfolios ....(617) 239-0445
Winthrop Focus Group................................(800) 225-8011
World Funds ....(800) 776-5455
WPG Mutual Funds ....(800) 223-3332
Zweig Series Trust.....................................(800) 444-2706

Source: Worth Magazine

Retail Stock Brokers

A. G. Edwards......................................(314) 289-3000
Advest..(203) 525-1421
Charles Schwab ....(415) 627-7000
Dain Bosworth ....(612) 371-2711
Dean Witter Reynolds..............................(415) 693-6000
Fidelity Investments ....(617) 570-7000
Kemper Securities...................................(800) 346-6616
Legg Mason...(410) 539-3400
Merrill Lynch ....(212) 236-1000
Olde Discount..(313) 961-6666
PaineWebber..(212) 713-2000
Prudential Securities................................(212) 214-1000
Quick & Reilly ....(312) 726-0010
The R. J. Forbes Group ....(800) 754-7687
Smith Barney...(415) 984-6500
Stock Cross ....(800) 225-6196
Tucker Anthony ....(212) 225-8000
Washington Discount Brokerage....................(800) 843-9838

Stock Analysts

CS First Boston......................................(212) 909-2000
Donaldson, Lufkin & Jenrette......................(212) 504-3000
Goldman Sachs.......................................(800) 323-5678
Lehman Brothers ....(212) 526-7000
Merrill Lynch ....(212) 236-1000
Morgan Stanley ....(212) 703-4000
PaineWebber..(617) 235-1177
Prudential Securities................................(212) 214-1000
Salomon Brothers ....(212) 783-7000
Smith Barney...(212) 816-6000

Stock Exchanges

American Stock Exchange, New York, NY.......(212) 306-1000
Boston Stock Exchange, Inc., Boston, MA ....(617) 723-9500
Chicago Board of Trade, Chicago, IL ....(312) 435-3500
Chicago Board Options Exchange,
     Chicago, IL ....(312) 786-5600
Chicago Mercantile Exchange (CME),
     Chicago, IL ....(312) 930-1000
Chicago Stock Exchange, Chicago, IL ....(312) 663-2222
Cincinnati Stock Exchange,
     Cincinnati, OH ....(312) 786-8803
Coffee, Sugar & Cocoa Exchange,

New York, NY..............................(212) 938-2966
Commodity Exchange (COMEX)
    New York, NY..............................(212) 938-2900
Commodity Futures Trading Commission,
    Washington, DC............................(202) 254-6970
New York Cotton Exchange,
    New York, NY..............................(212) 938-2650
New York Futures Exchange,
    New York, NY..............................(212) 656-4940
New York Mercantile Exchange,
    New York, NY..............................(212) 938-2222
New York Stock Exchange,
    New York, NY..............................(212) 656-3000
Pacific Stock Exchange ,
    San Francisco, CA........................(415) 393-4000
Philadelphia Board of Trade,
    Philadelphia, PA..........................(215) 496-5555
Philadelphia Stock Exchange,
    Philadelphia, PA..........................(215) 496-5000

Source: Securities Industry Association

The EYP 2000

Two thousand of the largest companies in the United States:

3COM..(408) 764-5000
3M..(612) 733-1110
20th Century Industries....................(818) 704-3700
2002 Target Term Trust ....(212) 713-2000
AAR ....(708) 439-3939
A. G. Edwards..................................(314) 289-3000
A. H. Belo.......................................(214) 977-6606
A. L. Pharma ....(201) 947-7774
A. M. Castle & Company ....(708) 455-7111
A. O. Smith.....................................(414) 359-4000
A. Schulman....................................(216) 666-3751
Abbey Healthcare Group ....(714) 957-2000
Abbott Laboratories ....(708) 937-6100
Abex ....(603) 926-5911
Acclaim Entertainment......................(516) 624-8888
Acme Metals....................................(708) 849-2500
Acordia ....(317) 488-6666
The Actava Group ....(404) 658-9000
Acuson..(415) 969-9112
ACX Technologies ....(303) 271-7000
Adams Resources & Energy ....(713) 797-9966
Adaptec...(408) 945-8600
ADC Telecommunications...................(612) 938-8080
Adelphia Communications ....(814) 274-9830
Adobe Systems ....(415) 961-4400
Adolph Coors ....(303) 279-6565
Advanced Marketing Services ....(619) 457-2500
Advanced Micro Devices ....(408) 732-2400
Advanced Technology Laboratories.....(206) 487-7000
ADVANTA ....(215) 657-4000
ADVO ....(203) 285-6100
The AES Corporation ....(703) 522-1315
Aetna Life & Casualty ....(203) 273-0123
Affiliated Computer Services..............(214) 841-6111
AFLAC..(706) 323-3431
AGCO ....(404) 813-9200
Air & Water Technologies..................(908) 685-4600

Air Express	(203) 655-7900
Air Products and Chemicals	(610) 481-4911
Airborne Freight	(206) 285-4600
Airgas	(610) 687-5253
AirTouch Communications	(415) 658-2000
AK Steel Holding	(513) 425-5000
Alaska Air Group	(206) 431-7040
Albany	(518) 445-2200
Albemarle	(504) 388-8011
Alberto-Culver	(708) 450-3000
Albertson's	(208) 385-6200
ALC Communications	(810) 647-4060
Alco Standard	(610) 296-8000
Alcoa	(412) 553-3042
Alexander & Alexander Services	(212) 840-8500
Alexander & Baldwin	(808) 525-6611
Alex. Brown	(410) 727-1700
Alfa	(205) 288-3900
Allegheny	(212) 752-1356
Allegheny Ludlum	(412) 394-2800
Allegheny Power System	(212) 752-2121
Allen Group	(216) 765-5818
Allergan	(714) 752-4500
Alliance Entertainment	(212) 935-6662
Alliant Techsystems	(612) 931-6000
ALLIED Group Insurance	(515) 280-4211
Allied Holdings	(404) 373-4285
AlliedSignal	(201) 455-2000
Allmerica Property & Casualty	(508) 855-1000
Allou Health & Beauty Care	(516) 273-4000
The Allstate Corporation	(708) 402-5000
ALLTEL	(501) 661-8000
Alltrista	(317) 281-5000
Allwaste	(713) 623-8777
Alumax	(404) 246-6600
ALZA	(415) 494-5000
AMBAC	(212) 668-0340
AMC Entertainment	(816) 221-4000
Amcast Industrial	(513) 291-7000
Amdahl	(408) 746-6000
Amerada Hess	(212) 997-8500
AMERCO	(702) 688-6300
America West Airlines	(602) 693-0800
American Annuity Group	(513) 333-5300
American Bankers Insurance Group	(305) 253-2244
American Brands	(203) 698-5000
American Building Maintenance Industries	(415) 597-4500
American Business Products	(404) 953-8300
American Colloid	(708) 392-4600
American Electric Power	(614) 223-1000
American Express	(212) 640-2000
American Freightways	(501) 741-9000
American General	(713) 522-1111
American Greetings	(216) 252-7300
American Heritage Life	(904) 992-1776
American Home Products	(201) 660-5000
American International Group	(212) 770-7000
American Maize Products	(203) 356-9000
American Management Systems	(703) 267-8000
American Media	(407) 586-1111
American Medical Holdings	(214) 789-2200

American Medical Response	(617) 261-1600
American National Insurance	(409) 763-4661
American Power Conversion	(401) 789-5735
American Premier Underwriters	(513) 579-6600
American President Companies	(510) 272-8000
American Publishing	(618) 937-6411
American Re-insurance	(609) 243-4200
American Stores	(801) 539-0112
American Water Works	(609) 346-8200
AmeriData Technologies	(203) 357-1464
Ameritech	(312) 750-5000
Ameron	(818) 683-4000
AMETEK	(610) 647-2121
Amgen	(805) 447-1000
Amoco	(312) 856-6111
AMP	(717) 564-0100
Amphenol	(203) 265-8900
AMR	(817) 963-1234
AMSCO	(412) 338-6500
AmSouth Bancorporation	(205) 320-7151
Amtran	(317) 247-4000
Anacomp	(317) 844-9666
Anadarko Petroleum	(713) 875-1101
Analog Devices	(617) 329-4700
Andrew	(708) 349-3300
Angelica	(314) 854-3800
Anheuser-Busch	(314) 577-2000
Ann Taylor Stores	(212) 541-3300
Antec	(708) 439-4444
Anthony Industries	(213) 724-2800
Aon	(312) 701-3000
Apache	(713) 296-6000
Apogee Enterprises	(612) 835-1874
Apple Computer	(408) 996-1010
Applied Magnetics	(805) 683-5353
Applied Materials	(408) 727-5555
Applied Power	(414) 781-6600
APS Holding	(713) 741-2470
AptarGroup	(815) 477-0424
Aquila Gas Pipeline	(210) 342-0685
Arbor Drugs	(810) 643-9420
Arcadian Partners	(901) 758-5200
Archer-Daniels-Midland	(217) 424-5200
ARCO Chemical	(610) 359-2000
Arctco	(218) 681-8558
Arden Group	(310) 638-2842
Argonaut Group	(310) 553-0561
Armco	(412) 255-9800
Armstrong World Industries	(717) 397-0611
Arnold Industries	(717) 274-2521
Arrow Electronics	(516) 391-1300
Arthur J. Gallagher & Co.	(708) 773-3800
Arvin Industries	(812) 379-3000
ASARCO	(212) 510-2000
Ashland	(606) 329-3333
Ashland Coal	(304) 526-3333
Associated Banc-Corp	(414) 433-3166
AST Research	(714) 727-4141
Astoria Financial	(516) 327-3000
Astrum	(305) 532-2426
AT&T	(212) 387-5400

AT&T Capital	(201) 397-3000
Atlanta Gas & Light	(404) 584-4000
Atlantic Energy	(609) 645-4500
Atlantic Richfield	(213) 486-3511
Atlantic Southeast Airlines	(404) 530-3838
Atmel	(408) 441-0311
Atmos Energy	(214) 934-9227
Audiovox	(516) 231-7750
Augat	(508) 543-4300
Autodesk	(415) 507-5000
Automatic Data Processing	(201) 994-5000
Automotive Industries Holding	(612) 332-6828
AutoZone	(901) 325-4600
Avery Dennison	(818) 304-2000
Aviall	(214) 956-5000
Avnet	(516) 466-7000
Avon Products	(212) 546-6015
Avondale Industries	(504) 436-2121
Aztar	(602) 381-4100
B M C West	(208) 387-4300
The B. F. Goodrich Co.	(216) 374-3985
Baker Hughes	(713) 439-8600
Baldor Electric	(501) 646-4711
Ball	(317) 747-6100
Bally Entertainment	(312) 399-1300
Ballys Grand	(702) 739-4900
Baltimore Gas & Electric	(410) 783-5920
Banc One	(614) 248-5944
Bancorp Hawaii	(808) 537-8111
BancTec	(214) 450-7700
Bandag	(319) 262-1400
Bank of Boston	(617) 434-2200
Bank of New York	(212) 495-1784
Bank South	(404) 529-4111
BankAmerica	(415) 622-3530
Bankers Life Holdings	(312) 396-6000
Bankers Trust New York	(212) 250-2500
Banponce	(809) 765-9800
Banta	(414) 751-7777
Barnes & Noble	(212) 633-3300
Barnes Group	(203) 583-7070
Barnett Banks	(904) 791-7720
Bassett Industries	(703) 629-6000
Battle Mountain Gold	(713) 650-6400
Bausch & Lomb	(716) 338-6000
Baxter	(708) 948-2000
Bay State Gas	(508) 836-7000
BayBanks	(617) 482-1040
BE Aerospace	(407) 791-5000
The Bear Stearns Companies	(212) 272-2000
Bearings	(216) 881-2838
Beazer Homes USA	(404) 250-3420
Beckman Instruments	(714) 871-4848
Becton, Dickinson and Co.	(201) 847-6800
Bed Bath & Beyond	(201) 379-1520
Belden	(314) 854-8000
Bell Atlantic	(215) 963-6000
Bell Industries	(310) 826-2355
Bell Microproducts	(408) 451-9400
BellSouth	(404) 249-2000
Bemis	(612) 376-3000

Ben Franklin Retail Stores	(708) 462-6100
Beneficial	(302) 425-2500
Bergen Brunswig	(714) 385-4000
Berkshire Hathaway	(402) 346-1400
Berlitz	(609) 924-8500
Best Buy	(612) 947-2000
Best Products	(804) 261-2000
Bethlehem Steel	(610) 694-2424
Betz Laboratories	(215) 355-3300
Beverly Enterprises	(501) 452-6712
BHC Communications	(212) 421-0200
BIC	(203) 783-2000
Big B	(205) 424-3421
Bindley Western Industries	(317) 298-9900
Bio-Rad Laboratories	(510) 724-7000
Biomet	(219) 267-6639
Birmingham Steel	(205) 970-1200
BJ Services	(713) 462-4239
The Black & Decker Corporation	(410) 716-3900
Blair	(814) 723-3600
Block Drug	(201) 434-3000
Blount	(205) 244-4000
BMC Software	(713) 918-8800
Boatman's Banking	(501) 378-1521
Boatmen's Bancshares	(314) 466-6000
Bob Evans Farms	(614) 491-2225
The Boeing Company	(206) 655-2121
Boise Cascade	(208) 384-6161
The Bombay Company	(817) 347-8200
The Bon-Ton Stores	(717) 757-7660
Borden	(614) 225-4000
Borden Chemicals & Plastics	(504) 673-6121
Borg-Warner Automotive	(312) 322-8500
Borland	(408) 431-1000
Boston Edison	(617) 424-2000
Boston Scientific	(508) 650-8000
Bowater	(803) 271-7733
Bowne & Company	(212) 924-5500
Boyd Gaming	(702) 792-7200
Brad Ragan	(704) 521-2100
Bradlees	(617) 380-8000
Breed Technologies	(813) 284-6000
Briggs & Stratton	(414) 259-5333
Brinker	(214) 980-9917
Bristol-Myers Squibb	(212) 546-4000
Broadway Stores	(213) 227-2000
Brooke Group	(305) 579-8000
Brooklyn Bancorp	(718) 780-0400
Brooklyn Union Gas	(718) 403-2000
Brown Group	(314) 854-4000
Brown-Forman	(502) 585-1100
Browning-Ferris Industries	(713) 870-8100
Bruno's	(205) 940-9400
Brunswick	(708) 735-4700
Brush Wellman	(216) 486-4200
Buffets	(612) 942-9760
Builders Transport	(803) 432-1400
Burlington Coat Factory Warehouse	(609) 387-7800
Burlington Industries	(910) 379-2000
Burlington Northern	(817) 333-2000
Burlington Resources	(713) 624-9000

Bush Boake Allen	(201) 391-9870
Butler	(201) 573-8000
Butler Manufacturing	(816) 968-3000
Buttrey Food & Drug Stores	(406) 761-3401
BW/IP	(310) 435-3700
C Tec	(609) 734-3700
CCH	(312) 583-8500
C. R. Bard	(908) 277-8000
Cabletron Systems	(603) 332-9400
Cablevision Systems	(516) 364-8450
Cabot	(617) 345-0100
Cabot Oil & Gas	(713) 589-4600
Cadence Design Systems	(408) 943-1234
Cadmus Communications	(804) 287-5680
Caesar's World	(310) 552-2711
Cagle's	(404) 355-2820
The Caldor Corporation	(203) 846-1641
Calgon Carbon	(412) 787-6700
California Federal Bank	(213) 932-4200
California Microwave	(408) 732-4000
Callaway Golf	(619) 931-1771
CalMat	(213) 258-2777
Cambrex	(201) 804-3000
Camco	(713) 747-4000
Cameron Ashley	(214) 340-1996
Campbell Soup	(609) 342-4800
Canandaigua Wine	(716) 394-7900
Capital Cities/ABC	(212) 456-7777
Capital One Financial	(804) 967-1000
Capitol American Financial	(216) 696-6400
Capstead Mortgage	(214) 874-2323
Carauster Industries	(404) 948-3101
Cardinal Health	(614) 761-8700
Career Horizons	(516) 496-2300
Caremark	(708) 559-4700
Carl Karcher Enterprises	(714) 774-5796
Carlisle Companies	(315) 474-2500
Carlisle Plastics	(602) 407-2100
Carmike Cinemas	(706) 576-3400
Carnival	(305) 599-2600
Carolina Freight	(704) 435-6811
Carolina Power & Light	(919) 546-6111
Carpenter Technology	(610) 208-2000
Carr-Gottstein Foods	(907) 561-1944
Carson Pirie Scott & Company	(414) 347-4141
Carter-Wallace	(212) 339-5000
Case	(414) 636-6011
Casey's General Stores	(515) 965-6100
Cash America	(817) 335-1100
Castle Energy	(610) 995-9400
Caterpillar	(309) 675-1000
Catherines Stores	(901) 363-3900
The Cato Corporation	(704) 554-8510
CBI Industries	(708) 572-7000
CBS	(212) 975-4321
CCB Financial	(919) 683-7500
CCP Insurance	(317) 573-6900
CDI	(215) 569-2200
CDW Computer Centers	(708) 465-6000
CellStar	(214) 323-0600
Centennial Cellular	(203) 972-2000

Centerior Energy	(216) 447-3100
Centex Construction Products	(214) 559-6500
Central and South West	(214) 777-1000
Central Fidelity Banks	(804) 782-4000
Central Garden & Pet	(510) 283-4573
Central Hudson Gas & Electric	(914) 452-2000
Central Louisiana Electric	(318) 484-7400
Central Maine Power	(207) 623-3521
Central Newspapers	(317) 231-9200
Central Tractor Farm & Country	(515) 266-3101
Central Vermont Public Service	(802) 773-2711
Centura Banks	(919) 977-4400
Century Telephone Enterprises	(318) 388-9500
Ceridian	(612) 853-8100
Chambers Development	(412) 242-6237
Champion	(203) 358-7000
Champion Enterprises	(810) 340-9090
Chaparral Steel	(214) 775-8241
The Charles Schwab Corporation	(415) 627-7000
Charming Shoppes	(215) 245-9100
Charter Medical	(404) 841-9200
Charter One Financial	(216) 589-8320
Chase Brass Industries	(419) 485-3193
The Chase Manhattan Corporation.	(212) 552-2222
Chemed	(513) 762-6900
Chemical Banking	(212) 270-6000
The Cherry Corporation	(708) 662-9200
Chesapeake	(804) 697-1000
Chevron	(415) 894-7700
Chic by H.I.S.	(212) 302-6400
Chicago & North Western Transporation	(312) 559-7000
Chipcom	(508) 460-8900
Chiquita Brands	(513) 784-8011
Chiron	(510) 655-8730
Chock Full O'Nuts	(212) 532-0300
Chrysler	(313) 956-5741
The Chubb Corp.	(908) 903-2000
Church & Dwight	(609) 683-5900
CIGNA	(215) 761-1000
CILCORP	(309) 675-8810
Cincinnati Bell	(513) 397-9900
Cincinnati Financial	(513) 870-2000
Cincinnati Milacron	(513) 841-8100
CINergy	(513) 381-2000
Cintas	(513) 459-1200
CIPSCO	(217) 523-3600
Circuit City Stores	(804) 527-4000
Circus Circus Enterprises	(702) 734-0410
Cirrus Logic	(510) 623-8300
Cisco Systems	(408) 526-4000
Citicorp	(800) 285-3000
Citizens Bancorp	(301) 206-6080
Citizens Utilities	(203) 329-8800
Claire's Stores	(305) 433-3900
CLARCOR	(815) 962-8867
Clark Equipment	(219) 239-0100
Clayton Homes	(615) 970-7200
Cleveland-Cliffs	(216) 694-5700
The Clorox Company	(510) 271-7000
The Clothestime	(714) 779-5881
Club Med	(212) 977-2100

CML Group	(508) 264-4155
CMS Energy	(313) 436-9200
CNA Financial	(312) 822-5000
Coachmen Industries	(219) 262-0123
Coast Savings Financial	(213) 362-2000
The Coastal Corporation	(713) 877-1400
Coca-Cola Bottling Consolidated	(704) 551-4400
The Coca-Cola Company	(404) 676-2121
Coca-Cola Enterprises	(404) 676-2100
Cold Metal Products	(216) 758-1194
Cole National	(216) 449-4100
Coleman	(303) 202-2400
Colgate-Palmolive	(212) 310-2000
Collective Bancorp	(609) 625-1110
Collins & Aikman Group	(704) 548-2350
Coltec Industries	(212) 940-0400
Columbia Gas System	(302) 429-5000
Columbia/HCA Healthcare	(502) 572-2000
Comair Holdings	(606) 525-2550
Comcast	(215) 665-1700
Comdata Holdings	(615) 370-7000
Comdisco	(708) 698-3000
Comerica	(313) 222-4000
Commerce Bancshares	(816) 234-2000
Commerce Group	(508) 949-4480
Commercial Federal	(402) 554-9200
Commercial Intertech	(216) 746-8011
Commercial Metals	(214) 689-4300
Commonwealth Energy System	(617) 225-4000
Community Health Systems	(713) 537-5230
Community Psychiatric Centers	(702) 259-3600
Compaq Computer	(713) 370-0670
Compass Bancshares	(205) 933-3000
CompuCom Systems	(214) 265-3600
CompUSA	(214) 383-4000
Computer Assocs.	(516) 342-5224
Computer Sciences	(310) 615-0311
Computer Task Group	(716) 882-8000
Computervision	(617) 275-1800
Compuware	(810) 737-7300
COMSAT	(301) 214-3000
ConAgra	(402) 595-4000
Cone Mills	(910) 379-6220
Connecticut Energy	(203) 579-1732
Connecticut Natural Gas	(203) 727-3000
Conner Peripherals	(408) 456-4500
Conrail	(215) 209-4000
Conseco	(317) 573-6100
Consolidated Edison of New York	(212) 460-4600
Consolidated Freightways	(415) 494-2900
Consolidated Natural Gas	(412) 227-1000
Consolidated Papers	(715) 422-3111
Consolidated Stores	(614) 278-6800
Contel Cellular	(404) 804-3400
Continental Airlines Holdings	(713) 834-5000
Continental Can	(516) 822-4940
The Continental Corporation	(212) 440-3000
Continental Homes Holding	(602) 483-0006
Continental Medical Systems	(717) 790-8300
The Continuum Company	(512) 345-5700
Control Data Systems	(612) 482-2401

Converse	(508) 664-1100
Cooper Industries	(713) 739-5400
Cooper Tire & Rubber	(419) 423-1321
Coram Healthcare	(303) 292-4973
Cordis	(305) 824-2000
CoreStates Financial	(215) 973-3827
Corning	(607) 974-9000
Corporate Express	(303) 373-2800
Countrywide Credit Industries	(818) 304-8400
Coventry	(615) 391-2440
CPC	(201) 894-4000
CPI	(314) 231-1575
Cracker Barrel Old Country Store	(615) 444-5533
Crane	(203) 363-7300
Crawford & Co. Risk Management Services	(404) 256-0830
Cray Research	(612) 683-7100
Crestar Financial	(804) 782-5000
Crompton & Knowles	(203) 353-5400
Crown Books	(301) 731-1200
Crown Central Petroleum	(410) 539-7400
Crown Cork & Seal	(215) 698-5100
CSF Holdings	(305) 577-0400
CSX	(804) 782-1400
CTS	(219) 293-7511
Cubic	(619) 277-6780
CUC	(203) 324-9261
Culbro	(212) 561-8700
Cullen/Frost Bankers	(210) 220-4011
Culp	(910) 889-5161
Cummins Engine	(812) 377-5000
Cygne Designs	(212) 354-6474
Cypress Semiconductor	(408) 943-2600
Cyprus Amax Minerals	(303) 643-5000
Cyrk	(508) 283-5800
Cytec Industries	(201) 357-3100
D. R. Horton	(817) 856-8200
Dairy Mart Convenience Stores	(203) 741-4444
Daisytek	(214) 881-4700
DAKA	(508) 774-9115
DAMARK	(612) 531-0066
Dames & Moore	(213) 683-1560
Dana	(419) 535-4500
Danaher	(202) 828-0850
Darling	(214) 717-0300
Data General	(508) 898-5000
Dauphin Deposit	(717) 255-2121
Dayton Hudson	(612) 370-6948
Dean Foods	(708) 678-1680
Dean Witter Reynolds	(212) 392-2222
DeBartolo Realty	(216) 758-7292
Deere & Co.	(309) 765-8000
DEKALB Genetics	(815) 758-3461
Del Webb	(602) 808-8000
Delchamps	(205) 433-0431
Dell Computer	(512) 338-4400
Delmarva Power & Light	(302) 429-3011
Delphi Financial Group	(302) 478-5142
Delta Air Lines	(404) 715-2600
Delta Woodside Industries	(803) 232-8301
Deluxe	(612) 483-7111
DENTSPLY	(717) 845-7511

Deposit Guaranty	(601) 354-8564
Designs	(617) 739-6722
Destec Energy	(713) 735-4000
Detroit Diesel	(313) 592-5000
The Detroit Edison Company	(313) 237-8000
The Dexter Corporation	(203) 627-9051
Diagnostek	(505) 345-8080
The Dial Corporation	(602) 207-4000
Diamond Shamrock	(210) 641-6800
The Diana Corporation	(414) 355-0037
Diebold	(216) 489-4000
Digital Equipment	(508) 493-5111
Dillard Department Stores	(501) 376-5200
Dime BanCorp	(212) 326-6170
Dimon	(804) 792-7511
Dixie Yarns	(615) 698-2501
Dole Food	(818) 879-6600
Dollar General	(615) 783-2000
Dominion Resources	(804) 775-5700
Donaldson	(612) 887-3131
Donnelly	(616) 786-7000
Doskocil Companies	(405) 879-5500
Douglas & Lomason	(810) 478-7800
Dover	(212) 922-1640
The Dow Chemical Company	(517) 636-1000
Dow Jones & Company	(212) 416-2000
Downey Financial	(714) 854-3100
DPL	(513) 224-6000
DQE	(412) 393-6000
Dr. Pepper/Seven-Up Companies	(214) 360-7000
Dravo	(412) 566-3000
Dress Barn	(914) 369-4500
Dresser Industries	(214) 740-6000
Dreyer's Grand Ice Cream	(510) 652-8187
Drug Emporium	(614) 548-7080
DSC Communications	(214) 519-3000
Duckwall-ALCO Stores	(913) 263-3350
Duke Power	(704) 594-0887
The Dun & Bradstreet Corporation	(203) 834-4200
Duplex Products	(815) 895-2101
Duracell	(203) 796-4000
The Duriron Company	(513) 476-6100
Duty Free	(203) 431-6057
Dynatech	(617) 272-6100
E-Systems	(214) 661-1000
E-Z Serve	(713) 684-4300
E. I. Du Pont de Nemours and Co.	(302) 774-1000
The E. W. Scripps Company	(302) 478-4141
Eagle Food Centers	(309) 787-7730
Eagle Hardware & Garden	(206) 431-5740
Eastern Enterprises	(617) 647-2300
Eastern Utilities Assocs.	(617) 357-9590
Eastex Energy	(713) 650-6255
Eastman Chemical	(615) 229-2000
Eastman Kodak	(716) 724-4000
Eaton	(216) 523-5000
Echlin	(203) 481-5751
Eckerd	(813) 399-6000
Ecolab	(612) 293-2233
Edison Brothers Stores	(314) 331-6000
Edisto Resources	(214) 880-0243

EG&G	(617) 237-5100
Egghead	(206) 391-0800
Ekco Group	(603) 888-1212
El Paso Electric	(915) 543-5711
El Paso Natural Gas	(915) 541-2600
Elco Industries	(815) 397-5151
Electronic Arts	(415) 571-7171
Electronic Data Systems	(214) 604-6000
Elek Tek	(708) 677-7660
Eli Lilly and Company	(317) 276-2000
Eljer Industries	(214) 407-2600
EMC	(508) 435-1000
Emerson Electric	(314) 553-2000
Emerson Radio	(201) 884-5800
Emphesys Financial Group	(414) 336-1100
Employee Benefit Plans	(612) 546-4353
Energen	(205) 326-2700
Energy Service	(214) 922-1500
Energy Ventures	(713) 297-8400
Engelhard	(908) 205-5000
Engle Homes	(407) 391-4012
ENRON	(713) 853-6161
ENSERCH	(214) 651-8700
Entergy	(504) 529-5262
EnviroSource	(203) 322-8333
EOTT Energy Partners	(713) 993-5200
Equifax	(404) 885-8000
The Equitable Companies	(212) 554-1234
Equitable of Iowa Companies	(515) 245-6911
Equitable Resources	(412) 261-3000
ERLY Industries	(213) 879-1480
Ernst Home Centers	(206) 621-6700
ESCO Electronics	(314) 553-7777
Esterline Technologies	(206) 453-9400
Ethan Allen Interiors	(203) 743-8000
Ethyl	(804) 788-5000
Exabyte	(303) 442-4333
Excel Industries	(219) 264-2131
EXECUTONE Information Systems	(203) 876-7600
Exide	(810) 258-0080
Exide Electronics Group	(919) 872-3020
Expeditors International of Washington	(206) 246-3711
Exxon	(214) 444-1000
F & M Distributors	(810) 758-1400
Fabri-Centers of America	(216) 656-2600
Fairchild	(703) 478-5800
Falcon Building Products	(312) 906-9700
Family Dollar Stores	(704) 847-6961
Farah	(915) 593-4444
Fay's	(315) 451-8000
Fedders	(908) 604-8686
Federal Express	(901) 369-3600
Federal Home Loan Mortgage	(703) 903-2000
Federal-Mogul	(810) 354-7700
Federal National Mortgage Association	(202) 752-7000
Federal Paper Board	(201) 391-1776
Federal Signal	(708) 954-2000
Federated Department Stores	(513) 579-7000
Ferrellgas Partners	(816) 792-1600
Ferro	(216) 641-8580
FFP Partners	(817) 838-4700

FHP	(714) 963-7233
Fibreboard	(510) 274-0700
Fidelity National Financial	(714) 852-9770
Fieldcrest Cannon	(910) 627-3000
Fifth Third Bancorp	(513) 579-5300
Figgie	(216) 953-2700
Filene's Basement	(617) 348-7000
FINA	(214) 750-2400
Fingerhut Companies	(612) 932-3100
Finova Group	(602) 207-6900
First American	(615) 748-2000
The First American Financial Corporation	(714) 558-3211
First Bancorporation of Ohio	(216) 384-8000
First Bank System	(612) 973-1111
First Brands	(203) 731-2300
First Chicago	(312) 732-4000
First Citizens BancShares	(919) 755-7000
First Colony	(804) 775-0300
First Commerce	(504) 561-1371
First Commercial	(501) 371-7000
First Data	(402) 222-2000
First Empire State	(716) 842-5445
First Fidelity Bancorporation	(201) 565-3200
First Financial	(715) 341-0400
First Financial Management	(404) 321-0120
First Hawaiian	(808) 525-7000
First Interstate Bancorp	(213) 614-3001
First Mississippi	(601) 948-7550
First of America Bank	(616) 376-9000
First Security	(801) 246-5706
First Tennessee National	(901) 523-4444
First Union	(704) 374-6565
First USA	(214) 746-8400
First Virginia Banks	(703) 241-4000
Firstar	(414) 765-4316
FirstFed Financial	(310) 319-6000
FirstFed Michigan	(313) 965-1400
FirsTier Financial	(402) 348-6000
FIserv	(414) 879-5000
Fisher Scientific	(603) 929-2650
Flagstar Companies	(803) 597-8000
Fleet Financial Group	(401) 278-5800
Fleet Mortgage Group	(803) 929-7900
Fleetwood Enterprises	(909) 351-3500
Fleming Companies	(405) 840-7200
FlightSafety	(718) 565-4100
Florida East Coast Industries	(904) 396-6600
Florida Progress	(813) 824-6400
Florida Rock Industries	(904) 355-1781
The Florsheim Shoe Company	(312) 559-2500
Flowers Industries	(912) 226-9110
Fluor	(714) 975-2000
FMC	(312) 861-6000
Foamex	(610) 859-3000
Food Lion	(704) 633-8250
Foodarama Supermarkets	(908) 462-4700
Foodmaker	(619) 571-2121
Ford Motor	(313) 322-3000
Foremost of America	(616) 942-3000
Forest City Enterprises	(216) 267-1200
Forest Laboratories	(212) 421-7850

Forstmann & Co.	(212) 642-6900
Foster Wheeler	(908) 730-4000
Foundation Health	(916) 631-5000
Fourth Financial	(316) 261-4444
FoxMeyer	(214) 446-4800
FPL Group	(305) 552-3552
Franklin Electric	(219) 824-2900
Franklin Quest	(801) 975-1776
Franklin Resources	(415) 312-2000
Fred Meyer	(503) 232-8844
Fred's	(901) 365-8880
Freeport-McMoran Copper & Gold	(504) 582-4000
Fremont General	(310) 315-5500
Fresenius USA	(510) 295-0200
Fretter	(810) 220-5000
Fritz Companies	(415) 904-8360
Frontier	(716) 777-1000
Frozen Food Express Industries	(214) 630-8090
Fruehauf Trailer	(317) 630-3000
Fruit of the Loom	(312) 876-1724
Fund American Enterprises Holdings	(802) 649-3633
Furon	(714) 831-5350
The Future Now	(513) 792-4500
G&K Services	(612) 546-7440
Galey & Lord	(212) 465-3000
Gander Mountain	(414) 862-2331
Gannett	(703) 284-6000
The Gap	(415) 952-4400
Gateway 2000	(605) 232-2000
GATX	(312) 621-6200
Gaylord Container	(708) 405-5500
Gaylord Entertainment	(615) 316-6000
GBC Technologies	(609) 767-2500
GC Companies	(617) 278-5600
GEICO	(301) 986-3000
GenCorp	(216) 869-4200
Genentech	(415) 225-1000
General Binding	(708) 272-3700
General Dynamics	(703) 876-3000
General Electric	(203) 373-2211
General Host	(203) 357-9900
General Instrument	(312) 541-5000
General Mills	(612) 540-2311
General Motors	(313) 556-5000
General Nutrition Companies	(412) 288-4600
General Public Utilities	(201) 263-6500
General Re	(203) 328-5000
General Signal	(203) 329-4100
Genesco	(615) 367-7000
Genesis Health Ventures	(610) 444-6350
Geneva Steel	(801) 227-9000
GENICOM	(703) 802-9200
The Genlyte Group	(201) 864-3000
Genovese Drug Stores	(516) 420-1900
Genuine Parts	(404) 953-1700
Genzyme	(617) 252-7500
The Geon Co.	(216) 447-6000
Georgia Gulf	(404) 395-4500
Georgia-Pacific	(404) 652-4000
Gerber Scientific	(203) 644-1551
Getty Petroleum	(516) 338-6000

Giant Food	(301) 341-4100
Giant Industries	(602) 585-8888
Gibson Greetings	(513) 841-6600
Giddings & Lewis	(414) 921-9400
Gilbert Assocs.	(610) 775-5900
The Gillette Company	(617) 421-7000
Glendale Federal Bank	(818) 500-2000
Global Marine	(713) 596-5100
Golden Poultry	(404) 393-5000
Golden West Financial	(510) 446-3420
The Good Guys	(415) 615-5000
Goody's Family Clothing	(615) 966-2000
The Goodyear Tire & Rubber Company	(216) 796-2121
Gottschalks	(209) 434-8000
Goulds Pumps	(315) 568-2811
Government Tech Services	(703) 502-2000
Graco	(612) 623-6000
GranCare	(404) 393-0199
Grand Casinos	(612) 449-9092
Granite Construction	(408) 724-1011
Graphic Industries	(404) 874-3327
The Great Atlantic & Pacific Tea Company	(201) 573-9700
Great Lakes Chemical	(317) 497-6100
Great Western Financial	(818) 775-3411
Green Tree Financial	(612) 293-3400
The Greenbrier Cos.	(503) 684-7000
Greenfield Industries	(706) 863-7708
Grey Advertising	(212) 546-2000
Greyhound Lines	(214) 789-7000
Grossman's	(617) 848-0100
Ground Round Restaurants	(617) 380-3100
Group Technologies	(813) 972-6000
Grow Group	(212) 599-4400
GTE	(203) 965-2000
GTECH	(401) 392-1000
Guaranty National	(303) 754-8400
Guidant	(317) 276-8734
Guilford Mills	(910) 316-4000
Guy F. Atkinson of California	(415) 876-1000
H&R Block	(816) 753-6900
H. B. Fuller	(612) 645-3401
H. F. Ahmanson and Co.	(818) 960-6311
H. J. Heinz	(412) 456-5700
Hadco	(603) 898-8000
Hadson	(214) 640-6800
Haemonetics	(617) 848-7100
Haggar	(214) 352-8481
Hahn Automotive Warehouse	(716) 235-1595
Halliburton	(214) 978-2600
Hancock Fabrics	(601) 842-2834
Handleman	(810) 362-4400
Handy & Harman	(212) 661-2400
Hannaford Bros.	(207) 883-2911
Hanover Direct	(201) 863-7300
Harcourt General	(617) 232-8200
Harley-Davidson	(414) 342-4680
Harleysville Group	(215) 256-5000
Harman International Industries	(202) 393-1101
Harnischfeger Industries	(414) 671-4400
The Harper Group	(415) 978-0600
Harris	(407) 727-9100

Harsco	(717) 763-7064
Harte-Hanks Comms.	(210) 829-9000
The Hartford Steam Boiler Inspection and Insurance Company	(203) 722-1866
Hartmarx	(312) 372-6300
Harvard Industries	(813) 288-5000
Hasbro	(401) 431-8697
Haverty Furniture Companies	(404) 881-1911
Hawaiian Electric Industries	(808) 543-5662
Hayes Wheels	(313) 941-2000
HBO & Co.	(404) 393-6000
HCA (Hospital Corp. of America)	(615) 327-9551
Health Care and Retirement	(419) 247-5000
Health Management Assocs.	(813) 598-3131
Health Systems	(818) 719-6978
Healthsource	(603) 268-7000
Healthsouth	(205) 967-7116
Healthtrust–The Hospital Co.	(615) 383-4444
Hechinger	(301) 341-1000
Heilig-Meyers	(804) 359-9171
Helene Curtis Industries	(312) 661-0222
Helmerich & Payne	(918) 742-5531
Herbalife	(310) 410-9600
Hercules	(302) 594-5000
Heritage Media	(214) 702-7380
Herman Miller	(616) 654-3000
Hershey Foods	(717) 534-6799
Hewlett-Packard	(415) 857-1501
Hexcel	(510) 847-9500
Hibernia National Bank	(504) 533-3333
Hillenbrand Industries	(812) 934-7000
The Hillhaven Corp.	(206) 572-4901
Hi-Lo Automotive	(713) 663-6700
Hills Stores	(617) 821-1000
Hilton Hotels	(310) 278-4321
Holly	(214) 871-3555
Hollywood Casino	(214) 392-7777
The Home Depot	(404) 433-8211
Home Holdings	(212) 530-6600
Home Shopping Network	(813) 572-8585
Homedco Group	(714) 755-5600
Homestake Mining	(415) 981-8150
HON Industries	(319) 264-7400
Honeywell	(612) 951-1000
Hooper Holmes	(908) 766-5000
Horace Mann Educators	(217) 789-2500
Horizon Healthcare	(505) 881-4961
Hormel Foods	(507) 437-5611
Hospitality Franchise Systems	(201) 428-9700
Host Marriott	(301) 380-9000
Houghton Mifflin	(617) 351-5000
House of Fabrics	(818) 995-7000
Household	(708) 564-5000
Houston Industries	(713) 629-3000
Hovnanian Enterprises	(908) 747-7800
Howell	(713) 658-4000
Hubbell	(203) 799-4100
Hudson Foods	(501) 636-1100
Huffy	(513) 866-6251
Hughes Supply	(407) 841-4755
Humana	(502) 580-1000

Hunt Manufacturing	(215) 732-7700
Huntington Bancshares	(614) 476-8300
Hutchinson Technology	(612) 587-3797
IBM	(914) 765-1900
IBP	(402) 494-2061
ICF Kaiser	(703) 934-3600
Idaho Power	(208) 383-2200
IDEX	(708) 498-7070
IES Industries	(319) 398-4411
Illinois Central	(312) 755-7500
Illinois Tool Works	(708) 724-7500
Illinova	(217) 424-6600
IMC Global	(708) 272-9200
Imo Industries	(609) 896-7600
Imperial Holly	(713) 491-9181
Inacom	(402) 392-3900
Independent Insurance Group	(904) 358-5151
Indiana Energy	(317) 926-3351
INDRESCO	(214) 953-4500
Infinity Broadcasting	(212) 750-6400
Information Resources	(312) 726-1221
Informix	(415) 926-6300
Ingersoll-Rand	(201) 573-0123
Ingles Markets	(704) 669-2941
Inland Steel Industries	(312) 346-0300
Inmac	(408) 727-1970
Inphynet Medical Management	(305) 475-1300
Insilco	(614) 792-0468
Insteel Industries	(910) 786-2141
Instrument Systems	(516) 938-5544
Integon	(910) 770-2000
Integra Financial	(412) 644-7669
Integrated Device Technology	(408) 727-6116
Integrated Health Services	(410) 998-8400
Intel	(408) 765-8080
Intelligent Electronics	(610) 458-5500
INTERCO	(314) 863-1100
Interface	(706) 882-1891
Intergraph	(205) 730-2000
Interim Services	(305) 938-7600
The Interlake Corp	(708) 852-8800
Intermet	(404) 431-6000
International Dairy Queen	(612) 830-0200
International Flavors & Fragrances	(212) 765-5500
International Game Technology	(702) 686-1200
International Jensen	(708) 317-3700
International Multifoods	(612) 340-3300
International Paper	(914) 397-1500
International Recovery	(305) 884-2001
International Rectifier	(310) 322-3331
International Shipholding	(504) 529-5461
International Specialty Products	(302) 429-8554
International Technology	(310) 378-9933
The Interpublic Group of Companies	(212) 399-8000
Inter-Regional Financial Group	(612) 371-7750
Interstate Bakeries	(816) 561-6600
Interstate Power	(319) 582-5421
Intertrans	(214) 830-8888
Intuit	(415) 322-0573
Invacare	(216) 329-6000
Iowa-Illinois Gas & Electric	(319) 326-7111

IPALCO Enterprises..(317) 261-8261
Itel...(312) 902-1515
ITT...(212) 258-1000
IVAX..(305) 590-2200
J&L Specialty Steel ....(412) 338-1600
J. B. Hunt Transport Services..............................(501) 820-0000
J. Baker..(617) 828-9300
J. C. Penney...(214) 431-1000
The J. M. Smucker Co. ....(216) 682-3000
J. P. Morgan & Co. ....(212) 483-2323
Jabil Circuit ....(813) 577-9749
Jacobs Engineering Group ....(818) 449-2171
Jacobson Stores..(517) 764-6400
James River of Virginia...(804) 644-5411
Jan Bell Marketing...(305) 846-8000
Jason..(414) 277-9300
Jefferies Group ....(310) 445-1199
Jefferson-Pilot ....(910) 691-3441
Jefferson Smurfit ....(314) 746-1100
Jenny Craig ....(619) 259-7000
John Alden Financial ....(305) 715-3767
John Fluke Manufacturing...................................(206) 347-6100
John H. Harland ....(404) 981-9460
John Wiley & Sons...(212) 850-6000
Johnson & Johnson ....(908) 524-0400
Johnson Controls...(414) 228-1200
Johnson Worldwide Assocs. ....(414) 884-1500
Johnstown America Industries ....(312) 280-8844
Jones Apparel Group ....(215) 785-4000
Jostens...(612) 830-3300
JP Foodservice...(410) 312-7100
Justin Industries ....(817) 336-5125
K Mart..(810) 643-1000
Kaiser Aluminum ....(713) 267-3777
Kaman..(203) 243-7100
Kansas City Power & Light...................................(816) 556-2200
Kansas City Southern Industries ....(816) 556-0303
Kasler Holding...(909) 884-4811
Kaufman & Broad Home......................................(310) 443-8000
KCS Energy ....(908) 632-1770
Keane ....(617) 241-9200
Kellogg...(616) 961-2000
Kellwood ....(314) 576-3100
Kelly Services ....(810) 362-4444
Kemet...(803) 963-6300
Kemper...(708) 320-4700
Kenetech..(415) 398-3825
Kennametal...(412) 539-5000
Kent Electronics ....(713) 780-7770
Kerr-McGee ....(405) 270-1313
KeyCorp..(216) 689-3000
Keystone ....(713) 466-1176
Keystone Consolidated Industries ....(214) 458-0028
Kimball ....(812) 482-1600
Kimberly-Clark ....(214) 830-1200
Kindercare Learning Centers ....(334) 277-5090
Kinetic Concepts..(210) 524-9000
King World Productions..(212) 315-4000
Kirby ....(713) 629-9370
KLA Instruments ....(408) 434-4200
KN Energy ....(303) 989-1740

Knight-Ridder	(305) 376-3800
Kohl's	(414) 783-5800
Komag	(408) 946-2300
Kroger	(513) 762-4000
The Krystal Co.	(615) 757-1550
KU Energy	(606) 255-2100
Kuhlman	(912) 598-7809
Kysor Industrial	(616) 779-2200
L. B. Foster	(412) 928-3400
L.A. Gear	(310) 452-4327
La Quinta Inns	(210) 302-6000
La-Z-Boy	(313) 241-4414
Laclede Gas	(314) 342-0500
Laclede Steel	(314) 425-1400
LADD Furniture	(910) 889-0333
Lafarge	(703) 264-3600
Lakehead Pipe Line Partners	(218) 725-0100
Lam Research	(510) 659-0200
Lamson & Sessions	(216) 464-3400
Lancaster Colony	(614) 224-7141
Lance	(704) 554-1421
Lands' End	(608) 935-9341
Landstar Systems	(203) 925-2900
Lawyers Title	(804) 281-6700
LCI	(614) 798-6862
LDDS Communications	(601) 360-8600
Lear Seating	(810) 746-1500
Leaseway Transportation	(216) 765-5500
Lechters	(201) 481-1100
Lee Enterprises	(319) 383-2100
LEGENT	(703) 708-3000
Legg Mason	(410) 539-0000
Leggett & Platt	(417) 358-8131
Lehman Bros. Holdings of Hannaford Bros.	(212) 526-7000
Lennar	(305) 559-4000
Leslie Fay Companies	(212) 221-4000
Leucadia National	(212) 460-1900
Levitz Furniture	(407) 994-6006
LG&E Energy	(502) 627-2000
Libbey	(419) 727-2100
The Liberty Corp.	(803) 268-8436
Life Partners Group	(303) 779-1111
Life Re	(203) 321-3000
Life Technologies	(301) 840-8000
Lilly Industries	(317) 687-6700
The Limited	(614) 479-7000
LIN Broadcasting	(206) 828-1902
Lincoln National	(219) 455-2000
Litton Industries	(818) 598-5000
Liuski	(516) 454-8220
Living Centers of America	(713) 578-4700
Liz Claiborne	(212) 354-4900
Lockheed	(818) 876-2000
Loctite	(203) 520-5000
Loews	(212) 545-2000
Logicon	(310) 373-0220
Lomas Financial	(214) 879-4000
Lone Star Industries	(203) 969-8600
Lone Star Technologies	(214) 386-3981
Long Drug Stores	(510) 937-1170
Long Island Lighting	(516) 755-6650

The Long Island Savings Bank ....(516) 547-2000
Longview Fibre ....(206) 425-1550
Loral..(212) 697-1105
Lotus Development ....(617) 577-8500
The Louisiana Land and Exploration Co. ....(504) 566-6500
Louisiana-Pacific..(503) 221-0800
Lowe's Companies ....(910) 651-4000
LSB Industries..(405) 235-4546
LSI Logic...(408) 433-8000
The LTV Corp. ....(216) 622-5000
The Lubrizol Corp. ....(216) 943-4200
Luby's Cafeterias ....(210) 654-9000
Lukens...(215) 383-2000
Lyondell Petrochemical ....(713) 652-7200
M/A-COM...(508) 442-5000
M.D.C. Holdings ....(303) 773-1100
M. A. Hanna ....(216) 589-4000
M/I Schottenstein Homes ....(614) 221-5700
M. K. Rail..(412) 237-2250
M. S. Carriers...(901) 332-2500
Mac Frugal's Bargains ....(310) 537-9220
Madison Gas & Electric ....(608) 252-7923
Magma Copper ....(602) 575-5600
Magna Group ....(314) 963-2500
MagneTek ....(615) 316-5100
Mallinckrodt Group ....(314) 854-5200
The Manitowoc Company ....(414) 684-4410
Manor Care...(301) 681-9400
Manpower...(414) 961-1000
Manville...(303) 978-2000
MAPCO ....(918) 581-1800
The Marcus Corporation.....................................(414) 272-6020
Mārion Merrell Dow ....(816) 966-4000
Mark IV Industries..(716) 689-4972
Mark VII Risk Management ....(816) 891-0500
Markel...(804) 747-0136
Marquette Electronics ....(414) 355-5000
Marriott..(301) 380-3000
Marsh & McLennan Companies.........................(212) 345-5000
Marsh Supermarkets ....(317) 594-2100
Marshall & Ilsley ....(414) 765-7801
Marshall Industries ....(818) 307-6000
Martin Marietta ....(301) 897-6000
Martin Marietta Materials...................................(919) 781-4550
Marvel Entertainment Group ....(212) 696-0808
Masco...(313) 274-7400
Mascotech...(313) 274-7405
Masland..(717) 249-1866
MasTec ....(305) 599-1800
Matlack Systems ....(302) 426-2700
Mattel ....(310) 252-2000
Maxicare Health Plans ....(213) 765-2000
Maxtor ....(408) 432-1700
Maxus Energy ....(214) 953-2000
MAXXAM...(713) 975-7600
May Department Stores..(314) 342-6300
Maybelline...(901) 324-0310
Mayflower Transit ....(317) 875-1000
Maytag ....(515) 792-8000
MBIA ....(914) 273-4545
MBNA ....(302) 453-9930

McClatchy Newspapers	(916) 321-1846
McCormick & Company	(410) 771-7301
McDermott	(504) 587-5400
McDonald's	(708) 575-3000
McDonnell Douglas	(314) 232-0232
McGraw-Hill	(212) 512-2000
MCI Communications	(202) 872-1600
McKesson	(415) 983-8300
MCN	(313) 256-5500
McWhorter Technologies	(708) 428-2657
MDU Resources Group	(701) 222-7900
The Mead Corporation	(513) 495-6323
Measurex	(408) 255-1500
Medaphis	(404) 319-3300
Media General	(804) 649-6000
Medtronic	(612) 574-4000
Medusa Cement	(216) 371-4000
Mellon Bank	(412) 234-5000
Melville	(914) 925-4000
Men's Wearhouse	(713) 295-7200
Mentor Graphics	(503) 685-7000
Mercantile Bancorporation	(314) 425-2525
Mercantile Bankshares	(410) 237-5900
Mercantile Stores	(513) 881-8000
Merck & Company	(908) 423-1000
Mercury Finance	(708) 564-3720
Mercury General	(213) 937-1060
Meredith	(515) 284-3000
Meridian Bancorp	(610) 655-2000
Merisel	(310) 615-3080
Merrill	(612) 646-4501
Merrill Lynch & Company	(212) 449-1000
Merry-Go-Round Enterprises	(410) 538-1000
Mesa	(214) 969-2200
Mesa Airlines	(505) 327-0271
Mestek	(413) 568-9571
Methode Electronics	(708) 867-9600
MFS Communications	(402) 271-2890
MGIC Investment	(414) 347-6480
MGM Grand	(702) 891-3333
Michael Baker	(412) 269-6300
Michael Foods	(612) 546-1500
Michaels Stores	(214) 714-7000
Michigan National	(810) 473-3000
Micro Warehouse	(203) 899-4000
MicroAge	(602) 968-3168
Micron Technology	(208) 368-4000
Micropolis	(818) 709-3300
Microsoft	(206) 882-8080
Mid Atlantic Medical Services	(301) 294-5140
The Midland Company	(513) 721-3777
Midlantic	(908) 321-8000
Midwest Resources	(515) 242-4300
Mikasa	(310) 886-3700
Millipore	(617) 275-9200
Mine Safety Appliances	(412) 967-3000
Minerals Technologies	(212) 878-1800
Minnesota Power & Light	(218) 722-2641
Mirage Resorts	(702) 791-7111
Mississippi Chemical	(601) 746-4131
Mitchell Energy & Development	(713) 377-5500

Mobil	(703) 846-3000
Modine Manufacturing	(414) 636-1200
Mohawk Industries	(404) 951-6000
Molex	(708) 969-4550
The Money Store	(908) 686-2000
Monk-Austin	(919) 753-8000
Monsanto	(314) 694-1000
The Montana Power Company	(406) 723-5421
Moog	(716) 652-2000
Moore Medical	(203) 826-3600
Morgan Products	(708) 317-2400
Morgan Stanley Group	(212) 703-4000
Morningstar Group	(214) 360-4700
Morrison Knudsen	(208) 386-5000
Morrison Restaurants	(205) 344-3000
Morton	(312) 807-2000
Mosinee Paper	(715) 693-4470
Motorola	(708) 576-5000
Mueller Industries	(316) 636-6300
The Multicare Companies	(201) 488-8818
Multimedia	(803) 298-4373
Murphy Oil	(501) 862-6411
Musicland Stores	(612) 931-8000
Myers Industries	(216) 253-5592
Mylan Laboratories	(412) 232-0100
Nabors Industries	(713) 874-0035
NAC Re	(203) 622-5200
NACCO Industries	(216) 449-9600
Nalco Chemical	(708) 305-1000
Nash Finch	(612) 832-0534
Nashua	(603) 880-2323
National Auto Credit	(216) 349-1000
National Beverage	(305) 581-0922
National City	(216) 575-2000
National Commerce Bancorporation	(901) 523-3242
National Computer Systems	(612) 829-3000
National Convenience Stores	(713) 863-2200
National Education	(714) 474-9400
National Fuel Gas	(212) 541-7533
National Gypsum	(704) 365-7300
National Health Laboratories	(619) 550-0600
National Healthcare	(615) 890-2020
National Medical Enterprises	(310) 998-8000
National Re	(203) 329-7700
National Sanitary Supply	(513) 762-6500
National Semiconductor	(408) 721-5000
National Service Industries	(404) 853-1000
National Steel	(219) 273-7000
National Western Life Insurance	(512) 836-1010
NationsBank	(704) 386-5000
Nautica Enterprises	(212) 541-5990
Navistar	(312) 836-2000
NBD Bancorp	(313) 225-1000
NCH	(214) 438-0211
The Neiman Marcus Group	(617) 232-0760
Nellcor	(510) 463-4000
Network Equipment Technologies	(415) 366-4400
Network Systems	(612) 424-4888
Nevada Power	(702) 367-5000
New Age Media Fund	(410) 547-2000
New England Business Service	(508) 448-6111

New England Electric System	(508) 366-9011
New England Investment Companies	(617) 578-3500
New Jersey Resources	(908) 938-1480
New World Communications Group	(404) 955-0045
New York State Electric & Gas	(607) 347-4131
New York Times	(212) 556-1234
Newell	(815) 235-4171
Newmont Gold	(303) 863-7414
Niagara Mohawk Power	(315) 474-1511
NICOR	(708) 305-9500
Nike	(503) 671-6453
Nine West Group	(203) 324-7567
NIPSCO Industries	(219) 853-5200
NL Industries	(713) 423-3300
Noble Affiliates	(405) 223-4110
Noble Drilling	(713) 974-3131
Noland	(804) 928-9000
NorAm Energy	(713) 654-5699
Nordson	(216) 892-1580
Nordstrom	(206) 628-2111
Norfolk Southern	(804) 629-2680
Norrell	(404) 240-3000
Norstan	(612) 420-1100
Nortek	(401) 751-1600
North American Mortgage	(707) 523-5000
Northeast Federal	(203) 280-1000
Northeast Utilities	(203) 665-5000
Northern States Power	(612) 330-5500
Northern Trust	(312) 630-6000
Northrop Grumman	(310) 553-6262
Northwest Airlines	(612) 726-2111
Northwest Natural Gas	(503) 226-4211
Northwestern Steel and Wire	(815) 625-2500
Norwest	(612) 667-1234
NovaCare	(610) 992-7200
Novell	(801) 429-7000
NPC	(316) 231-3390
NS Group	(606) 292-6809
Nucor	(704) 366-7000
NUI	(908) 781-0500
NVR	(703) 761-2000
NYNEX	(212) 395-2121
O'Sullivan	(703) 667-6666
O'Sullivan Industries Holdings	(417) 682-3322
Oak Industries	(617) 890-0400
Oakwood Homes	(910) 855-2400
Occidental Petroleum	(310) 208-8800
Oceaneering	(713) 578-8868
Octel Communications	(408) 321-2000
Office Depot	(407) 278-4800
Office Max	(216) 921-6900
Ogden	(212) 868-6100
Ohio Casualty	(513) 867-3000
Ohio Edison	(216) 384-5100
OHM	(419) 423-3529
Oklahoma Gas & Electric	(405) 553-3000
Old Dominion Freight Line	(910) 889-5000
Old Kent Financial	(616) 771-5000
Old National Bancorp	(812) 464-1434
Old Republic	(312) 346-8100
Olin	(203) 356-2000

Olsten	(516) 844-7800
Olympic Steel	(216) 292-3800
OM Group	(216) 781-0083
OMI	(212) 986-1960
Omnicare	(513) 762-6666
Omnicom Group	(212) 415-3600
ONBAN	(315) 424-4400
One Price Clothing Stores	(803) 433-8888
One Valley Bancorp of West Virginia	(304) 348-7000
Oneida	(315) 361-3636
ONEOK	(918) 588-7000
Oracle Systems	(415) 506-7000
Orange & Rockland Utilities	(914) 352-6000
Orchard Supply Hardware Stores	(408) 281-3500
Oregon Steel Mills	(503) 223-9228
Orion Capital	(212) 332-8080
OrNda Health	(615) 383-8599
Oryx Energy	(214) 715-4000
Oshkosh B'Gosh	(414) 231-8800
Oshkosh Truck	(414) 235-9151
Oshman's Sporting Goods	(713) 928-3171
Otter Tail Power	(218) 739-8200
Outback Steakhouse	(813) 282-1225
Outboard Marine	(708) 689-6200
Overseas Shipholding Group	(212) 869-1222
Owens & Minor	(804) 747-9794
Owens-Corning Fiberglas	(419) 248-8000
Oxford Health Plans	(203) 852-1442
Oxford Industries	(404) 659-2424
P. H. Glatfelter	(717) 225-4711
PACCAR	(206) 455-7400
Pacific Enterprises	(213) 895-5000
Pacific Gas & Electric	(415) 973-7000
Pacific Physician Services	(909) 825-4401
Pacific Scientific	(714) 720-1714
Pacific Telecom	(206) 696-0983
Pacific Telesis Group	(415) 394-3000
PacifiCare Health Systems	(714) 952-1121
PacifiCorp	(503) 731-2000
Paging Network	(214) 985-4100
Pall	(516) 484-5400
Pamida	(402) 339-2400
Panhandle Eastern	(713) 627-5400
Paragon Trade Brands	(206) 924-4509
Parametric Technology	(617) 398-5000
Park Electrochemical	(516) 354-4100
Parker & Parsley Petroleum	(915) 683-4768
Parker Hannifin	(216) 531-3000
Patrick Industries	(219) 294-7511
Patterson Dental	(612) 686-1600
Paul Revere	(508) 799-4441
Paychex	(716) 385-6666
Payless Cashways	(816) 234-6000
PECO Energy	(215) 841-4000
Pegasus Gold	(509) 624-4653
PennCorp Financial Group	(212) 832-0700
Pennsylvania Enterprises	(717) 829-8843
Pennsylvania Power & Light	(610) 774-5151
Pennzoil	(713) 546-4000
Pentair	(612) 636-7920
People's Bank	(203) 338-7171

Peoples Energy	(312) 240-4000
The Pep Boys	(215) 229-9000
PepsiCo	(914) 253-2000
Performance Food Group	(615) 391-0112
Perini	(508) 628-2000
The Perkin-Elmer Corporation	(203) 762-1000
Perrigo	(616) 673-8451
Perry Drug Stores	(810) 334-1300
Pet	(314) 622-7700
Petrie Stores	(201) 866-3600
Petroleum Heat & Power	(203) 325-5400
Petrolite	(314) 961-3500
PETsMART	(602) 944-7070
Pfizer	(212) 573-2323
Phelps Dodge	(602) 234-8100
PHH	(410) 771-3600
Philip Morris Companies	(212) 880-5000
Phillips Petroleum	(918) 661-6600
Phillips-Van Heusen	(212) 541-5200
Physicians of America	(305) 267-6633
Physicians Health Services	(203) 381-6400
Piccadilly Cafeterias	(504) 293-9440
PictureTel	(508) 762-5000
Piedmont Natural Gas	(704) 364-3120
Pier 1 Imports	(817) 878-8000
Pilgrim's Pride	(903) 855-1000
Pillowtex	(214) 333-3225
Pinkerton's	(818) 380-8800
Pinnacle West Capital	(602) 379-2500
Pioneer Financial Services	(815) 987-5000
Pioneer Hi-Bred	(515) 248-4800
Pioneer-Standard Electronics	(216) 587-3600
Piper Jaffray Companies	(612) 342-6000
Pitney-Bowes	(203) 356-5000
Pitt-Des Moines	(412) 331-3000
Pittston Minerals Group	(203) 978-5200
Pittway	(312) 831-1070
Plains Resources	(713) 654-1414
Playboy Enterprises	(312) 751-8000
Playtex Products	(203) 341-4000
Plexus	(414) 722-3451
Plum Creek Timber	(206) 467-3600
Ply-Gem Industries	(212) 832-1550
PNC Bank	(412) 762-2000
Polaris Industries	(612) 542-0500
Polaroid	(617) 386-2000
Policy Management Systems	(803) 735-4000
Pool Energy Services	(713) 954-3000
Pope & Talbot	(503) 228-9161
Portland General	(503) 464-8820
Potlatch	(415) 576-8800
Potomac Electric Power	(202) 872-2456
PPG Industries	(412) 434-3131
Pratt & Lambert United	(716) 873-6000
Pratt Hotel	(214) 386-9777
Praxair	(203) 837-2000
Precision Castparts	(503) 777-3881
Premark	(708) 405-6000
Premier Bancorp	(504) 332-4011
Premier Industrial	(216) 391-8300
The Presley Companies	(714) 640-6400

Price/CostCo...(206) 803-8100
Primark ....(617) 466-6611
The Procter & Gamble Company..................(513) 983-1100
Proffitt's...(615) 983-7000
Progressive ....(216) 461-5000
Promus Companies ....(901) 762-8600
Protective Life ....(205) 879-9230
Provident Bancorp....................................(513) 579-2000
Provident Life and Accident Insurance...........(615) 755-1011
Providian...(502) 560-2000
Public Service Company of Colorado..............(303) 571-7511
Public Service Company of New Mexico..........(505) 848-2700
Public Service Company of North Carolina......(704) 864-6731
Public Service Enterprise Group.....................(201) 430-7000
Puget Sound Power & Light ....(206) 454-6363
Pulitzer Publishing....................................(314) 340-8000
Pulte ....(810) 647-2750
Puritan-Bennett.......................................(913) 661-0444
QMS...(334) 633-4300
The Quaker Oats Company ....(312) 222-7111
Quaker State..(814) 676-7676
QUALCOMM...(619) 587-1121
Quality Food Centers ....(206) 455-3761
Quanex...(713) 961-4600
Quantum...(408) 894-4000
Questar..(801) 534-5000
The Quick & Reilly Group ....(407) 655-8000
Quorum Health Group..............................(615) 371-7979
R. P. Scherer ....(810) 649-0900
R. R. Donnelley & Sons............................(312) 326-8000
Radius..(408) 541-6100
Ralcorp..(314) 982-5900
Ralston Continental Baking Group...............(314) 982-1000
Raychem..(415) 361-3333
Raymond James Financial ....(813) 573-3800
Rayonier...(203) 348-7000
Raytheon...(617) 862-6600
The Reader's Digest Association.....................(914) 238-1000
Read-Rite...(408) 262-6700
Redman Industries....................................(214) 353-3600
Reebok ....(617) 341-5000
Regal-Beloit ....(608) 364-8800
Regions Financial ....(205) 326-7100
Regis...(612) 947-7777
Reinsurance Group of America....................(314) 453-7300
Reliance Group Holdings...........................(212) 909-1100
Reliance Steel & Aluminum.........................(213) 582-2272
Reliastar Financial.....................................(612) 372-5432
Republic New York...................................(212) 525-6100
Resorts..(609) 344-6000
Revco D.S..(216) 425-9811
REX Stores..(513) 276-3931
Rexel ....(305) 466-8000
Rexene ....(214) 450-9000
Reynolds & Reynolds ....(513) 443-2000
Reynolds Metals ....(804) 281-2000
Rhodes ....(404) 264-4600
Rhone-Poulenc Rorer................................(610) 454-8000
Richfood Holdings....................................(804) 746-6000
Riggs National ....(202) 835-6000
RightChoice Managed Care........................(314) 923-4444

Riser Foods...(216) 292-7000
Rite Aid...(717) 761-2633
The Rival Company.....................................(816) 943-4100
Riverwood..(404) 644-3000
RJR Nabisco...(212) 258-5600
Roadmaster Industries................................(303) 290-8150
Roadway Services..(216) 384-8184
Roberd's...(513) 859-5127
Robert Half...(415) 854-9700
Robertson-Ceco..(617) 424-5500
Rochester Community Savings Bank..............(716) 258-3000
Rochester Gas & Electric.............................(716) 546-2700
Rock-Tenn..(404) 448-2193
Rockwell..(310) 797-3311
Rohm & Haas..(215) 592-3000
Rohr...(619) 691-4111
Rollins...(404) 888-2000
Roosevelt Financial Group...........................(314) 532-6200
Rose's Stores..(919) 430-2600
Ross Stores...(510) 505-4400
Rouge Steel..(313) 390-6877
The Rouse Company....................................(410) 992-6000
Rowan Companies.......................................(713) 621-7800
Roy F. Weston...(610) 701-3000
Royal Appliance Manufacturing...................(216) 449-6150
Royal Caribbean Cruises..............................(305) 539-6000
RPM...(216) 273-5090
Rubbermaid..(216) 264-6464
Ruddick..(704) 372-5404
Russ Berrie & Company................................(201) 337-9000
Russell...(205) 329-4000
Rust...(205) 995-7878
Ryan's Family Steak Houses.........................(803) 879-1000
Ryder System..(305) 593-3726
Rykoff-Sexton...(213) 622-4131
The Ryland Group.......................................(410) 715-7000
SAFECO..(206) 545-5000
Safeguard Scientifics...................................(610) 293-0600
Safety-Kleen...(708) 697-8460
Safeway..(510) 891-3000
Sahara Gaming..(702) 737-2111
St. Jude Medical..(612) 483-2000
St. Paul Bancorp...(312) 622-5000
The St. Paul Companies................................(612) 221-7911
Salant..(212) 221-7500
Salomon Brothers..(212) 783-7000
San Diego Gas & Electric.............................(619) 696-2000
Santa Fe Energy Resources...........................(713) 783-2401
Santa Fe Pacific..(708) 995-6000
Santa Fe Pacific Gold...................................(505) 880-5300
Sara Lee...(312) 726-2600
Savannah Foods & Industries.......................(912) 234-1261
Sbarro...(516) 864-0200
SBC Communications..................................(210) 821-4105
SCANA...(803) 748-3000
SCEcorp...(818) 302-2222
Schering-Plough...(201) 822-7000
Schlumberger...(212) 350-9400
Schnitzer Steel Industries............................(503) 224-9900
Scholastic...(212) 343-6100
Schult Homes..(219) 825-5881

Schultz Sav-O Stores	(414) 457-4433
Scientific-Atlanta	(404) 903-5000
SCOR U.S.	(212) 978-8200
Scotsman Industries	(708) 215-4500
Scott Paper	(610) 522-5000
The Scotts Company	(513) 644-0011
Seaboard	(913) 676-8800
Seagate Technology	(408) 438-6550
Seagull Energy	(713) 951-4700
Sealed Air	(201) 791-7600
Sealright	(913) 344-9000
Sears, Roebuck & Company	(312) 875-2500
Seaway Food Town	(419) 893-9401
Security-Connecticut	(203) 677-8621
SEI	(610) 254-1000
Selective Insurance Group	(201) 948-3000
Seneca Foods	(716) 385-9500
Sensormatic Electronics	(305) 420-2000
Sequa	(212) 986-5500
Sequent Computer Systems	(503) 626-5700
Service	(713) 522-5141
Service Merchandise	(615) 660-6000
ServiceMaster	(708) 271-1300
SFFed	(415) 955-5800
Shared Medical Systems	(610) 219-6300
Shaw Industries	(706) 278-3812
Shawmut National	(203) 728-2000
Shelter Components	(219) 262-4541
The Sherwin-Williams Company	(216) 566-2000
Shiloh Industries	(419) 525-2315
Shoney's	(615) 391-5201
ShopKo Stores	(414) 497-2211
Shorewood Packaging	(516) 694-2900
ShowBiz Pizza Time	(214) 258-8507
Showboat	(702) 385-9123
Sierra Health Services	(702) 242-7000
Sierra Pacific Resources	(702) 689-5400
Sigma-Aldrich	(314) 771-5765
Signet Banking	(804) 747-2000
Silicon Graphics	(415) 960-1980
Silicon Valley Group	(408) 434-0500
Simon Property Group	(317) 636-1600
Simpson Industries	(810) 540-6200
Sithe Energies	(212) 450-9000
Sizzler	(310) 827-2300
Skyline	(219) 294-6521
SLM	(212) 675-0070
Smart & Final	(213) 589-1054
Smith	(713) 443-3370
Smith Corona	(203) 972-1471
Smithfield Foods	(804) 357-4321
Smith's Food & Drug Centers	(801) 974-1400
Snap-On	(414) 656-5200
Snyder Oil	(817) 338-4043
Software Spectrum	(214) 840-6600
Solectron	(408) 957-8500
Sonat	(205) 325-3800
Sonat Offshore Drilling	(713) 871-7500
Sonoco Products	(803) 383-7000
Sotheby's Holdings	(212) 606-7000
South Jersey Industries	(609) 561-9000

Southdown	(713) 650-6200
Southeastern Michigan Gas Enterprise	(810) 987-2200
Southern California Edison	(818) 302-1212
The Southern Company	(404) 393-0650
Southern Electronics	(404) 491-8962
Southern Indiana Gas and Electric	(812) 424-6411
Southern National	(910) 671-2000
Southern New England Telecommunications	(203) 771-5200
Southern Pacific Rail	(415) 541-1000
Southern Union Exploration	(512) 477-5981
The Southland Corporation	(214) 828-7011
SouthTrust	(205) 254-5000
Southwest Airlines	(214) 904-4000
Southwest Gas	(702) 876-7237
Southwestern Life	(214) 954-7111
Southwestern Public Service	(806) 378-2121
Sovereign Bancorp	(610) 320-8400
SpaceLabs Medical	(206) 882-3700
Spain Fund	(212) 969-1000
SPARTECH	(314) 721-4242
Specialty Equipment	(815) 544-5111
Spelling Entertainment Group	(213) 965-5700
Spiegel	(708) 986-8800
Sportmart	(708) 966-1700
Sports & Recreation	(813) 886-9688
The Sports Authority	(305) 735-1701
Spreckels Industries	(510) 460-0840
Springs Industries	(803) 547-1500
Sprint	(913) 624-3000
SPS Technologies	(215) 517-2000
SPS Transaction Services	(708) 405-3700
SPX	(616) 724-5000
Staff Builders	(516) 358-1000
Standard Commercial	(919) 291-5507
Standard Federal Bank	(810) 643-9600
Standard Microsystems	(516) 273-3100
Standard Motor Products	(718) 392-0200
Standard Pacific	(714) 668-4300
The Standard Products Company	(216) 281-8300
The Standard Register Company.	(513) 443-1000
Standex	(603) 893-9701
Stanhome	(413) 562-3631
The Stanley Works	(203) 225-5111
Stant	(317) 962-6655
Staples	(508) 370-8500
Star Banc	(513) 632-4000
Starbucks	(206) 447-1575
Starter	(203) 781-4000
State Street Boston	(617) 786-3000
Station Casinos	(702) 367-2411
Steel Technologies	(502) 245-2110
Stein Mart	(904) 346-1500
Stepan	(708) 446-7500
Sterling Chemicals	(713) 650-3700
Sterling Electronics	(713) 627-9800
Sterling Software	(214) 891-8600
Stewart & Stevenson Services	(713) 868-7700
Stewart Enterprises	(504) 837-5880
Stewart Information Services	(713) 625-8100
Stolt Neilsen	(203) 625-3608
Stone & Webster	(212) 290-7500

Stone Container	(312) 346-6600
Storage Technology	(303) 673-5151
Stratus Computer	(508) 460-2000
Strawbridge & Clothier	(215) 629-6000
The Stride Rite Corporation	(617) 491-8800
Stryker	(616) 385-2600
The Student Loan Corporation	(716) 248-7187
Student Loan Marketing Association	(202) 333-8000
Sudbury	(216) 464-7026
The Summit Bancorporation	(201) 701-2666
Sun	(215) 977-3000
Sun Distributors	(215) 665-3650
Sun Healthcare Group	(505) 821-3355
Sun Microsystems	(415) 960-1300
Sun Television and Appliances	(614) 445-8401
SunAmerica	(310) 772-6000
Sunbeam-Oster	(305) 767-2100
Sundstrand	(815) 226-6000
SunGard Data Systems	(610) 341-8700
Sunrise Medical	(619) 930-1500
SunTrust Banks	(404) 588-7711
Super Food Services	(513) 439-7500
Super Rite	(717) 232-6821
Superior Industries	(818) 781-4973
SUPERVALU	(612) 828-4000
Surgical Care Affiliates	(615) 385-3541
Swift Transportation	(602) 269-9700
Sybase	(510) 596-3500
Sybron	(414) 274-6600
Symantec	(408) 253-9600
Symbol Technologies	(516) 563-2400
Syms	(201) 902-9600
SynOptics Communications	(408) 988-2400
Synovus Financial	(706) 649-2311
SyQuest Technology	(510) 226-4000
Sysco	(713) 584-1390
System Software Assocs.	(312) 641-2900
T2 Medical	(404) 442-2160
The Talbots	(617) 749-7600
Talley Industries	(602) 957-7711
Tambrands	(914) 696-6000
Tandem Computers	(408) 285-6000
Tandy	(817) 390-3700
Tandycrafts	(817) 551-9600
TBC	(901) 363-8030
TCF Financial	(612) 661-6500
Tech Data	(813) 539-7429
TECO Energy	(813) 228-4111
Tecumseh Products	(517) 423-8411
Tejas Gas	(713) 658-0509
Tejas Power	(713) 597-6200
Tektronix	(503) 627-7111
Tele-Communications	(303) 267-5500
Teledyne	(310) 277-3311
Teleflex	(610) 834-6301
Telephone & Data Systems	(312) 630-1900
Tellabs	(708) 969-8800
Telxon	(216) 867-3700
Temple-Inland	(409) 829-2211
Tennant	(612) 540-1200
Tenneco	(713) 757-2131

Teradyne	(617) 482-2700
Terex	(203) 222-7170
Terra Industries	(712) 277-1340
Terra Nitrogen	(918) 660-0050
Tesoro Petroleum	(210) 828-8484
Texaco	(914) 253-4000
Texas Industries	(214) 647-6700
Texas Instruments	(214) 995-2011
Texas Utilities	(214) 812-4600
Texfi Industries	(919) 783-4736
Textron	(401) 421-2800
Thermadyne Holdings	(314) 721-5573
Thermo Cardiosystems	(617) 622-1000
Thermo Instrument Systems	(505) 438-3171
Thiokol	(801) 629-2000
Thomas & Betts	(901) 682-7766
Thomas Industries	(502) 893-4600
Thomas Nelson	(615) 889-9000
Thomaston Mills	(706) 647-7131
Thor Industries	(513) 596-6849
Thorn Apple Valley	(810) 552-0700
Tidewater	(504) 568-1010
Tiffany & Company	(212) 755-8000
TIG Holdings	(212) 446-2700
Timberland	(603) 926-1600
Time Warner	(212) 484-8000
The Times Mirror Company	(213) 237-3700
The Timken Company	(216) 438-3000
Titan Wheel	(217) 228-6011
TJ	(208) 345-8500
The TJX Companies	(508) 390-1000
TNP Enterprises	(817) 731-0099
TNT Freightways	(708) 696-0200
Toll Brothers	(215) 938-8000
Tootsie Roll Industries	(312) 838-3400
The Topps Company	(212) 376-0300
Tops Appliance City	(908) 248-2850
Torchmark	(205) 325-4200
The Toro Company	(612) 888-8801
Tosco	(203) 977-1000
Tower Air	(718) 553-4300
Town & Country	(617) 884-8500
TPI Enterprises	(407) 835-8888
Tracor	(512) 926-2800
Tractor Supply	(615) 366-4600
Trans World Entertainment	(518) 452-1242
Transamerica	(415) 983-4000
Transatlantic Holdings	(212) 770-2000
Transco Energy	(713) 439-2000
TransTexas Gas	(713) 447-3111
The Travelers	(212) 891-8900
Treadco	(501) 785-6000
Tredegar Industries	(804) 330-1000
Triangle Pacific	(214) 931-3000
Triarc Companies	(212) 230-3000
Tribune	(312) 222-9100
Trident NGL Holding	(713) 367-7600
TriMas	(313) 747-7025
Trinity Industries	(214) 631-4420
TRINOVA	(419) 867-2200
Truck Components	(815) 964-3301

True North Communications	(312) 751-7000
Trustmark	(601) 354-5111
TRW	(216) 291-7000
Tucson Electric Power	(602) 571-4000
Tultex	(703) 632-2961
Turner	(212) 229-6000
Turner Broadcasting System	(404) 827-1700
Tyco	(603) 778-9700
Tyco Toys	(609) 234-7400
Tyler	(214) 754-7800
Tyson Foods	(501) 290-4000
UAL	(708) 952-4000
UDC Homes	(602) 820-4488
UGI	(610) 337-1000
UJB Financial	(609) 987-3200
Ultramar	(203) 622-7000
UMB Financial	(816) 860-7000
UNC	(410) 266-7333
The Unicom Corp.	(312) 394-4321
Unifi	(910) 294-4410
UniFirst	(508) 658-8888
Uni-Marts	(814) 234-6000
Union Bank	(415) 705-7350
Union Camp	(201) 628-2000
Union Carbide	(203) 794-2000
Union Electric	(314) 621-3222
Union Pacific	(610) 861-3200
Union Planters National Bank	(901) 383-6000
Union Texas Petroleum Holdings	(713) 623-6544
Unisys	(215) 542-4011
United Asset Management	(617) 330-8900
United Carolina Bancshares	(910) 642-5131
United Cities Gas	(615) 373-5310
United Companies Financial	(504) 924-6007
United HealthCare	(612) 936-1300
The United Illuminating Company.	(203) 499-2000
United Insurance Companies	(214) 960-8497
United Retail Group	(201) 845-0880
United States Cellular	(312) 399-8900
The United States Shoe Corporation.	(513) 527-7000
United States Surgical	(203) 845-1000
United Stationers	(708) 699-5000
United Technologies	(203) 728-7000
United Water Resources	(201) 784-9434
United Wisconsin Services	(414) 226-6900
Unitrin	(312) 661-4600
Univar	(206) 889-3400
Universal	(804) 359-9311
Universal Foods	(414) 271-6755
Universal Forest Products	(616) 364-6161
Universal Health Services	(610) 768-3300
Unocal	(213) 977-7600
UNR Industries	(312) 341-1234
UNUM	(207) 770-2211
The Upjohn Company.	(616) 323-4000
U.S. Bancorp	(503) 275-6111
U.S. Can	(708) 571-2500
U.S. Healthcare	(215) 628-4800
U.S. Home	(713) 877-2311
US Robotics	(708) 982-5010
U.S. Trust	(212) 852-1000

US West	(303) 793-6500
U.S. Xpress Enterprises	(615) 697-7377
USAir Group	(703) 418-5306
USF&G	(410) 547-3000
USG	(312) 606-4000
USLIFE	(212) 709-6000
UST	(203) 661-1100
USX – Delhi Group	(412) 433-1121
UtiliCorp United	(816) 421-6600
V. F.	(610) 378-1151
Valassis Communications	(313) 591-3000
Valero Energy	(210) 246-2000
Valhi	(214) 233-1700
Valley National Bancorp	(201) 305-8800
Valmont Industries	(402) 359-2201
The Valspar Corporation	(612) 332-7371
Value City Department Stores	(614) 471-4722
Value Health	(203) 678-3400
Varian Assocs.	(415) 493-4000
Varity	(716) 888-8000
Varlen	(708) 420-0400
Vastar Resources	(713) 584-6000
Vencor	(502) 569-7300
Venture Stores	(314) 281-5500
VeriFone	(415) 591-6500
Viacom	(212) 258-6000
VICORP Restaurants	(303) 296-2121
The Vigoro Corporation	(312) 819-2020
Viking Office Products	(213) 321-4493
Vishay Intertechnology	(610) 644-1300
Vivra	(415) 348-8200
VLSI Technology	(408) 434-3000
Volt Information Sciences	(212) 704-2400
The Vons Companies	(818) 821-7000
Vulcan Materials	(205) 877-3000
VWR	(610) 431-1700
W. H. Brady	(414) 332-8100
W. R. Berkley	(203) 629-2880
W. R. Grace & Company	(407) 362-2000
W. W. Grainger	(708) 982-9000
Waban	(508) 651-6500
Wabash National	(317) 448-1591
Wachovia	(910) 770-5000
The Wackenhut Corporation	(305) 666-5656
Wainoco Oil	(713) 658-9900
Walbro	(517) 872-2131
Walgreen	(708) 940-2500
Wallace Computer Services	(312) 626-2000
Wal-Mart Stores	(501) 273-4000
The Walt Disney Co.	(818) 560-1000
Wang Laboratories	(508) 459-5000
The Warnaco Group	(212) 661-1300
Warner-Lambert	(201) 540-2000
Washington Energy	(206) 622-6767
Washington Federal	(206) 624-7930
Washington Gas & Light	(703) 750-4440
Washington Mutual	(206) 461-2000
Washington National	(708) 793-3000
The Washington Post Company	(202) 334-6000
The Washington Water Power Company	(509) 489-0500
Watkins-Johnson	(415) 493-4141

Watsco	(305) 858-0828
Watts Industries	(508) 688-1811
Wausau Paper Mills	(715) 845-5266
WCI Steel	(216) 841-8000
Weathersford	(713) 439-9400
Weirton Steel	(304) 797-2000
Weis Markets	(717) 286-4571
Wellman	(908) 542-7300
WellPoint Health Networks	(818) 703-4000
Wells Fargo & Company	(415) 477-1000
Wendy's	(614) 764-3100
Werner Enterprises	(402) 895-6640
West	(610) 594-2900
West One Bancorp	(208) 383-7000
Western Atlas	(310) 888-2500
Western Beef	(718) 821-0011
The Western Company of North America	(713) 629-2600
Western Digital	(714) 932-5000
Western Gas Resources	(303) 452-5603
Western National	(713) 888-7800
Western Publishing Group	(212) 688-4500
Western Resources	(913) 575-6300
Western Waste Industries	(310) 328-0900
Westinghouse Electric	(412) 244-2000
Westmoreland Coal	(215) 545-2500
WestPoint Stevens	(706) 645-4000
Westvaco	(212) 688-5000
Weyerhaeuser	(206) 924-2345
Wheelabrator Technologies	(603) 929-3000
Whirlpool	(616) 923-5000
Whitman	(708) 818-5000
Whole Foods Market	(512) 328-7541
WHX	(212) 355-5200
Wickes Lumber	(708) 367-3400
WICOR	(414) 291-7026
Willamette Industries	(503) 227-5581
The Williams Companies	(918) 588-2000
Williams-Sonoma	(415) 421-7900
Wilmington Trust	(302) 651-1000
Winn-Dixie Stores	(904) 783-5000
Winnebago Industries	(515) 582-3535
WinsLoew Furniture	(305) 858-2200
Wisconsin Electric	(414) 221-2345
Witco	(203) 552-2000
WLR Foods	(703) 896-7001
William Wrigley Jr.	(312) 644-2121
WMS Industries	(312) 961-1000
WMX Technologies	(708) 572-8800
Wolohan Lumber	(517) 793-4532
Wolverine Tube	(205) 353-1310
Wolverine World Wide	(616) 866-5500
Woolworth	(212) 553-2000
Worthington Industries	(614) 438-3210
WPL Holdings	(608) 252-3311
WPS Resources	(414) 433-1445
WTD Industries	(503) 246-3440
Wyle Electronics	(714) 753-9953
Wyman-Gordon	(508) 839-4441
Wynn's	(714) 938-3700
Xerox	(203) 968-3000
Xilinx	(408) 559-7778

Money

XTRA ....(617) 367-5000
Yankee Energy System.......................................(203) 639-4000
Yellow..(913) 967-4300
York...(717) 771-7890
Younkers..(515) 244-1112
Zale ....(214) 580-4000
Zeigler Coal Holding...(618) 394-2400
Zenith Electronics ....(708) 391-7000
Zenith National Insurance ....(818) 713-1000
ZEOS..(612) 623-9614
Zions Bancorporation ....(801) 524-4787
Zurn Industries...(814) 452-2111

Source: Based upon information compiled from sources including Hoover's MasterList of Major U.S. Companies. Copyright © 1995, The Reference Press, Inc. Reprinted with permission. Book and disk versions of this product are available from The Reference Press, 6448 Highway 290 East, E-104, Austin, TX 78723; Phone (800) 486-8666; Fax (512) 454-9401; email refpress6@aol.com. For more information see Hoover's Online on the Internet (http://www.hoovers.com).

Audio/Visual Rental Companies

ALABAMA
Holt Audio Visual & Video, Birmingham ....(205) 328-5231

ARIZONA
Ancha Audio Video Corporation,
   Scottsdale...(602) 860-9321
Audio Visual America, Phoenix ....(602) 275-6060
Timberline Productions, Phoenix ....(602) 277-7075

CALIFORNIA
American Video Comms.,
   Los Alamitos..(310) 493-3771
Ametron/American Electronic Supply,
   Los Angeles...(213) 466-4321
Audio Video West, Venice................................(310) 821-1391
Audio Visual Headquarters, Rancho.................(310) 885-4200
AV Images, Dublin ....(510) 828-2288
Background Engineers, Glendale ....(818) 500-0454
Crown Audio Visual, Coronado........................(619) 522-8078
Hi Tech Rentals, Burbank................................(818) 848-1010
Impact Corporate Comms., Ventura ....(800) 675-2200
Instructional Materials & Equipment
   Distributors, Los Angeles................................(213) 879-0377
Media Fabricators, Los Angeles ....(213) 937-3344
Meeting Services, San Diego ....(619) 299-6042
Photo & Sound, San Francisco........................(415) 703-8920
Riverview Systems Group, San Jose..................(408) 283-5930
Shoreline, Hollywood......................................(213) 461-9800
Video Applications, Irvine ....(714) 724-1700
Vision Master, Pomona ....(909) 622-3306

COLORADO
Ceavco Audio-Visual, Denver ....(303) 238-6493
Colorado Visual Aids, Denver ....(303) 778-1111
Davis Audio-Visual, Denver..............................(303) 455-1122
Image Audiovisuals, Denver..............................(303) 758-1818
Multimedia Audio Visual, Denver ....(303) 623-2324
Spectrum Audio Visual, Denver ....(303) 477-4456

CONNECTICUT
Everett Hall Assocs., Stamford ....(203) 325-4328
HB Communications, North Haven...................(203) 234-9246

DELAWARE
AAVCO Audio Visual Rentals, Newark ....(302) 733-7978
Showorks Audio Visual, Wilmington ....(302) 798-7999

DISTRICT OF COLUMBIA
AVCOM ....(202) 408-0444

FLORIDA
Audio Visual Support Service, Tampa...............(813) 872-7914
AV Services, Orlando..(407) 240-0694
Brandons, Jacksonville ....(904) 398-1591
Dial-A-Rent Audio Visual, Jacksonville............(904) 398-8175
Harmon's Audio-Visual Services,
   Fort Myers...(813) 481-9455
Hubbard Sight & Sound AV, Jacksonville.........(904) 645-7880
Matrix Audio Visual, Sarasota ....(813) 359-1111
Metro Audio Visual, Miami ....(305) 623-1300

Photosound of Orlando, Orlando......................(407) 898-8841
Presentation Resource, Jacksonville..................(904) 398-8179
Southern Audio Visual, Miami ....(305) 591-3888

GEORGIA

Audio Visual Resources, Savannah....................(912) 355-2020
Hi-Tech Computer & Data Display Rentals,
    Morrow..(404) 968-1652
Projexions Video Supply, Atlanta ....(404) 872-6247
Staging Directions, Norcross..............................(404) 409-9909
Tech Rentals, Atlanta ....(404) 457-0966
Total Audio Visual Services, Atlanta ....(404) 875-7555

HAWAII

Media Plus, Kihei ....(808) 879-6188

IDAHO

Aatronics, Boise..(208) 343-0900
Rocky Mountain Audio Visual, Boise................(208) 336-7655

ILLINOIS

Allen Visual Systems, Northbrook.....................(708) 498-9220
Media Control, Schiller Park.............................(708) 671-9670
Midwest Visual Equipment, Chicago.................(708) 673-4525
Presentation Services, Schiller Park ....(708) 671-6277
Rent Com, Schiller Park ....(708) 678-7000
The Show Dept., Chicago...................................(312) 384-7300
Sound & Stagecraft, Des Plaines ....(708) 699-9080
Swiderski Electronics, Elk Grove Village...........(708) 364-1900
United Visual, Bensenville.................................(708) 595-3544
Video Replay, Chicago ....(312) 467-0425

INDIANA

Markey's Audio Visual, Indianapolis..................(317) 783-1155
Rent-a-Bit, Osceda ....(219) 674-5973

IOWA

Pratt Audio-Visual & Video,
    Cedar Rapids...(319) 363-8144

KENTUCKY

Audio Visual Techniques, Lexington.................(606) 254-8954
Audio Visuals of Louisville, Louisville...............(502) 568-6030

MAINE

Headlight Audio Visual, Portland......................(207) 774-5998

MARYLAND

Audio Visual, Lanham...(301) 459-9010
Total Audio-Visual Systems,
    Silver Spring ....(301) 589-3337
Visual Aids Electronics Corporate Offices,
    Silver Spring ....(301) 680-8400

MASSACHUSETTS

A. D. Handy Co., Boston....................................(617) 542-3954
A/V Presentations, Northborough.....................(508) 393-9767
Advanced Media Technologies,
    Stoughton ....(617) 344-8770
Mass Audio Visual Equipment,
    Burlington...(617) 270-0027

MICHIGAN

Advanced Media Service, Livonia....................(313) 953-9221
Allied-Vision, Troy...(810) 585-0445
Carpenter Comms., Southfield ....(810) 350-1100

MINNESOTA

Blumberg Comms., Minneapolis.......................(612) 333-1271
Electronic Design, St. Paul.................................(612) 636-3550
Mid-Co TV Systems, Minneapolis....................(612) 544-3375

MISSOURI

Hoover's Audio Visual, Kansas City ....(816) 221-7663
Show-Me Audio-Visual, Raytown ....(816) 358-5222
Swank Audio Visuals, St. Louis ....(314) 534-1940
VMI Company of St. Louis, St. Louis................(314) 569-1334

NEVADA

Encore Productions, Las Vegas..........................(702) 739-8803
Source, Las Vegas ....(702) 876-4235

NEW JERSEY

Audio Visual Assocs., Denville..........................(201) 887-5521
Audio Visual Systems Rental Centres,
    Burlington..(609) 387-3636
Giant TV Rentals, Rockaway ....(201) 361-2563

NEW YORK

Audio Visual Productions, Riverdale................(718) 601-5944
CMI Comms., Rochester....................................(716) 424-1900
Colortone Audio Visual, Elmsford....................(914) 592-4151
Design Audio Visual, Farmingdale....................(516) 694-3334
King Cole Audio Visual Services,
    Woodside ....(212) 532-6780
KVL Audio Visual Services, Yonkers................(914) 965-8300
Michael Andrews Audio Visual Services,
    New York ....(212) 265-2660
Scharff Weisberg, New York...............................(212) 582-4705
Select Audio Visual, New York..........................(212) 290-4800
Specialized Audio-Visual, Clifton Park ....(518) 383-6501
Visual Aid Equipment, Syracuse ....(315) 423-9741
Visual Impact Productions, Rochester ....(716) 263-8650

NORTH CAROLINA

AV METRO, Raleigh ....(919) 233-1901
IVS Media, Charlotte..(704) 525-2380
Norman Sound & Productions, Charlotte ....(704) 334-1601
Sirtage, Raleigh ....(919) 828-3400

OHIO

Audio Visual Systems, Dayton ....(513) 294-2304
Colortone Audio Visual Staging & Rentals,
    Cleveland..(216) 581-5055
Hughie's Audio-Visual, Cleveland.....................(216) 241-7773
I.T.A. Meeting & Presentation Services,
    Cincinnati...(513) 631-7000
Singer Audio Visual Equipment Rental,
    Worthington ....(614) 436-5273

OKLAHOMA

Cory's Audio-Visual Services,
    Oklahoma City ....(405) 682-8800

Fairview-AFX, Tulsa ....(918) 664-8020

PENNSYLVANIA

Advanced Audio Visual, Philadelphia..............(610) 696-7700
A.L.N., Valley Forge...(610) 630-4523
The Visual Aids Center of Pittsburgh,
   Pittsburgh..(412) 566-1800

SOUTH CAROLINA

Premier Audio-Visual, Hilton Head ....(803) 681-1024
United States Audio-Visuals,
   Hilton Head...(803) 681-5000

TENNESSEE

Allied Audio-Visual Services, Nashville ....(615) 883-4000
Audio Visual Resources, Nashville ....(615) 871-9100
Memphis Comms., Memphis ....(901) 725-9271
Nolan's Audio Visual, Memphis........................(901) 527-4313

TEXAS

Alford Media Services, Dallas...........................(214) 241-9400
AVW Audio Visual, Dallas ....(214) 638-0024
Higginbotham Enterprises, Irving ....(214) 554-0481
J&S Audio Visual Comms., Dallas ....(214) 241-5444
Molloy Corp., Houston ....(713) 771-1824
Wagner's American Hi Tech Rentals,
   Houston...(713) 987-3355

VIRGINIA

American Audio Video, Falls Church ....(703) 573-6910
Projection Video Services, Springfield...............(703) 912-1333

WISCONSIN

A to Z RentAll and Sales, Madison...................(608) 222-5004

Source: This is a partial selection of the thousands of firms named in the
Directory of Video, Computer, and Audio Visual Products. *This*
annual directory, as well as an ICIA membership directory, is available
from the International Communication Industries Association. To order,
contact ICIA, 3150 Spring St., Fairfax, VA 22031-2399; phone
(703) 273-7200, fax (703) 278-8082.

Couriers/Messenger Services

ANCHORAGE, AK

Alaska Pony Express...(907) 562-7333
Aurora Courier Express ....(907) 522-3896

ATLANTA, GA

City Courier..(404) 454-7277
Classic Companies...(404) 246-9001
Courier Express..(404) 424-1100
Dependable Courier ....(404) 763-1100

ATLANTIC CITY, NJ

Jet Messenger Service..(800) 225-5538
Lightning Messenger Service ....(609) 347-7788

BALTIMORE, MD

Acme Delivery & Messenger Service ....(410) 945-3900
American Eagle Express ....(410) 536-0200
Maryland Messenger...(410) 837-5550

Office Management

BOSTON, MA

Expressit Courier	(617) 268-2600
First Call Courier	(617) 268-6700
Marathon Messenger Service	(617) 266-8990

BUFFALO, NY

ASAP Delivery Service	(716) 834-2727
Classic Transport	(716) 874-2100
Click Messenger Service	(716) 685-0494
MDS Express	(716) 893-8204

CHARLOTTE, NC

Dial Four Delivery	(704) 374-0444
Flash Courier Service	(704) 358-9971
Fleet Courier Service	(704) 535-1486
General Parcel Service	(704) 338-9000

CHICAGO, IL

Anderson Courier & Transportation Service	(800) 339-0300
Arrow Messenger Service	(312) 489-6688
Cannonball Courier Services	(312) 829-1234
Larson Express	(708) 342-1100

CINCINNATI, OH

City Dash	(606) 341-1000
Rapid Delivery	(513) 733-0500
Rush Package Delivery	(513) 771-7874
Urex Express	(513) 681-4608

CLEVELAND, OH

City Express Delivery	(216) 781-6500
J & L Kwik Delivery Service	(216) 431-1310
Midway Delivery	(216) 391-0700
Professional Delivery & Courier	(216) 234-2700

COLUMBUS, OH

Anthony's Delivery Service	(614) 274-7679
Columbus Corporate Courier	(614) 864-9797
Premier Courier	(614) 221-6433

DALLAS, TX

A Truck Express	(214) 741-2146
Access Couriers	(214) 350-4884
J & S Delivery	(214) 484-4800
Qwik Couriers	(214) 271-6770
Running Man Courier Service	(214) 946-4786

DENVER, CO

Concorde Express Messenger Service	(303) 771-7288
Direct Connection Executive Courier Service	(303) 740-8084
DTD Couriers	(303) 671-6371
Quicksilver Express Courier	(303) 595-8100

DETROIT, MI

Direct Delivery	(313) 389-2864
Metro Messenger	(313) 885-0280
Urban Transportation Specialist	(313) 864-8980

GRAND RAPIDS, MI

P & J Delivery	(616) 534-4490
Professional Courier Services	(616) 451-4445
West Michigan Delivery Service	(616) 538-2935

GREENVILLE, SC

Acme Courier Express	(803) 675-1500
Direct Express Courier Service	(803) 277-7706
Phillips Delivery Service	(803) 233-3400
Professional Express	(803) 242-0749
Tiger Transport	(803) 288-0988

HARRISBURG, PA

ASAP Courier	(610) 678-2727
Courier Unlimited	(717) 396-1299
Friendly Messenger Service	(717) 393-2222
Quik Trip	(717) 854-1120
Way Messenger Service	(717) 299-0991

HARTFORD, CT

Connecticut Delivery Service	(203) 234-7177
Corporate Courier	(203) 282-7840
Hartford Courier Service	(203) 561-5121
Meyer Courier Service	(800) 972-0008

HONOLULU, HI

Aloha Delivery Service	(808) 847-7322
Courier Xpress	(808) 955-0079
Padget Couriers Plus	(808) 524-5389
Rabbit Transit Honolulu	(808) 524-4273

HOUSTON, TX

Bayou City Express	(713) 864-3073
City Central Courier	(713) 623-0303
Pasadena Delivery Service	(713) 473-8378
Texas Transportation Service	(713) 464-8775
Yellow Cab Express Delivery	(713) 225-9500

INDIANAPOLIS, IN

Courier One & MP Racing	(317) 329-1873
Eagle Courier	(317) 547-3984

KANSAS CITY, KS

Cartwright Delivery Service	(913) 342-4900
Quick Delivery	(913) 888-4600

KANSAS CITY, MO

Action Delivery	(816) 474-0001
Flexfleet Couriers	(816) 241-3300
Sun Courier Service	(816) 452-2595

LAS VEGAS, NV

Express Direct Delivery Service	(702) 736-4315
Fleet Delivery Service	(702) 367-4555
UCI Distribution Plus	(702) 457-3934

LOS ANGELES, CA

Jet Delivery	(213) 749-0123
Minute Man Delivery	(800) 833-1776

MEMPHIS, TN

Action Express	(901) 794-4766
Bee Line Delivery & Courier Service	(901) 388-3648
Express Courier	(901) 521-8282
Road Runner Small Package Delivery	(901) 373-6047

MIAMI, FL

A Step Ahead	(305) 591-7410

Choice Courier Systems of Florida ....(305) 949-0909
Gator Express...(305) 949-1440
Lincoln Messenger Service................................(305) 945-7978

Milwaukee, WI

Action Express..(414) 549-3300
Arrow Express...(414) 649-8000
Bonded Messenger Service..................................(414) 933-4500
Day 1 Express...(414) 769-9600
Dispatch 10 Messenger Service............................(414) 468-1010

Minneapolis, MN

Ace Delivery & Courier....................................(612) 721-5666
Bicycle Express...(612) 340-0059
Silver Bullet Delivery...................................(612) 378-7550

Nashville, TN

AA Dispatch...(615) 329-4297
Bly Delivery Service......................................(615) 329-9866
Courier Systems...(615) 872-0111
Hot Shot Delivery Service.................................(615) 883-5840
Sisco Express Delivery....................................(615) 256-8727

New Orleans, LA

Choice Courier..(504) 522-2678
New Orleans Messenger Service.............................(504) 586-0036
Reliable Courier..(504) 469-7637

New York, NY

Able Motorized Delivery Service...........................(212) 687-5515
Bullit Motorized Delivery.................................(212) 855-5555
DeSantis Despatch...(212) 279-3669
Moonlite Courier..(212) 473-2246
Supersonic..(212) 944-6932

Norfolk, VA

Ace Courier...(804) 486-2016
B&C Courier Service.......................................(804) 479-5130
Commonwealth Courier Service..............................(804) 467-4166
Jack Rabbit Express Delivery..............................(804) 467-6080
Metro Courier...(804) 625-1311

Oklahoma City, OK

Ala Carte Courier Service.................................(405) 670-2000
Holton Express..(405) 948-2065
Martinaire of Oklahoma....................................(405) 946-0600
Rapid Delivery Service....................................(405) 793-1122
Speedy Delivery Service...................................(405) 787-5200

Orlando, FL

Ace Expediters..(407) 333-4223
Budget Couriers...(407) 339-8201
Florida Courier Express...................................(407) 298-9772

Philadelphia, PA

Able Network Courier Service..............................(800) 458-3332
Courier Unlimited...(610) 666-0660
Heaven Sent Couriers......................................(215) 545-9100
Quick Courier Service.....................................(610) 825-2603
Rapid Delivery Service....................................(215) 496-9600

Phoenix, AZ

Arizona Messenger...(800) 231-6768

Pro Courier & Messenger....................................(602) 272-0407

PITTSBURGH, PA

Courier Unlimited...(412) 765-3099
Dash Delivery...(412) 922-4426
Daytrooper..(412) 821-2028
First Courier..(412) 322-0300
Hurry Kwik Delivery Systems ....(412) 931-3300

PORTLAND, OR

Broadway Cab..(503) 227-1234
Executive Courier Service..................................(503) 236-0134
Express-It Delivery Services...............................(503) 228-6622
Transerve Systems..(503) 241-0484
Radio Cab ....(503) 227-1212

PROVIDENCE, RI

Current Carrier...(401) 728-3150
Expressman Courier Service...............................(401) 463-3200
Mr. Messenger..(401) 461-2240
Now Courier..(800) 543-9669

RALEIGH, NC

KBD Services...(800) 441-4703
Triangle Express...(919) 387-0052
Triangle Transit..(919) 419-8378

SACRAMENTO, CA

Action ASAP Delivery Service ....(209) 462-4163
Aerospeed Delivery Service ....(916) 922-4503
All Points Courier ....(916) 387-4001
B & G Delivery System.......................................(916) 971-4182
Express-It Couriers...(800) 882-1000

ST. LOUIS, MO

Access Courier..(314) 968-5800
ADCOM Express...(314) 432-4606
Sprint Courier...(314) 781-3322

SALT LAKE CITY, UT

Fast Pitch Courier...(801) 975-7777
Fleet Delivery Services ....(801) 263-3800
Kwik Courier ....(800) 946-5945
Miller Express ....(801) 321-6622

SAN ANTONIO, TX

CFI Delivery Service ....(210) 228-9772
Mission Courier ....(210) 377-2387

SAN DIEGO, CA

Bullet Express Couriers.......................................(619) 454-7439
Lightning Express ....(619) 293-0300
Western Express..(619) 565-9990

SAN FRANCISCO, CA

Express-It Couriers...(800) 882-1000
Lightning Express ....(415) 621-4900
Special T Delivery...(415) 284-1200

SEATTLE, WA

Bullet Delivery Service..(800) 696-3788
ENA Couriers..(206) 624-3200
Fleetfoot Messenger Service................................(206) 728-7700

Office Management (Courier-Fax/Copier)

TAMPA, FL

Central Courier Systems ....(800) 393-1007
Express-It Messenger and Delivery Service ....(813) 968-5757
Thunderbird Express..(813) 222-8070

WASHINGTON, DC

Best Messenger...(202) 986-0100
Deadline Express..(202) 543-6651
Dependable Courier Service ....(202) 638-0114
Grace Courier Service ....(703) 550-5000
Quick Messenger Service ....(202) 783-3600

WEST PALM BEACH, FL

Crown Courier..(407) 689-6662
Florida Courier Express ....(407) 737-5202
Palm Beach Express..(407) 689-7764
Personalized Messenger Service ....(407) 844-0990
Sunshine State Messenger....................................(407) 737-4444

Delivery Companies

Airborne Express ....(800) 247-2676
DHL Worldwide Express ....(800) 225-5345
Emery Worldwide ACF...(800) 443-6379
Federal Express ....(800) 238-5355
United Parcel Service..(800) 742-5877

Executive Gift Companies

Baekgaard...(708) 498-3040
Balducci's Bounty by Mail...................................(800) 225-3822
Balloon America..(800) 257-7880
Collector's Armoury ....(800) 336-4572
French & Pacific Trading ....(909) 902-1320
FTD Direct ....(800) 736-3383
Harry and David ....(800) 547-3033
Iris Arc Crystal ....(805) 963-3661
Lifedance Distribution..(503) 228-9430
Omaha Steaks..(800) 228-9055
Penco Industries ....(508) 999-6484
The Popcorn Emporium ....(800) 832-2676
Red Mill Manufacturing.......................................(304) 872-5231
Reuge Music U.S.A...(310) 474-5670
Sand Design..(801) 972-4775
SeaBear ....(800) 973-2232
Send-A-Song ....(800) 736-3276
Vagabond House..(818) 341-7616
Suzanne's Mail Order Muffins..............................(800) 742-2403
Vermont Teddy Bear Co..(800) 829-2327
Wolferman's..(800) 998-0169

*Partial Source: Gift & Decoratives Accessory Buyers Directory. For
an annual subscription call: (212) 689-4411, or write Geyer-
McAllister, Subscription Service Center, 51 Madison Ave., New York,
NY 10010.*

Fax Machine/Copier Dealers

ANCHORAGE, AK

Alaska Business Systems.......................................(907) 277-4525
Business Machine Center ....(907) 562-1080
Frontier Business Machines...................................(907) 276-6360

ATLANTA, GA

National Photocopy	(404) 934-5005
Panasonic Copier	(404) 491-8143
Southern Copy Machines	(404) 223-0456
Zeno MBM	(404) 446-7100

ATLANTIC CITY, NJ

Adrian-Lewis	(609) 344-4949
Copiers Plus	(609) 645-7587
Mossman's Business Machines	(609) 652-0600

BALTIMORE, MD

Action Business Systems	(410) 574-5555
Advance Business Systems	(410) 252-4800
Commonwealth Copiers & Business Machines.	(410) 684-6800
Danka Business Systems	(410) 536-1819

BOSTON, MA

New England Copy Specialists	(617) 935-4340
Northern Business Machines	(617) 451-5090
Offtech	(617) 451-9134

BUFFALO, NY

Central Copier Service	(716) 873-9010
Comdoc Office Systems	(716) 689-0202
United Business Systems	(716) 854-4122

CHARLOTTE, NC

American Photocopy	(704) 551-8650
Charlotte Copy Data	(704) 523-3333
White Business Machines	(704) 527-3790

CHICAGO, IL

American Office Equipment	(800) 837-2631
Coordinated Business Systems	(800) 882-2679
Des Plaines Office Equipment	(708) 924-7999
Kee Business Systems	(312) 334-0551

CINCINNATI, OH

Donnellon McCarthy	(513) 733-8700
REM Office Products	(513) 772-7156
Scot Business Systems	(513) 984-9898

CLEVELAND, OH

American Business Machines	(216) 328-0000
Meritech	(216) 459-8333
Ohio Business Machines	(216) 579-1345

COLUMBUS, OH

American Business Equipment	(614) 291-4661
Capitol Copy	(614) 846-1510
Gordon Flesch Company	(614) 876-1174

DALLAS, TX

A. Watson Copiers	(214) 484-5000
Danka Business Systems	(214) 621-0013
Innovative Office Systems	(214) 788-0800

DENVER, CO

Associated Business Products	(303) 295-1767
ATEO Copier & Fax Systems	(303) 778-0600
CDP Imaging Systems	(303) 639-3600

DETROIT, MI

Albin Business Centers	(313) 662-4915
American Photocopy	(313) 962-5090
CDP Imaging Systems	(810) 353-6460
Facsimile Systems	(313) 592-0066

GRAND RAPIDS, MI

Applied Imaging	(616) 531-1199
Hovinga Business Systems	(616) 538-8720
Multi-Line Business Systems	(616) 243-3600
Richardson Business Machines	(616) 949-1600

GREENVILLE, SC

Acme Business Products	(803) 297-3560
Advanced Business Systems	(803) 234-7722
Kearns Corp.	(803) 859-5013

HARRISBURG, PA

Colony Products	(717) 569-5900
Conestoga Copiers	(717) 299-5626
Sheaffer Office Products	(717) 394-1123

HARTFORD, CT

Bloom's Business Systems	(800) 282-9991
Copy-Rite Business Systems	(203) 529-9802
Prism Office Systems	(203) 488-7979
Ryan Business Systems	(203) 528-9881
Supreme Copy	(203) 239-6511

HONOLULU, HI

Hawaii Business Equipment/Savin	(808) 593-8230
Lanier Facsimile Systems	(808) 423-9657
Minolta	(808) 842-5146
Pacific Business Machines	(808) 946-5059
Sharp	(808) 847-1366

HOUSTON, TX

Canter Office Equipment	(713) 226-8377
TLC Office Systems	(713) 695-1616
Tonerland	(713) 695-1717

INDIANAPOLIS, IN

Braden Business Systems	(317) 580-0100
CopyRite	(317) 329-2679
HPS Office Systems	(317) 875-9000

KANSAS CITY, MO

Danka Business Systems	(913) 888-8840
DeCoursey Business Systems	(913) 492-2131
Modern Business Systems	(913) 371-8080

LAS VEGAS, NV

Associated Business Products	(702) 382-2666
Danka Business Systems	(702) 737-1510
Nevada Copy Systems	(702) 736-2679
Sun Office Systems	(702) 798-3366

LOS ANGELES, CA

American Office Equipment	(213) 664-4586
Astro Office Products	(213) 629-6700
California Copy Products	(213) 776-7700
Edgemont Business Systems	(213) 871-9222

MEMPHIS, TN

Danka Business Systems/B.B.M.........................(901) 382-1859
Diversified Copy Products ....(901) 683-1197
Mid-South Systems...(901) 365-1043

MIAMI, FL

Complete Business Systems...............................(305) 436-3810
Danka Business Systems ....(305) 264-5800
Delta Business Systems ....(305) 829-5454
Wood Business Products....................................(305) 592-5191
Xerotech ....(305) 238-8007

MILWAUKEE, WI

Copy Plus...(414) 353-2704
Office Copying Equipment.................................(414) 464-3070
Office Machine Showcase ....(414) 438-2729

MINNEAPOLIS, MN

Copy Duplicating Products ....(612) 861-0555
Metro Sales ....(612) 861-4000
Unicopy Advanced Imaging ....(612) 854-4900

NASHVILLE, TN

American Business Copiers...............................(615) 754-2233
Consolidated Copy Systems ....(615) 822-1422
Danka Business Systems ....(615) 781-8350

NEW ORLEANS, LA

Gulf Coast Office Products ....(504) 733-3830
Innovative Office Systems.................................(504) 455-2324
WJS Enterprises...(504) 838-6226

NEW YORK, NY

Alpha Business Machine ....(212) 643-5555
Home & Office Business Systems ....(718) 927-0443
Lexington Business Systems ....(212) 674-8548

NORFOLK, VA

Copy Data Group ....(804) 881-9400
The Copy Machine Store...................................(804) 523-5955
Danka Business Systems ....(804) 857-7285

OKLAHOMA CITY, OK

American Office Systems...................................(405) 787-9700
Central Business Equipment ....(405) 947-7743
Copysolutions ....(405) 842-4455

ORLANDO, FL

Copytronics..(407) 894-0999
Delta Business Systems.....................................(407) 299-7180
Universal Office Systems...................................(407) 297-1238

PHILADELPHIA, PA

Copi-Rite ....(215) 928-1770
Executive Imaging Systems ....(215) 922-2070
XTEC Office Systems..(215) 567-1532

PITTSBURGH, PA

Holzer Business Machines ....(412) 653-4677
Three Rivers Business Systems.........................(412) 373-4500
Von Renner Photocopy Repair ....(412) 673-3482

PHOENIX, AZ

Advanced Copy Systems	(602) 269-6700
Arizona Office Equipment	(602) 248-7778
CDP Imaging	(602) 929-7800

PORTLAND, OR

American Business Machines	(503) 226-1541
Automated Office Systems	(503) 620-2800
Intermountain Business Machines	(503) 641-3301

PROVIDENCE, RI

Copyrite	(401) 463-5400
Core Business Technologies	(401) 431-0700
Danka Business Systems	(401) 732-2540

RALEIGH, NC

Commercial Equipment Incorporated	(919) 489-2322
Omni Business Machines	(919) 872-9400
Uni-Copy	(919) 469-1102

SACRAMENTO, CA

Discovery Office Systems	(916) 443-0998
Network Office Systems	(916) 974-0100
Standard Office Systems	(916) 489-2679
Taylor Made Office Systems	(209) 952-9000

ST. LOUIS, MO

Mirex	(314) 968-5200
Modern Business Systems	(314) 739-7440
Suburban Business Products	(314) 567-0087

SALT LAKE CITY, UT

The Copy Man	(801) 486-9641
Les Olson Company	(801) 486-7431
Tri-City Business Products	(801) 263-0665

SAN ANTONIO, TX

Danka Business Systems	(210) 655-3330
Office Communications Systems	(210) 494-1110
Texas Copy	(210) 820-0334

SAN DIEGO, CA

Coastal Copy Systems	(619) 560-9600
Copyline	(619) 220-0500
Danka Business Systems	(619) 565-7551
ImageCom Business Systems	(619) 565-7440
Remco Business Products	(619) 571-1737

SAN FRANCISCO, CA

Golden Gate Office Systems	(415) 621-2222
Taylor Made Office Systems	(415) 777-0200
VOE	(415) 558-8878

SEATTLE, WA

Cascade Office Systems	(206) 625-9893
United Business Machines	(206) 827-0611
William Dierickx	(206) 822-8883

TAMPA, FL

Da-Tek Office Systems	(813) 875-1030
Delta Business Systems	(813) 888-7710
Racine Business Systems	(813) 443-2699
SOS Office Systems	(813) 961-2744

WASHINGTON, DC

Capitol Copyproducts...(202) 775-9494
Commonwealth ....(800) 624-2679
Item..(703) 971-5700

WEST PALM BEACH, FL

Complete Business Systems................................(407) 689-6500
Copyco ....(407) 832-6220
Wood Business Products.....................................(407) 588-9440

Mail Order Office Supply Companies

Adirondack Direct...(718) 932-4003
Atlantic Advertising ....(609) 439-0508
Caddylak Systems ....(800) 523-8060
Charrette...(617) 935-6000
City Office Supply ....(312) 559-0100
Deluxe Business Forms and Supplies..................(800) 843-4294
Fidelity Products ....(800) 544-3013
Frank Eastern ....(212) 219-0007
Franz Stationery ....(708) 593-0060
Garvey's Office Plus...(800) 621-1503
Ginns ....(301) 853-3000
Hill Specialties ....(800) 523-0163
Iroquois Products ....(312) 436-3900
Memindex...(716) 342-7890
Modern Service Office Supply ....(800) 672-6767
Raymark Office Products Center ....(800) 346-7100
Reliable..(800) 735-4000
Staples..(800) 333-3330
Viking Office Products ....(213) 321-4493
Wholesale Supply ....(800) 962-9162

Private Investigators

Able Investigations...(800) 423-0026
A.D.A. ....(800) 834-2512
AIS American Investigative Services................(800) 554-3463
All-Boro Investigations ....(800) 683-9966
All Private Investigations...................................(800) 999-0909
The Blackdog Group ....(800) 490-9777
Bradshaw Investigative ....(800) 786-9201
Capitol Detective Agency...................................(800) 346-0347
Global Information Systems...............................(800) 671-8001
International Counterintelligence Services.......(800) 828-9198
Investigators...(800) 543-3329
John T. Lynch Esq. ....(800) 421-2822
Marshall & Assocs...(800) 541-0634
Peace of Mind...(800) 222-4373
A Private Investigators Referral Service............(800) 867-7448
TCW Investigations ....(800) 664-3774
Triangle Investigative Services...........................(800) 334-0196

Security/Guard Agencies

ANCHORAGE, AK

Ahtna AGA Security ....(907) 272-8884
Alaska Security ....(907) 561-2221
Guardian Security Systems ....(907) 274-5275

ATLANTA, GA

Centurion Security & Detective Agency ....(404) 766-3423
Confidential Security Agency ....(404) 888-0801
Elite Investigations and Security ....(404) 607-1718
PSI Security Service ....(404) 850-1111

BALTIMORE, MD

CES Security ....(410) 922-8900
Phelps Protection Systems ....(410) 467-3169
Watkins Security Agency ....(410) 523-5080

BOSTON, MA

Alliance Security Service ....(617) 387-1261
Maximum Security ....(617) 244-1212
New World Security Assocs. ....(617) 427-0707
Ogden Allied Security Services ....(617) 367-0460

BUFFALO, NY

AAA Top Gun Security ....(716) 632-4141
Burns International Security Services ....(716) 874-4303
Doyle Alarm Services ....(716) 873-2264
Sentrex Security Systems ....(716) 693-5433

CHARLOTTE, NC

ABM Security Services ....(704) 525-0590
Stroupe Security Services ....(704) 332-5074

CHICAGO, IL

A & R Security Services ....(312) 282-0490
CSC ....(312) 482-9660
Industrial Patrol Service ....(312) 237-5882
National K-9 Security ....(312) 722-7070
Protection ....(708) 647-1044

CINCINNATI, OH

Cincinnati Security Service ....(513) 793-9578
National Security ....(513) 621-1447
Nuckols Security ....(513) 762-7614
Pennington International ....(513) 631-2130

CLEVELAND, OH

Metro Cleveland Security ....(216) 398-0924

COLUMBUS, OH

County Wide Security & Investigations ....(614) 231-5533
Moling & Assocs ....(614) 759-7433

DALLAS, TX

Accu-Guard ....(214) 637-6410
Executive Security Systems ....(214) 480-0101
Fort Knox Protection ....(214) 298-6991
Phasa Security ....(214) 530-9897
Texas Protection & Security ....(214) 688-4449

DENVER, CO

Continental Security ....(303) 837-1254

Firstwatch Security Services..............................(303) 871-0606
Reliant Security Services...................................(303) 773-9236
Twin City Security...(303) 691-8001

DETROIT, MI

Armor Protective Services ....(313) 864-4800
Century Security Guard Services.......................(313) 837-7760
Smith Security Cooperation ....(313) 965-0900

GRAND RAPIDS, MI

Burns International Security Services.................(616) 323-2020
Charles Services ....(616) 382-4800
D & R Security...(616) 774-4011
F & M Protection ....(616) 235-2602
Guardian Guard Services ....(616) 241-5115

GREENVILLE, SC

American Security...(803) 292-7450

HARRISBURG, PA

American Eagle Security....................................(717) 393-2733
Security Guards ....(610) 375-4747

HARTFORD, CT

Argus Security Group..(203) 528-7700
Murphy Security Service ....(203) 229-7727
Ogden Security Services....................................(203) 562-6132

HONOLULU, HI

Centurion Security Systems ....(808) 833-6631
Freeman Guards..(808) 521-9555
HIS...(808) 677-2400
Royal Guard Security ....(808) 596-0848
Star Protection ....(808) 532-3911

HOUSTON, TX

A & R Security Services ....(713) 781-1000
A.D.F. Security Service ....(713) 351-6463
B & B Protective Service ....(713) 464-3025
Professional Guard & Patrol ....(713) 448-4900
Twin City Security...(713) 952-4003

INDIANAPOLIS, IN

Action Security ....(317) 241-7088
Blue Line Security System.................................(317) 784-7103
Harrod Security Force ....(317) 254-9980
Protection Plus ....(317) 244-7569

KANSAS CITY, KS

Orion Security ....(913) 451-5657
Sentry Security Services....................................(913) 334-5017

LAS VEGAS, NV

Curtis Security Services.....................................(702) 251-7944
General Security & Protection Services.............(702) 259-2620
Greenvalley Security ....(702) 261-0440
Thunderbird Security Services...........................(702) 432-6062
Wells Fargo Guard Services...............................(702) 365-1585

LOS ANGELES, CA

Assured International Security ....(213) 977-0683
Intercept Private Security ....(213) 962-6228
Spear Security...(800) 773-2771

MEMPHIS, TN

A Certified Security	(901) 454-0667
ARC Security	(901) 360-9822
Federal Security	(901) 685-2378
Phelps Security	(901) 365-9728
Security One	(901) 346-7746

MIAMI, FL

The Eagle Security & Patrol Agency	(305) 649-2011
Feick Security	(305) 661-1390
U.S. Security	(305) 274-7753
Vanguard Security	(305) 592-9747

MILWAUKEE, WI

American K-9 Services	(414) 384-4540
Security Personnel	(414) 464-5300

MINNEAPOLIS, MN

Chase Security	(612) 755-9133
General Security Services	(612) 331-9456
Hannon Security Services	(612) 881-5865
Quality Protective Agency	(612) 639-9624
Twin Cities Security	(612) 784-4160

NASHVILLE, TN

O.P.P. Security Company	(615) 360-3800
Special Security Services	(615) 255-2656

NEW ORLEANS, LA

Louisiana Protection & Patrol Services	(504) 241-7300
New Orleans Private Patrol	(504) 525-7111
New South Security Service	(504) 277-4942
State Protection Agency	(504) 363-0089

NEW YORK, NY

Copstat Security	(718) 518-8055
Epic Security	(212) 580-3434
John C. Mandel Security Bureau	(718) 237-4000
VGI	(718) 665-1515
Web Security	(212) 289-6060

NORFOLK, VA

American International Security Specialists	(804) 490-3070
Global Security Specialists	(804) 463-6007
Key Security Services	(804) 855-5666

OKLAHOMA CITY, OK

Bureau of Professional Security	(405) 521-8834

ORLANDO, FL

Allied Security	(407) 629-6064
Argenbright & Assocs. Security	(407) 423-1477

PHILADELPHIA, PA

Burns International Security Services	(215) 625-8445
PA Security Services	(215) 945-2054

PHOENIX, AZ

Arizona Protection Agency	(602) 423-0187

PITTSBURGH, PA

AM-Gard	(412) 781-5800
Burns International Security Services	(412) 922-2331

C & C Security Agency ....(412) 628-1234

PORTLAND, OR
Jones Security ....(503) 227-4140
Northwest Protective Service ....(503) 274-4040
Swanberg & Assocs ....(503) 274-2060

PROVIDENCE, RI
AAA Security Task Force ....(401) 944-4443
Industrial Security & Investigators ....(401) 231-8130

RALEIGH, NC
American Protective Services............................(919) 469-4717
Faulkner Security..(919) 847-7300
North Carolina Detective Agency.....................(919) 286-7124
Security Forces...(919) 787-0749

SACRAMENTO, CA
AD Force ....(209) 465-8420
Lyons Security Service.......................................(916) 452-3381
Phoenix Operations...(800) 432-4465
Premium Patrol Services ....(916) 966-1200
State Investigations ....(916) 486-9175

ST. LOUIS, MO
Gateway Guard Service......................................(314) 621-7660
Stoehner Security Services.................................(314) 567-7200

SALT LAKE CITY, UT
American Protective Services............................(801) 262-5678
Command Protection Service ....(801) 547-0767
Independent Security & Investigations ....(801) 272-5082
Knight Protective Services.................................(801) 292-7080
Utah Detective & Security Service ....(801) 467-4416

SAN ANTONIO, TX
Acme Security ....(210) 599-3670
Ranger American Security ....(210) 694-7979

SAN DIEGO, CA
Rodgers Police Patrol ....(619) 283-3976
Southern California Security Services...............(619) 542-1994

SAN FRANCISCO, CA
King Security Services...(415) 433-5464
San Francisco Security Services.........................(800) 690-7707
Wolf Protective Services ....(415) 227-0827

SEATTLE, WA
Argus Security & Investigations ....(206) 878-3401
Northwest Protective Services ....(206) 448-4040
Puget Sound Security Patrol ....(206) 643-1300
Seattle King County Security ....(206) 323-1411

TAMPA, FL
Coastal Protective Services................................(813) 572-7578
DeSurety Security..(813) 738-6118
Securex ....(813) 933-5521
Sykes Security..(813) 684-2687

WASHINGTON, DC
Apex Security ....(202) 362-3292
CES Security..(301) 621-4105
MRL Enterprises...(202) 726-7579

O'Neal's Village Security Agency ....(202) 328-7029

WEST PALM BEACH, FL

ARM Security...(407) 533-1642
Sunrise Security..(407) 585-4704

Associations

Action Committee for Rural Electrification,
Washington, DC..............................(202) 857-9570
Aircraft Owners & Pilots Association,
Frederick, MD.................................(301) 695-2000
AMA International, New York, NY ....(212) 586-8100
American Academy of Actuaries,
Washington, DC..............................(202) 223-8196
American Accounting Association,
Sarasota, FL...................................(813) 921-7747
American Advertising Federation,
Washington, DC..............................(202) 898-0089
American Automobile Association,
Heathrow, FL ....(407) 444-7000
American Automobile Touring Alliance,
San Francisco, CA...........................(415) 777-4000
American Bankers Association,
Washington, DC..............................(202) 663-5000
American Bed & Breakfast Association,
Midlothian, VA ....(804) 379-2222
American Booksellers Association.....................(914) 591-2665
American Business Association,
New York, NY................................(212) 949-5900
American Business Women's Association,
Kansas City, MO.............................(816) 361-6621
American Compensation Association,
Scottsdale, AZ ....(602) 951-9191
American Culinary Federation,
St. Augustine, FL.............................(904) 824-4468
American Federation of Small Business,
Chicago, IL ....(312) 427-0207
American Floral Marketing Council,
Alexandria, VA...............................(703) 836-8700
American Hotel & Motel Association,
Washington, DC..............................(202) 289-3100
American Institute of Certified Public Accountants,
New York, NY................................(212) 596-6200
American Management Association,
New York, NY................................(212) 586-8100
American Marketing Association,
Chicago, IL ....(312) 648-0536
American Small Business Association,
Grapevine, TX................................(817) 488-8770
American Society for Industrial Security,
Arlington, VA..................................(703) 522-5800
American Society of Association Executives,
Washington, DC..............................(202) 626-2723
American Society of CLU and ChFC,
Bryn Mawr, PA ....(215) 526-2500
American Society of Interior Designers,
Washington, DC..............................(202) 546-3480
American Society of Travel Agents,
Alexandria, VA...............................(703) 739-2782
American Water Works Association,
Denver, CO....................................(303) 794-7711
Appraisal Institute, Chicago, IL........................(312) 335-4100
Associated General Contractors of America,
Washington, DC..............................(202) 393-2040
Associated Locksmiths of America,
Dallas, TX......................................(214) 827-1701

Association for Investment Management &
Research, Charlottesville, VA ....(804) 977-6600

Association of Records Managers &
Administrators, Prairie Village, KS ....(913) 341-3808

Automotive Service Association,
Bedford, TX ....(817) 283-6205

Bureau of Salesmen's National Associations,
Atlanta, GA..(404) 351-7355

Bureau of Wholesale Sales Representatives,
Atlanta, GA..(404) 351-7355

Caterpillar Club, Trenton, NJ ....(609) 587-3300

Club Méditerranée, New York, NY...................(212) 977-2100

Commercial-Investment Real Estate Council,
Chicago, IL ....(312) 321-4460

Continental Association of Resolute Employers,
Petaluma, CA ....(800) 327-4355

Co-Op America, Washington, DC ....(202) 872-5307

Cotton Incorporated, New York, NY................(212) 586-1070

Direct Marketing Association, New York, NY ..(212) 768-7277

Employee Relocation Council,
Washington, DC ....(202) 857-0857

Financial Executives Institute,
Morristown, NJ ....(201) 898-4600

Florists' Transworld Delivery Association,
Southfield, MI ....(810) 355-9300

The Funeral and Memorial Societies of
America, Egg Harbor, WI..............................(414) 868-3136

Future Aviation Professionals of America,
Atlanta, GA..(404) 997-8097

Golf Course Superintendents Association of
America, Lawrence, KS..................................(913) 841-2240

Ice Skating Institute of America,
Buffalo Grove, IL ....(708) 808-7528

Independent Insurance Agents of America,
Alexandria, VA..(703) 683-4422

Independent Truck Owner/Operator
Association, Stoughton, MA ....(617) 828-7200

Institute of Certified Travel Agents,
Wellesley, MA ....(617) 237-0280

Institute of Financial Education,
Chicago, IL ....(312) 946-8800

Institute of Internal Auditors,
Altamonte Springs, FL ....(407) 830-7600

Institute of Management Accountants,
Montvale, NJ ....(201) 573-9000

Interflora, Southfield, MI ....(313) 355-9300

International Association for Financial
Planning, Atlanta, GA....................................(404) 395-1605

International Association of Business,
Arlington, TX...(800) 275-1171

International Association of Business
Communicators, San Francisco, CA..............(415) 433-3400

International Association of Electrical
Inspectors, Richardson, TX ....(708) 696-1455

International Association of Printing
House Craftsmen, Minneapolis, MN ....(612) 560-1620

International Council of Shopping Centers,
New York, NY..(212) 421-8181

International Credit Association,
St. Louis, MO ....(314) 991-3030

International Fabricare Institute,
Silver Spring, MD..(301) 622-1900
International Foundation of Employee Benefit Plans,
Brookfield, WI...(414) 786-6700
International Maple Syrup Institute,
Swanton, VT ....(802) 868-7244
International Traders Association,
Woodland Hills, CA...(818) 884-4400
Invest to Compete Alliance,
Washington, DC...(202) 546-4991
Jewelers of America, New York, NY ....(212) 768-8777
Log House Builders' Association of
North America, Monroe, WA.........................(206) 794-4469
Manufacturers' Agents National Association,
Laguna Hills, CA...(714) 859-4040
Master Printers of America,
Alexandria, VA...(703) 519-8130
Million Dollar Round Table,
Park Ridge, IL..(708) 692-6378
National Academy of Television Arts and
Sciences, New York, NY..................................(212) 586-8424
National Aeronautic Association of the
USA, Arlington, VA ....(703) 527-0226
National Association for Cottage
Industry, Chicago, IL ....(312) 472-8116
National Association for Female
Executives, New York, NY ....(212) 477-2200
National Association for the Self-Employed,
DFW Airport, TX..(800) 232-6273
National Association of Beverage Retailers,
Bethesda, MD ....(301) 656-1494
National Association of Credit Management,
Columbia, MD...(301) 740-5560
National Association of Federally Licensed
Firearms Dealers, Ft. Lauderdale, FL ....(305) 561-3505
National Association of Home Builders of
the US, Washington, DC ....(202) 822-0200
National Association of Insurance Women—
International, Tulsa, OK..................................(918) 744-5195
National Association of Legal Secretaries,
Tulsa, OK ....(918) 493-3540
National Association of Manufacturers,
Washington, DC..(202) 637-3000
National Association of Professional Insurance
Agents, Alexandria, VA................................... (703) 836-9340
National Association of Purchasing Management,
Tempe, AZ...(602) 752-6276
National Association of Railroad Passengers,
Washington, DC..(202) 408-8362
National Association of Real Estate Appraisers,
Scottsdale, AZ ....(602) 948-8000
National Association of Realtors,
Chicago, IL ....(312) 329-8200
National Association of Retail Druggists,
Alexandria, VA...(703) 683-8200
National Association of Theater Owners,
North Hollywood, CA.:....................................(818) 506-1778
National Association of Wholesaler-Distributors,
Washington, DC..(202) 872-0885
National Automobile Dealers Association,
McLean, VA ....(703) 827-7407

National Beauty Culturists' League,
Washington, DC ....(202) 332-2695
National Business Association, Dallas, TX ....(214) 991-5381
National Contract Management Association,
Vienna, VA ....(703) 448-9231
National Cosmetology Association,
St. Louis, MO ....(314) 534-7980
National Funeral Directors Association,
Milwaukee, WI ....(414) 541-2500
National Independent Automobile Dealers
Association, Arlington, TX ....(817) 640-3838
National Licensed Beverage Association,
Alexandria, VA ....(703) 671-7575
National Management Association,
Dayton, OH ....(513) 294-0421
National Piggly Wiggly Operators Association,
Memphis, TN ....(901) 395-8215
National Restaurant Association,
Washington, DC ....(202) 331-5900
National Retail Federation,
New York, NY ....(202) 783-7971
National Retail Hardware Association,
Indianapolis, IN ....(317) 290-0338
National Small Business United,
Washington, DC ....(202) 293-8830
National Society of Public Accountants,
Alexandria, VA ....(703) 549-6400
National Well Water Association,
Dublin, OH ....(614) 761-1711
Owner-Operator Independent Drivers Association,
Oak Grove, MO ....(816) 229-5791
Photo Marketing Association International,
Jackson, MI ....(517) 788-8100
Printing Industries of America,
Alexandria, VA ....(703) 519-8100
Professional Secretaries International,
Kansas City, MO ....(816) 891-6600
Propeller Club of the U.S.,
Fairfax, VA ....(703) 691-2777
Public Relations Society of America,
New York, NY ....(212) 995-2230
Realtors National Marketing Institute,
Chicago, IL ....(312) 329-8200
Refrigeration Service Engineers Society,
Des Plaines, IL ....(708) 297-6464
Sales and Marketing Executives International,
Cleveland, OH ....(216) 771-6650
Service Corps of Retired Executives Association,
Washington, DC ....(202) 205-6762
Small Business Service Bureau,
Worcester, MA ....(508) 756-3513
Society for Advancement of Management,
Vinton, VA ....(703) 342-5563
Society for Human Resource Management,
Alexandria, VA ....(703) 548-3440
Society for Technical Communication,
Arlington, VA ....(703) 522-4114
Society of Actuaries, Schaumburg, IL ....(708) 706-3500
Society of American Florists,
Alexandria, VA ....(703) 836-8700

Society of Chartered Property &
   Casualty Underwriters, Malvern, PA ....(610) 251-2728
Souvenir and Novelty Trade Association,
   Upper Darby, PA...(610) 734-2420
Special Industrial Radio Service Association,
   Arlington, VA...(703) 528-5115
Support Services Alliance, Schoharie, NY........(518) 295-7966
TAPPI, Atlanta, GA ....(404) 446-1400
Telophase Society, San Diego, CA ....(619) 299-0805
Tobacco Assocs., Washington, DC ....(202) 828-9144
Two/Ten International Footwear Foundation,
   Watertown, MA..(617) 923-4500
Uniform Code Council, Dayton, OH ....(513) 435-3870
Vidion/International Association of Video,
   Washington, DC...(202) 328-9346
Women's Council of Realtors of the National
   Association of Realtors, Chicago, IL ....(312) 329-8483
World International Nail and Beauty Association,
   Anaheim, CA ....(714) 779-9883

Charitable Organizations

EDUCATION AND PUBLIC AFFAIRS GROUPS

Anti-Defamation League of B'nai B'rith,
   New York, NY...(212) 490-2525
Citizens' Scholarship Foundation of America,
   St. Peter, MN...(507) 931-1682
Mothers Against Drunk Driving, Irving, TX.....(214) 744-6233
National Association for the Advancement
of Colored People, Baltimore, MD ....(410) 358-8900
National Urban League, New York, NY............(212) 310-9000
United Negro College Fund, New York, NY.....(800) 331-2244

ENVIRONMENTAL AND ANIMAL-RELATED GROUPS

National Wildlife Federation,
   Washington, DC...(202) 797-6800
Natural Resources Defense Council,
   New York, NY...(212) 727-2700
Nature Conservancy, Arlington, VA ....(703) 841-5300
World Wildlife Fund, Washington, DC.............(202) 293-4800

HEALTH CHARITIES

American Cancer Society, Atlanta, GA ....(404) 320-3333
American Heart Association, Dallas, TX..........(214) 373-6300
American Lung Association, New York, NY.....(212) 315-8700
March of Dimes Birth Defects Foundation,
   White Plains, NY...(914) 428-7100
Muscular Dystrophy Association, Tucson, AZ ..(602) 529-2000
National Easter Seal Society, Chicago, IL.........(312) 726-6200
National Multiple Sclerosis Society,
   New York, NY...(800) 344-4867
Planned Parenthood Federation of America,
   New York, NY...(212) 541-7800
Shriners Hospital for Crippled Children,
   Tampa, FL ....(813) 972-2250

INTERNATIONAL RELIEF AND DEVELOPMENT GROUPS

Americares Foundation, New Canaan, CT ....(203) 966-5195
Catholic Relief Services, Baltimore, MD ....(410) 625-2220
Christian Children's Fund, Richmond, VA.......(804) 756-2700
World Vision, Monrovia, CA ....(818) 357-7979

YOUTH GROUPS

Big Brothers/Big Sisters of America,
Philadelphia, PA ....(215) 567-7000
Boy Scouts of America, Irving, TX...................(214) 580-2000
Boys and Girls Clubs of America,
Atlanta, GA..(404) 815-5700
Girl Scouts of the USA, New York, NY ....(212) 852-8000

OTHER GROUPS

Gifts in Kind America, Alexandria, VA............(703) 836-2121
United States Olympic Committee,
Colorado Springs, CO ....(719) 632-5551

Labor Unions

Actors' Equity Association ....(212) 869-8530
Amalgamated Clothing & Textile
Workers Union ....(212) 242-0700
Amalgamated Transit Union............................(202) 537-1645
American Association of
University Professors.....................................(202) 737-5900
American Federation of
Government Employees ....(202) 737-8700
American Federation of Grain Millers ....(612) 545-0211
American Federation of Musicians of the
United States & Canada ....(212) 869-1330
American Federation of State, County
& Municipal Employees ....(202) 429-1000
American Federation of Teachers ....(202) 879-4400
American Federation of Television &
Radio Artists..(212) 532-0800
American Nurses' Association ....(202) 554-4444
American Postal Workers Union ....(202) 842-4200
Associated Actors & Artistes of America ....(212) 869-0358
Association of Flight Attendants......................(202) 328-5400
Brotherhood of Locomotive Engineers ....(216) 241-2630
Brotherhood of Maintenance of
Way Employees...(810) 948-1010
California School Employees Association ....(408) 263-8000
Civil Service Employees Association.................(518) 434-0191
Communications Workers of America ....(202) 434-1100
Federation of Nurses & Health Professionals ....(202) 879-4491
Graphic Communications
International Union ....(202) 462-1400
Hotel Restaurant Employees
International Union ....(202) 393-4373
International Air Line Pilots Association ....(202) 797-4010
International Alliance of Theatrical Stage
Employees & Moving Picture Machine
Operators of the United States and Canada..(212) 730-1770
International Association of Bridge,
Structural & Ornamental Iron Workers ....(202) 383-4800
International Association of Fire Fighters ....(202) 737-8484
International Association of Machinists
& Aerospace Workers....................................(301) 967-4500
International Brotherhood of Boilermakers,
Iron Ship Builders, Blacksmiths,
Forgers & Helpers...(913) 371-2640
International Brotherhood of
Electrical Workers...(202) 833-7000

International Brotherhood of
Firemen & Oilers..(404) 933-9104
International Brotherhood of Painters &
Allied Trades of the United States
& Canada...(202) 637-0700
International Brotherhood of Teamsters............(202) 624-6800
International Chemical Workers Union............(216) 867-2444
International Ladies'
Garment Workers' Union.................................(212) 265-7000
International Longshoremen's &
Warehousemen's Union....................................(415) 775-0533
International Longshoremen's Association........(212) 425-1200
International Union of Aluminum, Brick
& Glass Workers..(314) 739-6142
International Union of Bricklayers and
Allied Craftsmen ....(202) 783-3788
International Union of Electronic, Electrical,
Salaried, Machine & Furniture Workers........(202) 296-1201
International Union of Glass Molders, Pottery,
Plastics & Allied Workers ....(610) 565-5051
International Union of Operating Engineers ....(202) 429-9100
International Union of Police Associations ......(703) 549-7473
International Union of United Automobile,
Aerospace & Agricultural Implement
Workers of America...(313) 926-5000
International Woodworkers of America ....(503) 656-1475
Laborers' International Union of
North America ....(202) 737-8320
National Association of Letter Carriers.............(202) 393-4695
National Education Association ....(202) 833-4000
National Federation of Federal Employees ....(202) 862-4400
National Fraternal Order of Police ....(615) 399-0900
National Marine Engineers'
Beneficial Association ....(202) 466-7060
National Rural Letters Carriers' Association.....(703) 684-5545
National Treasury Employees Union ....(202) 783-4444
The Newspaper Guild ....(301) 585-2990
Office & Professional Employees
International Union ....(212) 675-3210
Oil, Chemical & Atomic Workers
International Union ....(303) 987-2229
Operative Plasterers' & Cement
Masons' International Association of the
United States & Canada ....(202) 393-6569
Retail, Wholesale & Department
Store Union ....(212) 684-5300
Screen Actors Guild...(213) 465-4600
Service Employees' International Union...........(202) 898-3200
Sheet Metal Workers'
International Association................................(202) 783-5880
State Employees Association of
North Carolina ....(919) 833-6436
Transportation Communications
International Union ....(301) 948-4910
Transport Workers Union of America ....(212) 873-6000
United Brotherhood of Carpenters &
Joiners of America...(202) 546-6206
United Electrical, Radio & Machine
Workers of America...(412) 471-8919
United Food & Commercial Workers
International Union ....(202) 223-3111

Organizations

United Mine Workers of America ....(202) 842-7200
United Paperworkers International Union........(615) 834-8590
United Rubber, Cork, Linoleum &
   Plastic Workers of America............................(216) 869-0320
United Steelworkers of America.......................(412) 562-3400
United Transportation Union ....(216) 228-9400
Utility Workers Union of America....................(202) 347-8105
Workers' International Union of Bakery, Confectionery
   & Tobacco Workers.......................................(301) 933-8600

Airlines

Aer Lingus	(800) 223-6537
AeroMexico	(800) 237-6639
Air Canada	(800) 776-3000
Air France	(800) 237-2747
Alaska Airlines	(800) 426-0333
Alitalia	(800) 223-5730
All Nippon Airways	(800) 235-9262
Aloha Airlines	(800) 367-5250
America West Airlines	(800) 235-9292
American Airlines	(800) 433-7300
American Trans Air	(800) 225-2995
Austrian Airlines	(800) 843-0002
Avianca	(800) 284-2622
British Airways	(800) 247-9297
British Caledonian	(800) 543-7619
British Midland	(800) 788-0555
Canadian Airlines International	(800) 426-7000
Cathay Pacific Airways	(800) 233-2742
China Airlines	(800) 227-5118
Continental Airlines	(800) 525-0280
Delta Airlines	(800) 221-1212
EVA Airways	(800) 695-1188
Finnair	(800) 950-5000
Hawaiian Airlines	(800) 367-5320
Horizon Air	(800) 547-9308
Iberia Airlines	(800) 772-4642
Icelandair	(800) 223-5500
Japan Airlines	(800) 525-3663
Kiwi International Air Lines	(800) 538-5494
KLM Royal Dutch Airlines	(800) 374-7747
Korean Air	(800) 438-5000
Lufthansa German Airlines	(800) 645-3880
Markair	(800) 627-5247
Mesa Airlines	(800) 637-2247
Midwest Express	(800) 452-2022
Nations Air	(800) 248-9538
Northwest Airlines, domestic	(800) 225-2525
Northwest Airlines, international	(800) 447-4747
Olympic Airways	(800) 223-1226
Qantas Airways	(800) 227-4500
Reno Air	(800) 736-6247
Royal Jordanian	(800) 223-0470
Sabena Belgian World Airlines	(800) 873-3900
Scandinavian Airlines System	(800) 221-2350
Singapore Airlines	(800) 742-3333
Skywest	(800) 453-9417
Southwest Airlines	(800) 435-9792
Swissair	(800) 221-4750
TAP Air Portugal	(800) 221-7370
Thai Airways	(800) 426-5204
Tower Air	(800) 452-5531
Transbrazil Airlines	(800) 872-3153
TWA, domestic	(800) 221-2000
TWA, international	(800) 892-4141
United Airlines	(800) 241-6522
USAir	(800) 428-4322
Varig Brazilian Airlines	(800) 468-2744
Virgin Atlantic	(800) 862-8621
Westair	(800) 253-9378

Airline Paging

ANCHORAGE, AK

Alaska Air	(907) 266-7710
Delta	(800) 354-9822
Northwest	(907) 266-5639
United	(907) 243-5836

ATLANTA, GA

American	(404) 530-3170
Continental	(404) 530-3530
Delta	(404) 714-7250
Northwest	(404) 530-3960
TWA	(404) 530-2620
United	(404) 765-1266
USAir	(404) 530-3300

ATLANTIC CITY, NJ

Continental	(609) 646-8769

BALTIMORE, MD

All	(410) 859-7111

BOSTON, MA

All	(617) 561-1806

BUFFALO, NY

American	(800) 433-7300
Continental	(716) 852-1233
Delta	(800) 354-9822
Northwest	(800) 225-2525
United	(800) 241-6522
USAir	(800) 428-4322

CHARLOTTE, NC

All	(704) 359-4013

CHICAGO, IL (MIDWAY)

Continental	(312) 918-7676
Delta	(312) 735-9041
Northwest	(312) 471-4692
TWA	(312) 471-8820
USAir	(312) 735-3056

CHICAGO, IL (O'HARE)

American	(312) 686-4477
Continental	(312) 601-5305
Delta	(312) 686-8635
Northwest	(312) 686-5575
TWA	(312) 938-9000
United	(312) 601-3100
USAir	(312) 686-7171

CINCINNATI, OH

All	(606) 283-3144

CLEVELAND, OH

All	(216) 265-6030

COLUMBUS, OH

All	(614) 239-4083

DALLAS, TX

American	(214) 425-2477
Continental	(214) 574-6673
Delta	(214) 574-2247
Northwest	(214) 574-6673
TWA	(214) 574-6673
United	(214) 574-6673
USAir	(214) 574-6673

DENVER, CO

All	(303) 342-2300

DETROIT, MI

American	(800) 433-7300
Continental	(313) 963-4600
Delta	(313) 942-2643
Northwest	(313) 942-4268
TWA	(313) 962-8650
United	(313) 942-4062
USAir	(313) 942-2460

GRAND RAPIDS, MI

American	(800) 433-7300
Delta	(616) 336-4663
Northwest	(616) 336-4682
TWA	(800) 221-2000
United	(616) 949-2330
USAir	(800) 428-4322

GREENVILLE, SC

All	(803) 877-7426

HARRISBURG, PA

American	(800) 433-7300
Continental	(717) 944-2323
Delta	(717) 948-2923
Northwest	(717) 948-3749
United	(717) 948-3696
USAir	(717) 948-3620

HARTFORD, CT

American	(800) 433-7300
Continental	(203) 627-3974
Delta	(203) 627-3824
Northwest	(203) 627-3530
TWA	(203) 627-0631
United	(203) 627-3722
USAir	(800) 428-4322

HONOLULU, HI

American	(800) 433-7300
Continental	(808) 834-7262
Delta	(800) 354-9822
Northwest	(800) 225-2525
TWA	(808) 834-2581
United	(808) 836-6411

HOUSTON, TX

All	(713) 230-3000

INDIANAPOLIS, IN

All	(317) 487-9594

Kansas City, MO
All ....(816) 243-5237

Las Vegas, NV
All ....(702) 261-5743

Los Angeles, CA
American ....(310) 646-3533
Continental ....(310) 568-3131
Delta ....(310) 417-7335
Northwest ....(310) 646-7700
TWA ....(310) 646-2424
United...(310) 646-3116
USAir ....(310) 646-2020

Memphis, TN
American ....(800) 433-7300
Delta ....(901) 922-8241
Northwest ....(901) 922-8451
Trans World Express ....(901) 922-8152
United...(800) 241-6522
USAir ....(901) 922-8261

Miami, FL
All ....(305) 876-7000

Milwaukee, WI
All ....(414) 747-5245

Minneapolis, MN
American ....(612) 726-5843
Continental ....(612) 726-5818
Delta ....(612) 725-4931
Northwest ....(612) 726-3007
TWA ....(612) 726-5642
United...(612) 726-5075
USAir ....(612) 726-5373

Nashville, TN
All ....(615) 275-1675

New Orleans, LA
All ....(504) 464-0831

New York, NY (JFK)
American ....(718) 632-3100
Delta ....(718) 632-4180
Northwest ....(718) 244-5636
TWA ....(718) 244-2000
United...(800) 241-6522
USAir ....(800) 428-4322

New York, NY (LaGuardia)
Continental ....(718) 334-7132
Delta ....(718) 565-3940
Northwest ....(718) 476-7191
TWA ....(718) 803-6810
United...(800) 241-6522
USAir ....(718) 533-2634

Norfolk, VA
All ....(804) 444-3040

OKLAHOMA CITY, OK
All..(405) 680-3317

ORLANDO, FL
All..(407) 825-2000

PHILADELPHIA, PA
All..(215) 492-3222

PHOENIX, AZ
All..(602) 273-3455

PITTSBURGH, PA
All..(412) 472-3525

PORTLAND, OR
All..(503) 335-1040

PROVIDENCE, RI
All..(401) 737-4000

RALEIGH, NC
All..(919) 840-2123

SACRAMENTO, CA
All..(916) 929-5411

ST. LOUIS, MO
All..(314) 426-8000

SALT LAKE CITY, UT
All..(801) 575-2600

SAN ANTONIO, TX
All..(210) 821-3411

SAN DIEGO, CA
All..(619) 231-2294

SAN FRANCISCO, CA
All..(415) 876-2377

SEATTLE, WA
Continental ....(206) 624-1740
Delta ....(206) 439-4324
Northwest ....(206) 433-3603
TWA...(206) 433-5722
United...(206) 433-4324
USAir ....(206) 433-7850

TAMPA, FL
All..(813) 870-8770

WASHINGTON, DC (DULLES)
All..(703) 661-8636

WASHINGTON, DC (NATIONAL)
All..(703) 419-3972

WEST PALM BEACH, FL
All..(407) 471-7420

Car Rental Companies

Advantage	(800) 777-5500
Agency	(800) 321-1972
Airways	(708) 671-7070
Alamo	(800) 327-9633
Avis	(800) 831-2847
Budget	(800) 527-0700
Dollar	(800) 800-4000
Enterprise	(800) 325-8007
Hertz	(800) 654-3131
National	(800) 328-4567
Payless Car Rental	(800) 237-2804
Practical	(800) 233-1663
Rent A Wreck	(800) 822-1662
Sears	(800) 527-0770
Thrifty	(800) 367-2277
U-Save	(800) 438-2300
Value	(800) 327-2501

Hotels

Best Western	(800) 528-1234
Budgetel Inns	(800) 428-3438
Budget Host	(800) 283-4678
Central Reservation Service	(800) 257-4477
Choice Hotels	(800) 424-6423
Comfort Inns	(800) 221-2222
Condotels	(800) 852-6636
Courtyard by Marriott	(800) 321-2211
Days Inn	(800) 325-2525
Doubletree Hotels	(800) 528-0444
Hilton	(800) 445-8667
Holiday Inn	(800) 465-4329
Hospitality Inns	(800) 424-5338
Howard Johnson	(800) 654-2000
Hyatt	(800) 233-1234
Journey's End Hotels	(800) 668-4200
Knights Lodging	(800) 843-5644
La Quinta Inn	(800) 642-4279
Loews Hotels	(800) 235-6397
Marriott	(800) 228-9290
Motel 6	(800) 440-6000
Radisson	(800) 333-3333
Ramada	(800) 228-2828
Red Roof Inns	(800) 843-7663
Sheraton	(800) 325-3535

Taxi/Limousine Services

ANCHORAGE, AK

A Touch of Class Limousine Service	(907) 562-2498
Alaska Cab & Handicap Dispatch	(907) 258-3434
Prestige Limousine Service	(907) 243-6669

ATLANTA, GA

Atlanta Limousine	(404) 351-5466
Carey Executive Limousine	(404) 681-3366
Checker Cab Company	(404) 351-1111

ATLANTIC CITY, NJ

Atlantic City Airport Taxi	(609) 383-1457

Metro Cab..(609) 344-0100

BALTIMORE, MD

A Better Limousine Service ....(410) 841-5455
Royal Cab ....(410) 327-0330
Yellow Cab ....(410) 685-1212

BOSTON, MA

Checker Taxi ....(617) 536-5200
Independent Taxi Operators Association ....(617) 426-8700
Town Taxi ....(617) 536-5000

BUFFALO, NY

Action Taxi & Limo...(716) 639-0648
Airport Taxi Service...(716) 633-8294
Liberty Cab ....(716) 877-7111
Radio Express Taxi Service ....(716) 633-4200

CHARLOTTE, NC

A Classy Affair Limousine Service ....(704) 364-5006
Bush Limousine Service ....(704) 394-0131
Crown Cab ....(704) 334-6666
Yellow Cab Co. of Charlotte...............................(704) 332-6161

CHICAGO, IL

Checker Taxi Association ....(312) 243-2537
Chicago Limousine..(312) 726-1035
Flash Cab ....(312) 561-1444
O'Hare Midway Limousine Service ....(312) 558-1111
Yellow Cab..(312) 829-4222

CINCINNATI, OH

Cincinnati Limousine Service.............................(513) 388-3808
Queen City Limousine ....(513) 861-9949

CLEVELAND, OH

Americab ....(216) 429-1111
Hollywood Limousines ....(216) 461-8686
Carey Limousine..(216) 267-8282
Yellow Cab Co. of Cleveland..............................(216) 623-1550

COLUMBUS, OH

Aladdin Limousine ....(614) 891-3440
Carey of Columbus Limousine Service ....(614) 228-5466
Northway Taxicab ....(614) 299-8022
Yellow Cab..(614) 221-3800

DALLAS, TX

Airport Limousine Service ....(214) 243-8880
American Luxury Transportation.......................(214) 905-9999
West End Cab ....(214) 902-7000
Yellow Checker Cab...(214) 565-9132

DENVER, CO

American Cab ....(303) 777-5200
DTC Boulevard Cars & Limousines ....(303) 773-1757
Metro Taxi ....(303) 333-3333
Yellow Cab..(303) 777-7777

DETROIT, MI

Bloomfield Hills Limousine................................(313) 271-7829
Checker Cab...(313) 963-7000
Michigan Limousine Service...............................(810) 546-6112

Southfield Cab..(810) 356-1090

GRAND RAPIDS, MI
Yellow Cab...(616) 458-4100

GREENVILLE, SC
Airport Limo Service..(803) 879-2315
Diamond Cab ....(803) 235-1713
Royal Cab ....(803) 271-2887
Yellow Cab...(803) 232-5322

HARRISBURG, PA
Keystone Limousine Service ....(717) 653-8141
Penn Harris Taxi Service.....................................(717) 238-7377
West Shore Taxi ....(610) 795-8294
Yellow Cab...(717) 238-7252

HARTFORD, CT
Ace Taxi Service ....(203) 291-0850
Buckley Limousine Service ....(203) 953-8787
Connecticut Limousine Group ....(203) 878-6867
Yellow Cab...(203) 666-6666

HONOLULU, HI
Aloha Limousine Service ....(808) 949-3636
Exclusive Limousines...(808) 946-7905

HOUSTON, TX
A-1 Limo & Airport Service.................................(713) 789-9789
Comet Cab & Limousine Service ....(713) 729-1001
Liberty Cab ....(713) 692-8080
Yellow Cab...(713) 236-1111

INDIANAPOLIS, IN
Indy Connection Limousines ....(317) 241-2522
Lafayette Limousine ....(317) 497-3828
Yellow Cab...(317) 487-7777

KANSAS CITY, MO
Adriene Exclusive Limousines ....(816) 822-7919
Amour Limousine Service....................................(816) 223-3901
Metropolitan Transportation Services ....(816) 471-6050
Yellow Cab...(816) 471-5000

LAS VEGAS, NV
Checker Cab..(702) 873-2227
Presidential Limousine Service ....(702) 731-5577
Whittlesea Blue Cabs...(702) 384-6111
Yellow Cab Co. of Nevada ....(702) 873-2227

LOS ANGELES, CA
Carey Huntington Limousine ....(310) 275-4153
Diva Limousine...(310) 278-3482
Fox Limousine ....(310) 641-9626
Metropolitan Express/Skycar..............................(310) 417-5050

MEMPHIS, TN
Checker Cab..(901) 577-7700
City Wide Cab..(901) 324-4202
Yellow Cab/Limousine..(901) 577-7700

MIAMI, FL
Aladdin's Limousine ....(305) 758-8400
Carey South Florida/Regal Limousine ....(800) 262-9299

Metro Taxi ....(305) 888-8888

MILWAUKEE, WI

Beverly Hills Limousine Service ....(414) 358-1900
City Veterans Taxicab ....(414) 291-8080
Limousines ....(414) 671-5466

MINNEAPOLIS, MN

All City Cab..(612) 222-8294
Airport Express ....(612) 827-7777
LCL Transportation ....(612) 888-6600
Suburban Taxi...(612) 588-0000

NASHVILLE, TN

Accent Limousines ....(615) 847-9857
Allied Taxi ....(615) 244-7433
Black Tie Limousines...(615) 254-1254
Music City Taxi ....(615) 262-0451

NEW ORLEANS, LA

Landry's Limousine Service ....(800) 344-0127
Limousine Livery ....(504) 561-8777
New Orleans Limousine Service ....(504) 529-5226
United Cabs...(800) 323-3303

NEW YORK, NY

London Towncars ....(212) 988-9700
Manhattan International ....(718) 729-4200
Sabra ....(212) 410-7600
Tel Aviv ....(212) 505-0555

NORFOLK, VA

Airport Shuttle..(804) 857-1231
Norfolk Checker Taxi...(804) 855-3333
Norfolk VIP & Celebrity Limousine..................(804) 853-5466
Yellow Cab..(804) 622-3232

OKLAHOMA CITY, OK

Airport Limousine ....(405) 685-2638
Checker Cab ....(405) 239-7710
Safeway Cab ....(405) 235-1431
Yellow Cab..(405) 232-0202

PHILADELPHIA, PA

Car One ....(215) 551-5500
Carey Limousine...(215) 492-8402
Quaker City Cab ....(215) 728-8000
United Cab Association.......................................(215) 238-9500

PHOENIX, AZ

Alpha Cab ....(602) 232-2000
Arizona Limousines ....(602) 267-7097
Carey Limousine...(602) 996-1955
Courier Transportation.......................................(602) 244-1818
Executive Transportation ....(602) 980-2081
Statewide Transportation Services.....................(602) 994-1616

PITTSBURGH, PA

American Eagle Limousine Service ....(412) 788-0338
Carey of Pittsburgh..(412) 731-8671
People's Cab..(412) 681-3131
Yellow Cab..(412) 665-8100

Travel/Transportation (Taxi)

PORTLAND, OR
Hut Airport Limousine.......................................(503) 378-7039
Metropolitan Airport Shuttle ....(503) 331-2335
Raz Transportation ....(503) 246-3301

PROVIDENCE, RI
Arrow Cab ....(401) 946-5333
Checker Cab...(401) 273-2222
Yellow Cab...(401) 941-1122

RALEIGH, NC
Allstar Limousine & Transportation..................(919) 846-1061
American Dream Limousine &
   Transportation..(919) 876-0657

SACRAMENTO, CA
Allard Limousine Service....................................(916) 486-8133
Checker Cab...(916) 457-2222
Paramount Limousine Service............................(916) 925-5881
Sacramento Cab ....(916) 331-4141
Yellow Cab...(916) 444-2222

ST. LOUIS, MO
Admiral Limousine...(314) 731-1707
Carey St. Louis/Show Me Limousine.................(314) 946-4114
Country..(314) 991-5300
Yellow Cab...(314) 361-2345

SALT LAKE CITY, UT
Interwest Limousine ....(801) 268-8856
Yellow Cab...(801) 521-2100

SAN ANTONIO, TX
Aladdin's Limousine ....(210) 436-1178
Carey Limousines ....(210) 525-0007
Checker Cab...(210) 222-2151
National Cab ....(210) 434-4444
Yellow Cab...(210) 226-4242

SAN DIEGO, CA
Advantage Limousine Service.............................(619) 563-1651
Ambassador Limousine Service..........................(619) 720-0201
San Diego Cab..(619) 226-8294
Silver Cabs...(619) 280-5555
Yellow Cab...(619) 234-6161

SAN FRANCISCO, CA
Carey/Nob Hill Limousine ....(415) 468-7550
Luxor Cab ....(415) 282-4141
Veteran's Taxicab...(415) 552-1300

SEATTLE, WA
Farwest Taxi...(206) 622-1717
Seattle Limousine ....(206) 762-3339
Washington Limousine..(206) 523-8000
Yellow Cab...(206) 622-6500

TAMPA, FL
Carey Limousine...(813) 228-7927
United Cab of Tampa..(813) 251-2844
Yellow Cab Co. of Tampa...................................(813) 253-8871

WASHINGTON, DC

Capitol Cab ....(202) 546-2400
Diamond Cab DC..(202) 387-6200
Dulles Taxi & Sterling .... (202) 333-8181
Red Top Executive Sedan ....(202) 882-3300
Washington Executive Car ....(202) 244-4606
Yellow Cab..(202) 544-1212

WEST PALM BEACH, FL

City Cab ....(407) 689-9999
County Cab ....(407) 688-2222
Gold Coast Limousines ....(407) 689-7117
Park Limousine Service......................................(407) 832-5866
Yellow Cab.. (407) 689-2222

Travel Agencies

American Express ....(800) 937-2639
Arrington..(800) 634-4146
Associated Travel Services ....(800) 969-9015
BTI America..(800) 243-6620
BTZ...(800) 888-8225
Carlson Wagonlit ....(800) 227-5766
Corporate Travel Consultants............................(800) 777-3242
IAP Travel ....(800) 354-4272
Maritz...(800) 553-0668
Northwestern..(800) 942-1316
Omega World Travel ....(800) 654-5398
Supertravel..(800) 637-5572
Travel & Transport ....(800) 832-2630
VTS...(800) 223-1632
World Travel Partners ....(800) 892-2335
World Wide Travel Service.................................(800) 372-8367
Worldtek ....(800) 892-2320

Topic Index

Topic Index